BEFORE
AMELIA

ALSO BY EILEEN F. LEBOW

Cal Rodgers and the Vin Fiz:
  The First Transcontinental Flight

A Grandstand Seat:
  The Army Balloon Corps in World War I

The Bright Boys:
  A History of Townsend Harris High School

BEFORE
AMELIA

Women Pilots in the Early Days of Aviation

EILEEN F. LEBOW

BRASSEY'S, INC.
Washington, D.C.

Library of Congress Cataloging-in-Publication Data
Lebow, Eileen F.
   Before Amelia : women pilots in the early days of aviation /
Eileen F. Lebow.—1st ed.
     p. cm.
Includes bibliographical references and index.
ISBN 1-57488-482-4
1. Women air pilots—Biography. 2. Aeronautics—History. I. Title.
TL539 .L42 2002
629.13'092'2—dc21

                                2002002635

ISBN 1-57488-482-4 (alk. paper)

Printed in the United States of America on acid-free paper that meets
the American National Standards Institute Z39-48 Standard.

Brassey's, Inc.
22841 Quicksilver Drive
Dulles, Virginia 20166

First Edition

10 9 8 7 6 5 4 3 2 1

For Therese,
whose courage matches that of
the pioneer women aviators

Contents

Acknowledgments

MANY PEOPLE HAVE contributed to this book. I am indebted to each one. In France, George Bourinet helped arrange appointments and wrote letters of introduction, and, with his wife, Simone, provided hospitality and comfort. Martine and François Faber welcomed me in Nancy and provided me with some excellent material from several sources on Marie Marvingt. At Musée de l'Air et l'Espace, Stéphane Nicolaou, Gilbert Deloizy, and Armel Brault were interested in my project and most helpful. Alain Marchant assisted me at the archives of the Fédération Aéronautique Internationale.

German museums and archives were particularly helpful in finding information on early German women fliers. I especially want to thank Monika Niese at Heimatmuseum Treptow, in Berlin; Dr. Eva A. Mayring and Dr. Bettina Gundler at the Deutsches Museum, in München; Veronika Mantei of Staatsbibliothek zu Berlin; and the staff of Frauen Stadt Archiv, in Dresden; Daimler-Benz Aerospace, in München; and Lufthansa, in Köln. Their responsiveness and interest were encouraging. Petr Cenker at the National Technical Museum in Prague supplied useful information on Bozena Láglrová.

In England, Christine Benson visited the staff at Brooklands Museum and paved the way for my meeting Gail and Anthony Hewlett, who shared family reminiscences of "The Old Bird." Julian C. Temple, curator of aviation at Brooklands, was interested and helpful, and introduced me to Michael Goodall, also at Brooklands, who generously shared his knowledge and photographs. Derek Judge shared information on Edith Maud Cook, his research subject for the past four years. The staffs at the Hendon Royal Air Force Museum, the Royal Aeronautical Society, and the British Library were most helpful during several visits.

For assistance in finding photographs of Lilian Bland, I am indebted to Stella O'Leary for putting me in touch with Thomas E. Fitzgerald, Norman Houston, and Jackie Hogg of the Northern Ireland Bureau in Washington, who led me to Dr. Ann McVeigh of Reader Services, Public Record Office of Northern Ireland, in Belfast.

In the United States, librarians and archivists around the country have assisted with research. The staffs of the Library of Congress, at the Manuscript Reading Room, the Photograph and Print Division, and, particularly, the Science Reference Section under Connie Carter, were helpful and invariably creative in solving problems. John Buydos suggested Russian references and helped translate them. Kate Igoé, Marilyn Graskowiak, Kristine Kaske, and Dan Hagedorn at the National Air and Space Museum were most accommodating and resourceful. Juanita Hartman, the librarian at Langley Air Force Base, found a special report on Russian women fliers for me—thank you. Special thanks go to Joan L. Hrubec and Lynn Johnson of the International Women's Air & Space Museum, Inc., in Cleveland. Rebecca Looney, assistant curator of the Cradle of Aviation Museum, in Garden City, New York, helped with information and photographs of women fliers. Casey Smith at the San Diego Aerospace Museum also assisted with photographs, as did Lygia Ionnitiu and Giacinta Bradley Koontz. Ned Preston, Federal Aviation Administration (FAA) historian, and Jim McMullen at Women in Aviation, International, in Daytona Beach, Florida, supplied current figures on women in aviation. (A special thank-you should be given to the unknown FAA telephone operator who, when told the purpose of my call, said: "Wait. Let me think a minute; who would be the right person?" She found the right person.) Nora Sullivan described the course of aeronautics she took at college. Judith Wells of the Lynn Public Library, in Lynn, Massachusetts, sent material from the reference department on Ruth Law. Mitch Yockelson and Ken Tessendorf were dependable for tips on possible sources and ideas on where to look next. William W. Lowe shared information on Katherine Stinson; Eileen Sullivan and Edward Strudwicke facilitated financial arrangements overseas. Marilyn Wisoff introduced me to Therese Gluecksmann, who became my friend and a fine German translator. Her help was invaluable. Michele Wolf did a fine editing job, for which I thank her. Finally, my husband, Morton Lebow, has edited, printed, schlepped, and comforted, all with rare good humor. I am most grateful.

1
In the Beginning

ON OCTOBER 22, 1909, at Châlons, France, a fragile aeroplane maneuvered across the field, turned, and, with motor at full gas, rushed and lifted into the air for a distance of some three hundred meters before settling down again. With roars of approval, the ground crew ran to help the pilot out, and a tall, elegant woman, smiling broadly, stepped into history.

Raymonde de Laroche had just driven a heavier-than-air machine into the air alone and is generally recognized as the first woman in the world who did so. Five months later she was issued license No. 36—35 men preceded her—by the Aero Club of France, joining the growing number of men licensed in Europe and the United States.

Her sisters in Europe and America were quick to follow in her footsteps. They knew they could ride bicycles and motorcycles, and drive automobiles—balloons were tame—and now here was this marvelous machine with its promise of speed, adventure, financial gain, and overall pure pleasure. The fact that they were invading a man's world didn't worry them; it never occurred to them.

By the end of 1910, France had three more licensed women pilots, and elsewhere adventuresome women had taken to the skies in 1911: Lydia Zvereva in Russia, Melli Beese in Germany, Hilda Hewlett in England, and Harriet Quimby in the United States. Like Laroche, each was the first licensed woman pilot in her country, followed soon after by other intrepid women.

Their appearance on the flying field, at first a surprise, came to be accepted in spite of early opposition from male aviators. Like most trailblazers, these pioneer women fliers learned to ignore criticism that claimed woman were unsuited for aviation, taunts that women were interested only in catching a man, and dirty tricks that sometimes resulted in crash landings, and focused on their goal. Adventurers at heart, individualists, definitely too large for the pigeonhole for women in that period, the first women fliers were caught up in the excitement aeroplanes generated. They had to fly and experience for themselves the intoxication of flight; they were courageous beyond imagining to step into flimsy machines, with disaster a constant risk. They were assured—most were familiar with wheels and motors—and viewed the aeroplane as a continuation of the new century's progress.

Melli Beese, Lydia Zvereva, and Hilda Hewlett were among the lucky women who had the financial and familial backing that allowed them to pursue the new craze; Lyubov Golanchikova and Hélène Dutrieu worked hard to achieve their wings and the possibility of a better living that aviation offered. Raymonde de Laroche, Lyubov Golanchikova and the Americans, Blanche Scott and Katherine Stinson, understood the show-business aspect of aviation exhibitions and did not hesitate to

France's Raymonde de Laroche and her pilot's license, the first ever issued to a woman. She received it on March 8, 1910. DIE LADYS IN DEN FLIEGENDEN KISTEN

promote their career like any star of the theater. If male stars received a larger sum for an appearance, women pilots hid their annoyance behind a smile, collected their fee, and put on a good show. Perhaps because of the predominant male attitudes, some of the early female pilots quickly lost interest in exhibitions and competitions, devoting their energy instead to teaching or building aeroplanes. Lydia Zvereva, Hilda Hewlett, Melli Beese, and Marjorie Stinson (Katherine's sister), an American, taught students to fly; the first two also built aeroplanes for their respective countries in the First World War.

Women were used to advertise aeroplanes as well as fly them. In Germany, the Rumpler Taube builder wanted Melli Beese to fly his aeroplane to show the military how easy it was, and in America Alfred Moisant sent Bernetta A. Miller to Washington, D.C., to demonstrate his company's monoplane, using the pitch: If a woman can fly it, anybody can! Elsewhere, the aeroplane builders Anthony Fokker and Henry Farman recruited Lyubov Golanchikova and Hélène Dutrieu because they believed women pilots were well suited to the fragile, unstable machines of the time; the women's lighter weight and size were assets; their smaller hands moved more dexterously than a man's; and despite criticism from aviation star Claude Grahame-White that they lacked coolness— sangfroid, so loved by the French—women's reactions in emergency situations proved him wrong repeatedly.

Courageous beyond belief, with confidence and eagerness, the early women fliers climbed off their bicycles and motorcycles, out of their automobiles, into the flimsy contraptions fashioned from bamboo, wire, and fabric that first carried people aloft. Seated precariously between the wings of the earliest machines, sometimes below the wing, lacking any protection from the elements, these intrepid women, by their example, pointed the way for women to attempt the unusual. For them, it was conquering the skies to reach for the horizon.

One thing was certain: Most of the early women fliers had no qualms about being in the public eye. Some, like Marie Marvingt and Raymonde de Laroche of France, Lyubov Golanchikova of Russia, and Harriet Quimby and Katherine Stinson of the United States, reveled in it and went out of their way to promote their careers.

One deterrent that women thought unfair was the Aero Club regulations that prevented women from competing with men. As the gentler sex, women were limited to flying circuits at aerodromes with their own sex or alone. No speed races, no cross-country competitions for them, because, as Grahame-White, England's foremost aviator, announced publicly, "Women lack qualities which make for safety in aviation. They are temperamentally unfitted for the sport." Apparently, there were similar thinking men in the international Aero Clubs. Hélène Dutrieu, Melli Beese, Lilly Steinschneider, who was from Hungary, and Jeanne Pallier, from France, were the only women to compete with men. These four women gave creditable performances against men, and Dutrieu beat all competitors to win the King of Italy Cup in 1911.

According to Grahame-White, the sense of balance, essential in flying, comes naturally to the aviator—a man, of course. "One elevates or lowers his planes almost instinctively, the same as one turns the handle-bars in bicycling or varies the stroke in swimming or tennis," he said, believing this was a quality women lacked, forgetting that women had proved their ability in all of these things. This kind of male arrogance was a major hurdle for women fliers, especially in Germany and England, less so in America, Russia, and France. The Wright Brothers opposed women flying at first; American aviator Glenn Curtiss didn't think they should attempt such an activity. The German aviator Hellmuth Hirth at Johannisthal resisted women as aviators, claiming they were physically unsuited for the role. Hirth and other aviation stars of the period worried about loss of public esteem if women were seen performing the same feats. After all, how difficult could they be?

Arnold Kruckman, the aviation editor for the *New York American,* was typical of the critics. In 1911, he expressed the attitude of male aviators who, though willing to assist female aviators in every way, held, deep down, a "defined feeling" that aeroplane sport was not for women. Women were too emotional, they were not mentally equipped to withstand the intense nervous strain of flying, they lacked discipline, "the natural heritage of many men."

Kruckman lamented the lack in 1911 of "one real first-class woman flier in the world." Women were unable to compete with men equally. In fact, Kruckman reported, when men knew a woman was flying on the field, they refrained from notable feats. French aviator Louis Blériot strenuously opposed women competing, and the Wrights declined "to sell their machine to a woman." Why? Because women lacked "coolness and judgment."

The beginning of the Aero Club of the United Kingdom is a fine example of male behavior of the period. According to historian Patricia Stroud, the idea for the club, born in the basket of a balloon somewhere between the Crystal Palace and Sidcup, was the brainchild of Vera Hedges Butler, a passenger on the flight. Once on the ground again, the gentlemen went off to Somerset House to register the name of the club. Miss Butler's name was not listed among those of the organizing committee. Later, "the magnanimous men" allowed her to become a member along with several other ladies. Writing in 1954, Stroud commented, "Even now women are tolerated (though not encouraged) to take part in the Club's activities."

Harry Harper, an English journalist who observed and wrote about the early years of flying, was a rare champion of women in aviation. He ticked off the reasons: Their instructors found them quick to learn; they took nothing for granted; they did not mind being told their mistakes; they were punctual and eager to master every phase of the subject. Once they had the knack of maneuvering a machine, "their quickness of movement and lightness of touch prove assets of the utmost value." According to Harper, maneuvering an aeroplane required small, swift, accurate movements, which women were adept at.

The British author Stella Murray, writing on women in aviation in 1929, had these points to add: Women drank less than men, a major factor in aeroplane safety, and they withstood cold altitudes better than men because of years spent enduring chilly temperatures dressed in wispy dresses.

The first women aviators had their own thoughts on the suitability of women in aviation. Hélène Dutrieu wrote that women could enter the male world of aviation and not lose their natural femininity, a rebuttal of the unwomanly criticism that was prevalent. The Americans Matilde Moisant and Harriet Quimby were almost self-consciously feminine, appearing for photographers in long gauzy gowns with picture hats when not dressed for flying. Like the French women who preceded them, Moisant and Quimby's size and weight were suited to the fragile aeroplanes they flew, their smaller hands moved more dexterously than a man's, their brain was just as able to concentrate on the levers as a man's was, and women like Melli Beese and Hilda Hewlett were quite capable of working with machinery. Lydia Zvereva, Harriet Quimby, and

Katherine Stinson spoke out clearly: Their goal was equality with men in the air. The Russians, out of necessity, would be the first to allow women to serve as military aviators.

Tragic accidents predictably caused the *New York Times* to editorialize: "It would be well to exclude women from a field of activity in which their presence is unnecessary from any point of view," a sentiment that lurked within some males, much as they might be entranced by a woman's performance in the air. Males dropped out of the sky all too frequently, but that was to be expected—they were men. But a woman, and a young one to boot, was outside the realm of what was natural. Women pilots, while saddened by the loss of a friend, did not dwell on the dangers of flying. Matilde Moisant put the thought of death out of her mind when she flew. The worst that can happen is to be killed, and, she reasoned, "there is only one death."

When the first two American women, Harriet Quimby and Matilde Moisant, became pilots, the *New York Times* observed, "Aviation is not for a favored few." If two women had earned a license, "almost anybody, man or woman, after a week or two or three of instruction and practice, can fly." At the same time, the editorial cautioned that the women's success "can hardly be taken as the opening of a great and promising as well as new 'career' for all their ambitious sisters." The editorial was quick to point out that one drawback remained: the high mortality rate from accidents, due often to needless risks, and the fact that cautiousness was not usually an aviator's trait.

If the press sometimes questioned women's place in aviation, other journalists searched for nouns and adjectives and apt nicknames for the new breed of pilots. Was a woman pilot an aviator, an aviatrix, or an aviatress? "Female *oiseau,*" "Girl Hawk," "Tomboy of the Air," "The Flying School Marm" were some of the nicknames; "daring," "fatalistic," "girlish" were favorite adjectives. Journals discussed the appropriate dress style for women pilots: Pants were a shocking departure from long skirts, and the absence of a corset was scandalous. The French, particularly, were fascinated by the costumes—pants and bloomers, divided skirts, leather suits, some all of one piece, and headgear—worn by various pilots.

If some writers thought women's presence was "unnecessary," the public didn't think so—excited spectators cheered themselves hoarse—and other journalists, much taken with the female "birds," wrote a lot that was sheer invention for the delight of their readers. The women aviators collaborated happily.

The pioneer era of aviation took on a circus mentality within several years, particularly in the United States. To the average person on the ground, early aviators were special, performing acts so extraordinary that they seemed superhuman. Harriet Quimby was the first woman to fly across the English Channel, and she did it under circumstances that would have tried the stamina and nerves of any man. Melli Beese competed in the same sphere with her male competitors until she found she was being cheated. Ruth Law set a distance record from Chicago to Hornell, New York, that beat every American male pilot at the time.

When the public became jaded with flying exhibitions, the need for more daring, more exciting maneuvers co-opted the air scene. Europeans looked askance at this development; their effort went into longer cross-country and international flights, requiring stronger motors and more stable machines. For too long, Americans were content to entertain, and technical development was left to overseas developers.

This had an effect on women fliers. Those who realized the increasing danger in straining for aerial acrobatics switched their interests elsewhere or gave up aviation altogether. Those with special technical experience, like Lydia Zvereva, Melli Beese, Hilda Hewlett, and Marjorie Stinson, turned to building aeroplanes or teaching. Blanche Scott went into the movies. The promise of the very early days gradually dissipated.

Once Europe was enveloped by war, civilian flying ended. Women were not allowed to use their aviation ability, but they could drive ambulances or do hospital work—safe activities for women. Those who had gone into building aeroplanes continued to do so during the war. When the war ended, the coterie of women fliers, never large in number but exemplary in their performance, with rare exceptions, never returned to aviation. They were older, technology had passed them by, and new lives claimed them.

Raymonde de Laroche, the world's first woman pilot, was one of the exceptions. She renewed her love of aviation and planned to become a test pilot. Her death in 1919 as a passenger in the crash of a new model aeroplane was an apt closing to the era of pioneer women aviators.

2
L'Aéroplane est là!

IN AN EARLIER DAY, following the male lead, women had stepped into baskets to travel aloft in balloons, and by 1909 they had formed their own club in France, the Stella Society, to promote an interest in aeronautics. A socially prominent group, the members of Stella reported their doings in a special column in the French journal *L'Aérophile*. Although they encouraged aeronautical exploration, few of the Stellas made the leap from balloon to aeroplane.

The first women pilots, on the other hand, a more adventuresome group, climbed into aeroplanes as the logical next step from bicycles and automobiles. As a group they were remarkably unconcerned about negative attitudes or prejudices that claimed women were unsuited for such activity. Aviation offered excitement, monetary gain, and freedom; joined with their enthusiasm, confidence, and courage, it was a splendid match.

RAYMONDE DE LAROCHE
She was a most unlikely candidate for an aviator. Tall, elegant, a standout in the theater and fashion worlds, the first woman in the world to receive a pilot's license to drive a heavier-than-air machine into the air was Raymonde de Laroche. A glamorous brunette, she was a natural for the theater and she had numerous friends in the Parisian art world. When Alberto Santos-Dumont, the Brazilian-born French aeronaut,

fired French imagination with his 1906 flight, Raymonde along with millions of others was caught up in the excitement of this marvelous new plaything, the aeroplane. Not content to be a shining light of the Belle Époque, she would learn to fly!

Born Élise Deroche on August 22, 1886, in a Paris neighborhood that, according to one source, smelled heavily of creosote and beer, her early years were ordinary for the time, as the daughter of a plumber. Her education was the usual elementary grades, and, as family circumstances were limited, the precocious young girl made her mind up early to achieve success. Nature had been kind to her; she had an alluring figure, eloquent brown eyes, and bountiful dark hair. The theater and the worlds of art and fashion would be her entry to the wider world of fame. By the time she was twenty, she had adopted the name Raymonde de Laroche—it was modern with a hint of social cachet, to which *Flight* attached the title "Baroness" on the occasion of her first solo. Her stylish clothes were the envy of the fashion world; her theatrical appearances won approval, though detractors claim her experience was more burlesque than drama; she had entrée to the art world. Reportedly, Léon Delagrange, an artist and one of the early stars of French aviation, fathered her son, André.

In an interview following her success as France's first woman pilot, Laroche confided that she had always loved sports. As a child she rode a pony, and as she grew older she took up, successively, tennis, rowing, ice-skating, skiing, and the bicycle, followed in turn by the motorcycle. There may have been some exaggeration in her account, but whatever she did she embraced wholeheartedly. When automobiles became the vogue, Laroche began driving and raced enthusiastically before switching to the aeroplane.

Wilbur Wright's flights at Hunaudières racetrack near Le Mans in August 1908 astonished the French aviation world, which hadn't really believed in the brothers' invention. He had come to France to interest the government in the Wright aeroplane. Invited by the military authorities to use a military field at Auvours seven miles east of Le Mans, Wright proved the biplane's ability to rise quickly, circle with ease at sharp angles, and land "like a bird." In a series of flights with the elite of Paris watching, Wilbur lengthened his flying time to an incredible one hour and thirty-one minutes on September 21. Impressed by his performance, the French government signed a contract with the Wright Company,

and that winter Wilbur Wright opened the first aviation school for training military fliers at Pau, in the southwest of France.

To demonstrate the safety of aeroplane travel, Wright carried a number of women aloft as passengers, among them Mrs. Hart Berg, wife of
the European manager of the Wright Company, who shared her impressions with the press. She had been warned she might feel seasick while
the machine was running down the rail (the original launching device),
but she had no distress. As the aeroplane soared upward, it felt like "a
boat sailing on air waves." Best of all was taking the curves, which was
how she had always imagined real flying would be. Her only wish was
that the flight "would go on for hours."

Mrs. Berg's attire did not go unnoticed by fashion-conscious Paris.
Her full skirt was tied at the ankle to prevent it from billowing up during the flight, an adjustment promptly adopted by fashion designers as
the hobble skirt. The style, denounced as a "fad" and a "freak" by the
American National Cloak, Suit and Skirt Manufacturers' Association,
proved short-lived and gave way by 1910 to a freer and "dignified use of
feet and limbs."

The sheer beauty of Wright's aerial maneuvers and a ride as a passenger convinced Laroche that flying was superior to the automobile for
travel. Already an accomplished motorist, she eagerly embraced this new
invention, which had caught the public's attention and offered greater
speed and the chance of stardom.

She was familiar with the efforts of the French aviation pioneers—
Alberto Santos-Dumont, Henry Farman, and Léon Delagrange. Santos-
Dumont had pointed the way in 1906 when his fragile machine, looking
like a large butterfly, took to the air. Farman flew the first closed circuit
in January 1908; Delagrange piloted the first passenger flight, with Farman aboard, in March of that year. Now, Laroche prevailed upon the
Voisin brothers, Gabriel and Charles—the latter was a special friend,
who had built aeroplanes for Santos-Dumont and Farman and were successfully established as aeroplane builders—to give her instruction.

Schools of aviation were just beginning to emerge; builders taught
interested students on machines of their own construction using whatever method they chose. Other builders quickly followed the Wrights'
example, usually on national land provided by the Ministry of War. The
range of differences in training made for a chaotic state—"anarchy" was

the term the Aero Club of France used to describe the carnage caused by aviation accidents—which forced the club to establish the first standards for a brevet, or license, in January 1909. Instructors would take their task more seriously and give students proper training. What form that took was left to the aeroplane builders.

Beginning on January 7, 1909, the test for a pilot's license required three closed circuits of five kilometers each; altitude was not mentioned. By the following year, the test included landing and stopping within 150 meters of a designated point to show adequate control of the aeroplane. Further refinement in 1911 required two circuits around a course, making figure eights to prove the candidate's ability to make right and left turns; a third test required the candidate to reach an altitude of fifty meters above the departure point, and to land and come to a stop within fifty meters of a designated spot. Very shortly the altitude was raised to one hundred meters. When war began in 1914, the number of fliers breveted was 1,720. Of that number, women were a very small part.

At the Voisin camp at Châlons, M. Château, a company engineer responsible for training new pilots, took Laroche in charge, supervised by Charles Voisin, who was already captivated by her charms. Charles was a tall, handsome man, and Raymonde was equally impressed with him. The two were inseparable, which did not please Gabriel, who complained that Charles was giving too much time and attention to the young student instead of concentrating on his work. Both brothers were experienced pilots who tested their own machines, but they were not interested in competitions. Their business was lucrative enough.

Raymonde proved a deft pupil. Learning to fly was very much an individual matter; one had a talent for it, or not. Instruction consisted of a few comments from a mentor on the ground on what made an aeroplane go up, how to bring it down, how to keep it balanced in the air. Technology was so primitive that such information could be given in a few short sessions. Would-be pilots learned by doing, especially what not to do, by making many short flights over time. With a good measure of luck, they gained the seasoning necessary to earn a pilot's brevet without smashing the machine or themselves.

Raymonde listened attentively to M. Château's instruction and soon was steering the Voisin training aeroplane across the ground to get the feel of the machine. Later, when her success won headlines, she endorsed

La Baronne de Laroche seated in the first plane she flew, a Voisin. MUSÉE DE L'AIR
ET DE L'ESPACE, LE BOURGET

the Voisin aeroplane for its manageability and stability, two important qualities for a machine. Her first attempts showed aptitude: She could drive the machine across the field in a straight line, have it turned by a mechanic, and bring it back to where she started. From that beginning, she progressed to making short hops. On her first try, she revved up the fifty-horsepower motor and taxied across the field, turned into the wind, and with full power raced back across the field. Suddenly, her wheels left the ground, and she continued in the air for three hundred meters before gently settling down. There were loud cheers from the ground crew, and M. Cháteau nodded approvingly to his pupil, who was flushed with happiness at her first "getting off." For the record books, it was the first female flight. The date was October 22, 1909, a day she never forgot.

Four days before, the Comte de Lambert had flown over Paris in a Wright biplane and circled the Eiffel Tower twice at an altitude of four hundred meters before returning to his landing site. For the Parisian public, the flight proved that aviation was no longer entertainment but a serious reality, "truly the French science" predicted by *La Petite République* following Blériot's Channel flight the previous summer.

Laroche continued making hops, gradually lengthening them in the weeks that followed, as she gained confidence. The tests for the Aero Club demanded the ability to land precisely and to achieve distance. Besides learning to maneuver the machine smoothly, students learned to judge the air, whose currents are never constant. A maneuver that worked well one day would be hazardous the next because of shifting air currents, or a sudden gust that could tip the aeroplane over. Early morning and late afternoon were usually the calmest times for flights, but not always. Judging distance was another essential requirement; other aeroplanes and obstacles must be avoided, especially when landing. In each case, the pilot must move instinctively to avoid disaster, an adeptness that would come only with experience.

Laroche learned the hard way on January 4, 1910. On that day, wind conditions required her to approach the Châlons field for a landing over a row of poplars. After a turn at the far end of the field, she approached the trees but misjudged their height. As she flew over, the tail of her machine brushed a tree branch before she could pull up, causing the machine to drop heavily some twenty feet, throwing her from her seat. The machine was shattered, but its pilot, at first unconscious, received only a broken collarbone and bruises. The fall did not discourage her; she was determined to be the first woman aeroplane pilot in the world. Through the weeks of recovery, aware that other women—Hélène Dutrieu, Marie Marvingt, Marthe Niel, and Jeanne Herveux—were learning to fly, she worried that one of them would beat her to it.

As soon as she was well enough to climb into an aeroplane and work the controls, Laroche was planning her next move. She would join a troop from the Voisin company and travel to Egypt to compete in the Heliopolis air meet in February. After that seasoning, she would take her tests for a pilot's license.

The Heliopolis meet was not a great success. The weather was difficult for flying, with three days of storms followed by two days of heavy wind that kept all but the most intrepid fliers on the ground. Twelve aviators competed, driving five monoplanes and seven biplanes. The Grand Prix d'Egypte for aggregate distance was won by Henri Rougier, who flew his Voisin 153.5 kilometers in spite of the weather. Madame de Laroche was listed as eighth, with twenty kilometers flown on February 10. Hubert Latham and Hubert Lablon, known in France for their aerial ability, each totaled five kilometers on the same day. Raymonde had plenty of courage.

On March 8, 1910, Fédération Aéronautique Internationale issued the world's first female pilot's brevet, No. 36, to Madame Laroche after successful flights before club officials. Her satisfaction was evident, as was her fatalism about facing risks. Questioned by crowds of reporters, who were delighted with aviation's new star, *la femme-oiseau* ("female bird"), Laroche declared flying to be ideal for women. It didn't rely on strength as much as physical and mental coordination. As for the risks, she insisted she knew no fear when she flew. She philosophized that many people spread danger over a lifetime; others pack it into a matter of only minutes or hours. With a strug of her shoulders, she observed: "In any case, what is to happen will happen." Her matter-of-factness won praise; she had courage and sangfroid.

Eighth place at Heliopolis did not bring financial rewards, but Raymonde was content with her appearance. She had made her debut in the aviation world; there would be other opportunities for prizes. Winning her brevet established her in aviation, and she had beaten her competitors to become the first woman pilot in the world.

Thérèse Peltier, a sculptor and protégée of Léon Delagrange, almost certainly flew an aeroplane alone, but she never received a pilot's license, although she was pictured seated in a Farman biplane on several occasions. She made headlines in 1908, first as a passenger with Delagrange when he broke the record for duration in a flight—thirty minutes and twenty-seven seconds—when he flew in Turin and, later, Rome. Peltier reported on the aviator's success in Rome for the French press and his meeting with the queen mother. Delighted with the aviator's aerial feats, the queen mother anticipated that in two or three years "we shall have a royal aeroplane." However, for her part, she preferred a new automobile.

In September 1908, Delagrange was listed in the press as head of a new commercial organization, Compagnie d'Aviation, to encourage aviation technology and promote exhibition flights. At the same time, he presented one thousand francs to the French National Aerial League as a prize for the first woman aviator to fly one kilometer, operating the machine on her own, with or without a passenger. Peltier, according to the same story, was continuing her training to try for the prize. When Delagrange was killed in January 1910, she gave up flying. France lost one of its heroes; his death plunged the country into mourning.

Following Laroche's success, there was a burst of female activity. Hélène Dutrieu piloted a fragile Santos-Dumont machine in 1908–9 trial tests, but didn't try for her brevet until August 1910. Her certificate, No. 27, was issued by the Aero Club of Belgium. Marthe Niel won brevet No. 226, issued August 29, followed by Marie Marvingt, who passed her tests and earned license No. 281, issued November 8. Jeanne Herveux passed her tests before the end of the year, earning certificate No. 318, issued on December 7. The number of French pilots had grown steadily from Raymonde's No. 36 nine months earlier. By 1910, the Aero Club of France ruled that aviators without a brevet, or one from the proper agency in a foreign country, were prohibited from entering aviation meets organized by the club. The carefree days of early flying were fast disappearing.

With confidence gained from her pilot's license, Laroche flew in meets around Europe during the spring. In St. Petersburg she was congratulated by Czar Nicholas II. Writing about her appearance there, Raymonde described the aviation ground as small, less than thirty meters wide, which made all the fliers hesitant to fly. Once she was up, she discovered that smoke from surrounding chimneys poured skyward, causing uncertain shifts in air currents and poor visibility. Mounting higher, she flew over houses and forests until she was about a hundred meters high. Circling in four broad turns, she turned off her motor and volplaned (glided) down. To her surprise, "nothing broke." The czar was much impressed by her performance, although Raymonde admitted her heart was in her mouth. Following her Russian appearance, where she was presented as la Baronne de Laroche, the title was used habitually in the press. There were hints that Czar Nicholas had "entitled" her, but Raymonde was using the title before her visit. It was good for publicity and set her apart in a title-conscious society.

Budapest followed St. Petersburg on the spring tour. Here, again, chimneys acting like pylons on the flying field belched smoke into the air, causing dangerous currents. She won first place in a consolation prize; there were no takers for a cross-country flight of 110 kilometers. The memory of Budapest's hazardous air currents haunted the Baronne until she flew at Rouen, which she discovered was even worse for dangerous currents. Feeling her Voisin caught in a tempest, she immediately started down and landed head-on; the machine upended, into the fence enclosing the aerodrome. Commenting later, Raymonde was thankful she had the wits to keep the motor running. Otherwise, the biplane would have fallen on the crowd. Happenings like these made flying an ongoing learning experience.

The Seconde Grande Semaine at Rheims, in July 1910, brought the flying world together again in hopes of repeating the success of the 1909 meeting. Raymonde, the only representative of her sex, would fly along with Hubert Latham; Jan Lindpaintner; Etienne Buneau-Varilla; Charles Weymann, the American; and other established pilots. On opening day the press wondered if these professionals of the infant aviation world would prevent the emergence of new stars in the short time since the previous year's first international meet.

Raymonde flew for short periods each day, to applause from the grandstand. The number of aeroplanes flying at one time was sometimes as many as thirty, a large number for the small area of the field. On July 4 an unusual series of mishaps occurred. Two aviators collided, followed almost immediately by the collapse of three or four machines, as if, according to the London *Times,* "they had been poisoned." While the wounded machines lay on the ground in disarray, fresh machines flew over them on their way up. Despite the sharp-eyed vigilance of the Aero Club officials, congestion was a critical factor. Penalties were assigned for infractions of the rules, and the press called for a limit to the number of machines that could safely fly at one time. Raymonde was fined twenty francs for not observing the rule of the road; Jan Olieslagers, one hundred francs for passing too near another flier. Flying over the heads of spectators was forbidden.

On the sixth day of the meet, dressed in her distinctive white sweater, white hood, and gray divided skirt, Raymonde took to the air for the five thousand–franc ladies' prize, for which she was the lone competitor. Passing in front of the grandstand, where the convivial crowds cheered her loudly, her machine was pitching uneasily in a seven- to eleven-mile-an-hour wind. On the second lap she rose high and wide as she rounded the pylon at the far end of the field, some nine hundred yards from the grandstand, leading a field that included Lindpaintner, Bartolomeo Cattaneo, and Latham. What happened next depends on the viewer reporting.

Suddenly, Raymonde's machine was seen to dip earthward and hit the ground with terrific force. According to one account, she was rattled when another aeroplane cut across her in the turn; the Voisin shuddered and swerved, side-slipped, and hit the ground. Another version blamed the draft from a machine that passed over her, causing her to turn off her ignition. Her machine glided briefly, then fell "like a meteorite" two hundred feet to the ground, shattering on impact. Another reporter wrote that two aeroplanes swung out to pass her, one on each side, without realizing the effect on the Voisin's pilot. Startled, she either pulled the wrong lever or let go of both levers, causing the elevation planes to tilt downward and the machine to plunge to earth out of control. The correspondent for the London *Times* observed the scene through strong glasses and reported that following Raymonde's exceptionally wide turn more than one machine was taking the turn closer than she had. She apparently started to come down from two hundred feet in a gentle slope that changed suddenly "to a sharp dive, and she shot down the last 150 feet at an angle of 60 degrees." The crowds shrieked in terror, women fainted, and scores of men rushed to the wreckage, where the bloodied pilot lay beside her machine. Lindpaintner, who had flown his Sommer biplane near her, was nearly lynched by angry Voisin men on landing, but an investigation by a committee of judges cleared him of wrongdoing.

On regaining consciousness, the severely injured baroness blamed the backwash from an aeroplane that cut in front of her for bringing her machine down. In her woozy state, she was more incensed that the aviator had not been punished for flying close to her than worried about her own condition. First reports indicated she had multiple fractures of the arms and legs and possible internal injuries. One Paris newspaper had her fatally injured, but most of the press focused on the terrible wreck and their wishes for her recovery. Her fall in January was retold with hints that bad luck was pursuing her, that she had lost her coolheadedness. More measured accounts pointed out the danger of crowding at air meets, especially "inconsiderate driving," which was blamed for other recent accidents by a competitor's backdraft.

The shock of the accident led *Le Monde* to contact Raymonde's parents and reveal that she had a son, André, a boy of seven, who lived with his grandparents. Raymonde's mother, who was stricken by the news, said the boy was the spitting image of his mother, whom he worshiped. In fact, the child had gone to Rheims with his godmother to watch the meet. This one mention of a son is the only one in all the articles about his mother, showing that it was still possible in 1910 for famous people to have a private life shielded from public scrutiny.

The crash triggered critical comments from aviation writers, who pointed to it as proof that in an emergency women were not suited to fly. Their training usually kept them circling a course free of other machines without permitting them to gain the kind of experience that competition flying demanded. Exhibition flying was a different matter; there was no competitive hustle in the air. It was polite and ladylike, not in the same category as competition.

André Beaumont, who flew as Lieutenant Jean Conneau, described in his 1912 memoir the qualities needed in an aviator: a grown man (too young or too old was not desirable), alertness, strength, sturdiness, good health, and, above all, endurance. He then went on to say: "Such qualities are not often to be found in women, and it is a pity, for the few bold 'aviatresses' who are regular visitors to the aerodromes bring with them a charm and brightness not to be despised; and we men are always ready to applaud their womanly bravery, for though we may be man-birds we remain none the less men." His comments, meant to be supportive, had a patronizing tone that the ladies did not miss.

In the aftermath of the crash, long months of recuperation followed surgery, but Raymonde's tenacity and the caring support of Charles Voisin helped her recover. She had lost none of her love for flying. By 1912 she was in the air again, showing more confidence and better judgment. Her white sweater and pulled-down cap were a common sight on the airfield at Châlons as she prepared to compete for the Coupe Fémina, established for women in 1910. Thanks to Pierre Lafitte, owner of the magazine of the same name, a prize of two thousand francs, designed to encourage women in aviation, would be awarded to the woman who flew the longest distance alone, without a stop, before sunset of December 31 of that year. Raymonde, showing her old vitality, would give it a try.

In the meantime, she went to court in April to obtain redress from a company, Office d'Aviation, for breach of contract, contending that the company was to furnish her an aeroplane and book engagements for her, none of which happened. The Commercial Tribunal found for the company, declaring the contract did not specify an aeroplane for her use, nor could the company be held responsible for not securing engagements. Furthermore, Raymonde had gone to two meets, in Tours and St. Petersburg, without the company's authorization. She was ordered to pay eight thousand francs in damages. On Raymonde's appeal of the judgment, the Fourth Chamber found in her favor and ordered the Office d'Aviation to pay her ten thousand francs. No doubt, Raymonde needed money; she had earned nothing in 1911.

On September 25, tragedy struck again. Charles and Raymonde were driving near Belleville-sur-Saone, not far from Lyons, on the way to visit his parents, when their automobile collided with another vehicle at a crossroads. Charles was killed instantly, and Raymonde was "desperately injured." The aviation world mourned the loss of one of France's foremost aeroplane builders and pilots; the irony of his death on the ground was not lost on the public, nor on his brother, Gabriel, who lost the courageous half of their partnership.

Raymonde was devastated. Once again she faced weeks of recuperation, but her indomitable spirit, though saddened, wouldn't quit. A letter written November 19 to her friend Jacques Mortane revealed that she was learning to fly a Sommer biplane at Mourmelon, outside of Paris and if all went well she would try for the Coupe Fémina. She admitted to sadness, but, happily, aviation helped her forget the pain, the feeling of being alone, that was especially bad at night.

By the end of November, the aviation journals reported that she was making good progress on the Sommer aeroplane. The move from the Voisin camp was probably due to Gabriel's refusal to extend the company's courtesy to her after Charles's death. It meant learning the idiosyncracies of another machine, also a biplane, almost as if it were the first. Observers reported that she was flying the machine with complete assurance in flights of fifteen to twenty minutes, but not competitive for the Coupe. Still, the *femme-oiseau* was spreading her wings again.

By the next spring, Raymonde had changed aeroplanes again. This time she was learning to fly a Farman biplane at the school near Buc. This machine was more compatible; it was dependable and stable. By the end of May she was making flights of over an hour in the country around Buc. In June she was slightly injured in another car crash when an automobile driven by M. Vial collided with a van. It didn't slow her down. She took a joyride as a passenger in a Farman military machine, and with Vial gave an exhibition at Granville using a Farman hydroaeroplane. Her confidence showed in her handling of the machine and her ability to bring it down perfectly in limited space on the beach.

By late October, la Baronne was flying at Mourmelon preparing for the Coupe Fémina competition on an eighty-horsepower Farman. The duration of her flights was lengthening to one and a half hours. On November 29, she took the lead for the Coupe with a flight of 323.5 kilometers in four hours. She stopped then only because of a gas-line problem. At the year's end, none of the competing women fliers had bettered her record. The Coupe Fémina was hers. Like the phoenix, Raymonde had risen again, despite grief and physical problems.

The First World War put an end to civilian flying in 1914. Raymonde, like other women pilots, offered her services to her country but was refused. She could drive an automobile, taking officers of rank from the rear zones to the front, exposed to artillery and shells, yet government officials considered this safer than piloting an aeroplane.

When the war ended after four terrible years, France's first woman pilot took to the air again, intrigued by the developments in aeroplanes.

Sleeker machines were powered by engines capable of speeding through the skies at 120 to 150 miles per hour. There was new interest in aviation; an anticipated increase in aeroplane production would require more test pilots. Raymonde envisioned a new career for herself.

On June 7 at Issy-les-Moulineaux, flying a new Caudron G3, she broke the women's altitude record at 3,900 meters. Three days later, the American flier Ruth Law captured the record with a height of 4,270 meters. On June 12, her competitive spirit in high gear, Raymonde soared to 4,800 meters and another record. The French press hailed her as "la femme la plus haute du monde." For the moment, she was.

Shortly after, she visited Le Crotoy airport to look over some of the new models. M. Barrault, a test pilot, recognized her and invited her to come along while he tried a machine with new features. Raymonde was strapped into the rear cockpit, the pilot was up front, and very quickly the powerful machine was in the air. It climbed quickly, its operation vastly different from the prewar models she knew, and the ground below was reduced to miniature size. The pilot turned and headed back toward the field, the aeroplane moving gracefully. As it lowered for a landing, it was seen to swerve to one side, lose speed, and go into a spinning dive before crashing heavily. The first people to reach the wreckage found la Baronne dead; the pilot died on the way to the hospital.

The ground crew shook their heads. She died doing what she loved, but it was a tragic waste. Raymonde, who believed that "what will be, will be," whose life was a pattern of success and tragedy at a time when records came and went daily, knew one title was securely hers for all time—world's first woman aeroplane pilot.

HÉLÈNE DUTRIEU

Belgian-born Hélène Dutrieu should have been France's second licensed woman pilot, but a dispute about her tests and more than a little national chauvinism interfered. She belonged to that extraordinary group of talented women who were flying in France before the end of 1910.

Born in Tournai, Belgium, July 10, 1877, to Florent Dutrieu and his wife, Clothilde van Thieghem, her early years were comfortable as the daughter of a former artillery officer in the Belgian army. The good fairy in attendance at her birth had smiled on the baby and predicted she would do great things. By the time Dutrieu was approaching young womanhood, that prediction seemed to have gone off course as the family's finances took a turn for the worse. Hélène would have to earn a living to contribute to the family purse.

At that time the customary work for Belgian women was lace making and embroidery, but neither skill interested her. Instead, she took a cycle course and was soon riding alone or in tandem with her brother through the countryside near Tournai. A diminutive, compact figure, almost elfin, her movements were well coordinated and capable of strength and speed not apparent in such a small figure. The hours spent cycling in these early years were good training for a career that would bring her fame.

In 1895 and again in 1897, Hélène won the Belgian cycling hour record (distance covered in one hour on a bicycle); she won the world speed record for women in 1897 and 1898 at Ostende, capped off by the Grand Prix d'Europe, riding from Paris to London in twelve days. That same year, Léopold of Belgium recognized her achievements with the Cross of St. André with diamonds. With these successes, Paris—the hub of entertainment, excitement, and fame—beckoned.

Hélène was soon established as a comedian in the theater, where her spectacular feats on a bicycle and motorcycle were a sensation. Her looping the loop attracted hundreds of viewers. Billed as "the human arrow," an act that proved electrifying, she defied catastrophe. Riding a motorcycle at full speed, Hélène launched herself from an inclined plane through the air. When this lost public interest, she took up the automobile, performing the same act in an automobile to enthusiastic crowds in many of the larger towns in Europe. Accidents and explosions were routine as her fearlessness led her to perform ever more sensational acts.

In Berlin, while performing as "the human arrow," the auto fell on her, and she spent the next six months in a hospital recovering from multiple injuries. Lying quiet for long periods, Hélène had time to think; had she used up her ordained number of lives? She recalled later that this was when the idea of flying first occurred to her. Watching Wilbur Wright's performance in 1908, she was inspired to become a pilot.

Her decision coincided with developments in French aviation. The Clément-Bayard Company was building another Santos-Dumont aeroplane, the Demoiselle, and needed a lightweight pilot to manage the fragile machine. A woman would be just right, and would be good publicity for the machine, considering its feminine name. Hélène, whom Clément-Bayard had met earlier, filled the order, and the young performer signed a contract in mid-1908 with the company for two thousand francs a month, which included an automobile, mechanics, and all hotel expenses.

In the fall of 1908 and early 1909, she was making test flights on the *Demoiselle* at Issy-les-Moulineaux. *L'Intransigeant,* a journal of the period, wrote that her "guileless eyes and timid voice" suited a young convent girl rather than a budding pilot of thirty-one years. The lightweight, unstable *Demoiselle* made for uncertain, demanding work, calling for all the skills Hélène had developed on cycles. Neither the designer, Santos-Dumont, nor the builder, Clément-Bayard, provided instructions for handling the aeroplane. The day before her first flight, a mechanic advised her to push the *manche* (literally "handle") forward to come down, and to pull back to go up. That was all she needed to know. He forgot to mention the warping belt that fitted over the shoulders to raise or lower the wings.

Armed with this advice, the petite pilot climbed into her seat, determined not to show her uncertainty before the curious onlookers, and started the motor. She concentrated hard on getting up, and the machine responded marvelously, except for one wing, which drooped and made straightening out impossible. She tried to look behind to see what was wrong; perhaps she should go down a bit and push up again to correct the machine. She pushed the stick forward a little and, to her surprise, landed abruptly in a marshy area. The machine was destroyed, but, miraculously, the mud absorbed much of the shock and the pilot was unhurt.

Made wiser by this experience, Hélène was determined to manage the aeroplane, but its fragility caused it to blow here and there with passing currents like a paper toy. In spite of numerous experiments—Hélène was game to try anything—the result was splintered wood, fractures, and contusions. Finally she had had enough; she canceled her contract.

She wrote to Roger Sommer, who was building a biplane at Mouzon in the Ardennes. Convinced by the eager pilot of her ability, Sommer signed a contract with her. Before her first flight, he instructed her briefly on his aeroplane, a heavier and larger machine than the *Demoiselle*. Takeoff was fine. The aeroplane rose in the air, a much more stable apparatus than the *Demoiselle,* and Hélène had a good view of the surrounding landscape, with the Meuse River straight ahead. She reacted immediately; she did not want to fly over it. She would have to turn, something she didn't want to do quite so soon. Gripping the controls—there was little time—she turned, successfully, and headed back over the landscape where she had gone up. Sommer and a few spectators below were gesturing to her, but the dubious pilot was hesitant to land. As she explained years later, it was easier to keep flying than to land. Hélène flew for twenty minutes, a women's record for the time, before deciding she had no choice. Luckily, the dreaded landing was perfect. The journals hailed her April 9 flight, but Hélène knew she had much to learn. Ten days later, she carried a passenger for the first time, another first for women, a claim made by several other French women pilots.

Her career was progressing nicely; Hélène, at last, was satisfying her *"terrible soif de voler"* (terrible thirst to fly). The following month she took part in an air meet at Odessa with Sommers. All went well until one day, coming down to a lower altitude at the end of a flight, she clipped the chimney of a house. In the next instant, she found herself on the ground, the aeroplane smashed. Sommer canceled her contract, convinced that she would never be a pilot.

Back in France again, the unhappy flier turned to Dick Farman, brother of Henry, who knew her from her cycling days. He agreed to the loan of an aeroplane, but without a motor, because the motor was equal to the cost of a machine and then some. Unperturbed, Hélène next went to Louis Seguin, the director of Gnome, manufacturer of the best motor available in France. She got her motor.

One of the hardships of early flying was exposure to motor oil, particularly with the motor up front. Castor oil, smelly and reminiscent of childhood sickness, was the oil of choice for the Gnome and most motors of the period because it was light. Hélène once said the combination of smelly oil—often pilots were spattered with it—and bobbing machine caused bouts of nausea until she got used to it.

The Farmans made one demand: Hélène must get her pilot's license, her brevet. Working with the Farmans was the wisest career decision Hélène made. Henry Farman was interested in building machines that would expand the primitive aviation technology. With Dutrieu he had a pilot as interested in the improvement of flying machines as in making a name for herself.

Belgian-born Hélène Dutrieu learning the ropes from Henry Farman on a Farman plane in France. MUSÉE DE L'AIR ET DE L'ESPACE, LE BOURGET

Writing in 1910 about his aeroplane, Farman explained that the machine's ailerons maintained lateral stability. A single lever controlled movements: forward to go down; back to go up. If the machine leaned to the left, move the lever to the right, and vice versa. The aeroplane was a marvel of simplicity, very practical for training fliers; Farman concluded that pupils required fewer lessons to learn to fly it because "the essential movements are instinctive."

Accordingly, Hélène practiced the required skills and on August 23, 1910, took her test. Because of confusion among the officials, she was asked to redo the test, but a scheduled appearance in Belgium made that impossible. It would be three months before she received French Aero Club recognition.

At Blankenberge, on the coast of Belgium, the first three days of the exhibition were a washout, with heavy rain and wind so strong that Hélène at times feared for her Farman biplane in the shaking hangar. On the fourth day, the ire of the customers and the promoters of the exhibition, who had no appreciation of the influence of weather on flying, had reached a climax. Late in the afternoon, Hélène's young mechanic, Beau, came running with news—the weather was great! She should take off at once, before officials declared she didn't know how to fly. That did it; the machine was rolled out. Beau, who was crazy about flying, begged to accompany her, and at 6:30 they were off, the brave Beau seated behind the pilot.

Years later, the elderly Hélène remarked, "It was a great imprudence" to carry two people on that machine, but, obviously, she never regretted it. As soon as they gained altitude and circled for the excited crowds below, Beau suggested it would be more interesting to fly across the countryside than the sea. Hélène was thinking in terms of a short flight, but Beau shouted encouragement to go on, pointing out the sights below. Ostende passed quickly, then Bruges appeared, as an excited Beau called out, "There is the belfry!" The marvelous spire of the cathedral reached to the sky as the biplane with its two passengers made a grand circle of it.

Hélène confided much later that if she had been alone in the aeroplane, she might have come undone at that point, realizing where she was and what she had done. But because of Beau, she felt something like a mother's need to protect her child, and she gathered her strength for the return to Blankenberge as day turned to night. In the gathering dusk it was a great relief to see the lights of the town; they weren't lost. For the first time in Hélène's experience, lights along the edge of the sea guided her to land, where fifty arms waited to help her from her aeroplane and carry her in triumph to her hotel.

The flight with Beau had chalked up a remarkable number of "firsts":
- first Belgian woman aeroplane pilot
- first woman in the world to make a cross-country flight
- first flight by a woman to go and return nonstop
- first woman to carry a passenger cross-country
- official record for altitude, four hundred meters
- official record for duration, thirty-five to forty minutes
- official record for distance, forty-five kilometers

Following this performance, the Aero Club of Belgium awarded her her pilot's brevet, No. 27. Hélène was hailed the next day by the international press for her extraordinary flight carrying Beau, who, she always said, gave her the courage to accomplish it.

Feeling more secure with each flight, Hélène made appearances at several meets in England, probably arranged for her by Henry Farman, whose machines were appearing throughout Europe. At Folkestone, Burton-on-Trent, and Doncaster, she made successful flights, sometimes with a passenger, when the weather permitted. At Burton she carried a passenger over the town to the delight and cheers of fourteen thousand people assembled in Bass's meadows, a performance hailed by the English press as the "first woman's flight with passenger." The press loved articles hailing "firsts." *Le Petit Journal* had it right when it observed: "Les aéroplanes montent et les records tombent." ("The aeroplanes go up and the records fall.") Back on the continent, Hélène appeared in Holland and Belgium, flying at Liége, Anvers, Braisne-le-Comte, and Menin with one or two passengers.

In England, Hélène's flights over towns raised concern in aviation circles. A notice in the *Daily Mail* stated that the Aero Club of England would penalize its members, or certified pilots, for flights over towns or populated areas because of the "present state of the science of aviation." The club reasoned that such flights did not contribute to the development of aviation and could be hazardous to the public.

Finally, in November, the Aero Club of France, recognizing Hélène's proven ability, issued her a pilot's license. The administrative debate was resolved; on November 25 she received license No. 27, the number given to her earlier by the Belgian Aero Club. Marthe Niel had won a license August 29, the second French woman to do so; Marie Marvingt was brevetted on November 8; and Jeanne Herveux would follow Hélène with a license on December 7. They were competent fliers and very competitive.

In December, the newly brevetted pilot resolved to try for the recently established Coupe Fémina. On the 22nd, taking off from Étampes in midafternoon after last-minute advice from Farman, Hélène circled the airfield in a steady wind, showing remarkable skill in handling her aeroplane. The distance tabulated by Aero Club representatives was 60.8 kilometers flown in one hour and nine minutes. (The reporting on early fliers in the press was far from accurate. Distance and time often differed from the official records, and a "new record" was a familiar claim when flights lengthened almost daily.) Marie Marvingt was second to Hélène, with a distance of forty-two kilometers, flown in fifty-three minutes. Because her flight was made first, Marvingt mistakenly claimed she won the Coupe. Not so.

In 1911, Hélène did not rest on her records. Most of the year was spent in competitions and appearances, and the press began to refer to her as *la femme épervier,* "the female sparrow hawk." In May she competed at Florence in the speed race for the King of Italy Cup against fourteen men, including Emile Védrines, Maurice Tabuteau, Eugène Renaux, and Romulo Manissero, and won. Other meets found her in Spain, Belgium, and France.

Flying at Le Mans in August, Hélène had a rare mishap. The day had gone well for all attending the meet, until near the end, when Charles Weymann's machine, after winning a speed race, suddenly fell to the ground. Shortly after, Hélène took off in her Farman biplane with Léon Bollée, president of the Aero Club of the Sarthe. Newspaper accounts reported that as the aeroplane flew in front of the grandstand, one wing struck a post, and in the next instant, the machine toppled over, shattering into pieces among some of the spectators. Fortunately, both pilot and passenger jumped free without injury, but three spectators hit by flying debris were taken by ambulance to the hospital. Never mind the injured spectators, and the near miss for the pilot and her passenger—the gossip papers seized on the fact that Hélène was not wearing a corset when she crashed. She explained that a corset is confining, and she needed freedom of movement when flying. Among the old biddies all the talk was of "the scandal," another shocking display by the day's young women. Hélène was not making a feminist statement; her concern was comfort.

In September an enthusiastic American public gathered at Nassau Boulevard at Mineola, Long Island, and cheered the French visitor in her first visit to America. She planned to compete against Harriet Quimby, the first American woman to receive a pilot's license, in a cross-country flight but lost by default because her machine was not ready. On Sunday, September 24 a record crowd surged through the gates at Nassau Boulevard to watch the assembled aviators compete, probably because of the dispute about Sunday flying. Cash prizes were forbidden on order of Sheriff Charles Mott in response to pressure from the Episcopal bishop of Long Island, but the aviators were spirited in their performances, and the press hinted that they expected to receive their awards in an indirect way.

The most important event of the day for the women in the audience was the contest for the Rodman Wanamaker Trophy, offered for the highest altitude flown by a woman. Matilde Moisant, the second American licensed pilot, dressed in a gray sweater and a leather helmet, was the uncontested winner of the trophy, flying a Blériot-type monoplane built by the Moisant Company. Rising in wide circles, she reached a height of twelve hundred feet and remained there for half an hour before coming down. Harriet Quimby and Hélène Dutrieu were grounded, waiting for their machines to be readied.

Hélène used the afternoon to familiarize herself with the field and the countryside nearby. The press noted that she was dressed in a light-brown divided skirt, especially adapted for flying while seated on the lower wing of a biplane facing into the wind. The petite pilot was pleased with the flying field, the best she had seen, commenting for the *New York Herald* that it was "like a billiard table, so smooth, so fine."

The following day, the French visitor again failed to fly. Her Farman was rolled out, but reports in the press indicated she was unhappy because the two thousand–dollar guarantee she had received from the meet organizers precluded winning prizes. Hélène thought that was expense money for travel. The management announced all women's events were postponed until the next day, because of the weather. Finally, dressed in a "chic brown khaki costume"—another newsman thought her suit was

After a three-day delay, Dutrieu was finally ready to fly her Farman at the Nassau meet on Long Island, September 1911. CRADLE OF AVIATION MUSEUM, GARDEN CITY, NEW YORK

a "drab brown" that couldn't compare with Harriet Quimby's plum-colored satin—the Farman ready, Hélène broke the U.S. duration record for women, thrilling the crowds with a thirty-seven-minute, twenty-two-second flight in a steady wind. According to the *New York American,* it was the most popular event of the day. Spectators had a good look at the pilot, seated on what looked like two skids jutting out from the machine, as she circled regularly, working her machine.

She was interviewed by the press, who were fascinated by her jewelry. Ashby Deering of the *Morning Telegraph* wrote that Dutrieu was vastly superior to "the feminine locust native to this continent," a reference to Harriet Quimby and Matilde Moisant. Hélène stated that she was not a feminist, but she believed women should not remain inferior because of their sex. Admitting that she found men "all very interesting" as aviators, and that they had steadier nerves and a firmer grip, she added that women had a finesse, an inborn tact, and a sense of the fitness of things that "men lack utterly—some men that is." Earlier, when questioned by French reporters on women in aviation, Hélène did not hesitate to say that women could fly as competently as men without losing the grace usually associated with females.

Besides a recalcitrant engine, there were other problems for the visitor. Dick Farman had arranged her contract in France, which guaranteed her two thousand dollars for her appearance, but, unbeknownst to her, she was not eligible for cash prizes unless she won more than her guarantee—an impossible feat. The management did not pay expenses, another unhappy surprise. Hélène's discontent was shared by others at the meet. American aviators claimed there was a bias favoring foreign visitors and that decisions were changed in their favor. Certainly, Claude Grahame-White and T.O.M. Sopwith garnered most of the prizes, but it may have been a reflection of the greater speed of foreign aeroplanes. Harriet Quimby departed for an appearance at the Trenton Inter-State Fair in New Jersey, since the majority of events were for men. As a result, the anticipated competition between four women pilots never materialized. At the meet's end, the tally of women's prizes was meager (Quimby, six hundred dollars; Dutrieu, five hundred dollars), in contrast with the winnings of male stars such as Grahame-White (forty-two hundred dollars) and Sopwith (forty-eight hundred dollars). The women's prizes were about what one would expect for a meet whose advertising featured male stars and women's events as curiosities.

Home in France again, Hélène capped her success of the previous year by winning the Coupe Fémina in December, extending her distance to 254.8 kilometers in two hours and fifty-eight minutes, to beat her nearest competitor, Jeanne Herveux. Each time she tried for the Coupe, Henry Farman was present with advice. Before she left for the United States, her first try resulted in a flight of 230 kilometers in two hours and forty-five minutes. Another record. Farman was on the ground giving encouragement as Hélène flew in a strong wind that reduced speed from 100 to an average of 84 kilometers per hour. A clattering screw in the engine did not bode well, and the wind's strength made the pilot apprehensive for her machine. Prudence counseled her to land, but there would be no record, and she flew on. At last, with a great sigh of relief, she saw Farman's signal from the ground—she had broken both distance and duration records for women; she could land.

In 1912 honors rained on Hélène. She received the Médaille d'Or from the Aero Club of France; the Grande Plaque of the Belgian Aero

Club, presented by King Albert I; and later in the year the Médaille de l'Aviation from the Sorbonne. Not content to rest on her honors, by summer Hélène was busy testing a hydro-aeroplane that Farman had built for her. The pilot was as interested in developing this new machine as Farman was. Tests were made at Lake Enghien with Farman handling the machine first and Hélène as passenger before she took over the controls. The new aeroplane required getting used to, and, as always, a new motor could be difficult. One day in a flight from Geneva to Lausanne, the motor suddenly stopped. Hélène was thrown from her seat as the machine dropped and floated in the water like so much flotsam. Hélène was none the worse for the adventure—a motorboat soon picked her up—but the machine had to be rebuilt.

Earlier that summer, she had experienced another near miss when she misjudged distance on landing. Dropping down rapidly to the ground, she smashed into two monoplanes parked ahead. All three machines were badly smashed, but Hélène was only slightly injured.

In September, the pilot was traveling by automobile from Roanne to Lapalisse when her vehicle crashed trying to avoid a farmer's cart. The driver swerved to the right, but the speed of the auto propelled it into a tree. The driver had leaped from the car an instant before the crash, but Hélène was seriously injured, the farmer slightly so. The aviatrix was taken to the hospital in Lapalisse. It was déjà vu all over again; she spent weeks recuperating.

The French government, realizing her place in aviation and her role in demonstrating French technology abroad, announced early in 1913 that she would be named a chevalier of the Legion of Honor. She would wear the red ribbon, the first woman aviator ever! Reportedly, President Raymond Poincaré protested that she was too young for such an honor, but several prominent women convinced him it was appropriate. It was pointed out to him that "women pilots hardly have time to grow old."

The *New York Times* acknowledged her distinction in aviation, noting that of all the women flying, "she is the only one who has kept pace with the leading aviators, and in many instances surpassed them in her achievements." It was a grand exit line.

The year 1913 was a quiet one for Hélène. There is no mention of activities in the air. Perhaps she was having second thoughts about how many lives she had. A year later the increasing tension in Europe curbed

A beaming Dutrieu learns in 1913 that she will be named a Chevalier of the Legion of Honor by the French government for her accomplishments. She was the first woman aviator to receive this prestigious award. LA VIE AU GRAND AIR.

civilian flying, and once the war began, flying ended. Hélène drove Red Cross ambulances to the front, where she helped run a surgical hospital for the wounded. She was reported to have taken part in the aerial defense of Paris against zeppelin attacks, but there is no verification of this. She never mentioned it, and her friends knew nothing of such activity. We do know that the military, generally, opposed allowing women in the air in wartime.

In 1915, Hélène returned to America under the auspices of the French Red Cross to promote American aid. She stayed for a month in New York City, living at the Knickerbocker Hotel and lecturing to interested groups. By all accounts, she was "an excellent propagandist." New York City press reports credited her with making unofficial flights to warn Paris of the Germans' approach. The articles made exciting reading but weren't based on fact. Hélène organized ambulance work and served as director of a military hospital in the later war years.

When peace finally came, like many of the early pioneer fliers, Hélène realized that technology had progressed beyond her former expertise. It would take time and money to learn new skills, and there were already too many aviators just when the demand for them had ended. Hélène became engaged, and the responsibilities of marriage to Pierre Mortier, a member of the French Assembly and a publisher, overshadowed aviation. For many years, Hélène took an active role in her husband's publishing business and public-health concerns.

In 1955, she received the insignia of the Légion d'Honneur, witnessed by Henry Farman and Gabriel Voisin, of the Aero Club of France. Her continued interest in aviation led her to establish the Coupe Franco-Belge Hélène Dutrieu-Mortier to promote interest in aviation among women. The rules set the competition, from January 1 to December 31 of each year, for the longest flight, touching down in three designated airports of the countries involved, by a licensed private pilot. The machine had to be a certain size with standard equipment, all properly inspected; the stops at the three airports had to meet certain conditions; and the pilot had to fly alone (this had to be verified on stopping). The first prize was ten thousand francs; second prize was four thousand francs. It was a gallant offer to a new generation of women.

This remarkable woman died on June 27, 1961, at her home in Paris. A. Van Hoorebeeck, the aviation journalist, observed: *"Elle a rejoint le Paradis des Pionniers."*

MARIE MARVINGT

A legendary figure almost from birth, Marie Marvingt puts most of us to shame with her lifetime of achievements. "Wonder Woman" is perhaps an apt description for someone who tried almost everything in the worlds of sports, aeronautics, the sciences, and literature, and did each one well.

Marie Félicie Elisabeth Marvingt was born in Aurillac in the Cantal on February 20, 1875. Her parents, Felix Marvingt and Elisabeth Brusquin, had met and married in Metz in 1861 before the German annexation of that region in the Franco-Prussian War sent them fleeing to Aurillac, where Felix was in charge of the local post office.

Felix and Elisabeth's marriage was a happy one, despite the deaths of three infant sons before Marie was born. It was a hopeful sign when the new baby cried with energy and thrived. Three years later, another son, Eugène, was born, a baby delicate from birth. Marie at three years was the constant companion of her father, who enjoyed sports of all kinds, and who delighted in the child's enthusiastic response to his instructions.

He began teaching her how to swim, and shortly she moved like a little fish in the water. By the time she was four, reportedly, she could swim four kilometers. Felix was overjoyed.

In 1880 the family moved back to Metz to be near Elisabeth's family; Felix took his place again with the PTT (Post, Telegraph, and Telephone). The Germans still occupied the city, and business and education were conducted in German. Marie learned a new language when she started school with the sisters of Sainte-Chrétienne de Saint-Vincent, but, a rebel at heart, she answered class questions to herself and voiced her inner thoughts in French.

The Moselle River was a place of enchantment for swimming, canoeing, and walking its length, none of which Eugène could do with his sister. She was loving toward him and amused him with stories, hoping that one day he could join her. Felix, resigned to the boy's condition, concerned himself even more with Marie's education. He recognized early on her unusual ability and spirit, so unlike that of the fragile female in need of protection, which was the contemporary attitude. Elisabeth, worried that her daughter was being pushed into activities too masculine, was partly mollified when Marie started school with the sisters, but as Marie observed years later, it isn't easy to change the leopard's spots. She remained an active, daredevil performer who accompanied her father in swimming, hiking, and mountain climbing while Eugène stayed with mother, who, like her son, was delicate.

When Marie was fourteen, her mother died after a period of debilitating illness, during which Marie had taken over much of the activity of running a household, hoping this would restore her mother. But it was not to be. Felix, overcome by his loss, retired and moved the family to Nancy, where they settled into the top-floor apartment at 8 place de la Carrière. Nancy was a delight to Marie; she became a thorough Nancéienne and remained one all her life. On a free day, she enjoyed strolling through the Place Stanislas, watching the well-dressed taking the afternoon air, followed by tea at the café in the Place Thiers.

At home, Marie assumed the role of housekeeper with all its responsibilities, a demanding task on top of her schooling. Reading became her refuge; she devoured books on exploration and science that explained the world outside. At school, she entertained and delighted her classmates with her spirited antics, such as taking over the control of one of the new locomotives running between Metz and Nancy as it pulled into the stop where her classmates waited to board. The good sisters, who liked docile young girls, were less than pleased.

When the Circus Rancy came to Nancy, Marie begged her father to be allowed to go, eager to learn how to vault into a net like the performers. Ever a loving father, Felix agreed, and Marie, age fifteen, learned gymnastics like a circus performer. She had the body, the agility, and the required discipline. Reportedly, Alphonse Rancy, the celebrated horseman and circus owner, gave Marie her training, including lessons in *la haute école,* the complicated horse maneuvers performed without any visible or audible command from a rider. At one unannounced performance, Marie astonished the spectators by doing a vault at a gallop, the first feat of its kind.

In 1897, Eugène died. It was not a shock, but it was a loss for father and sister, both of whom loved the gentle young man with the ready smile. Marie apparently made up her mind that she would pursue a life of sports; marriage, with its incumbent housework, was not for her. She had had enough of that!

Marie's decision was opportune. The newly organized Olympic Games were strictly for men, but the efforts of Marie and women like her gradually opened the door for feminine sports in the new world evolving in the twentieth century. During 1908–10, Marie dominated winter sports, winning prizes in skiing, ice-skating, luge, and bobsledding. Earlier she had opened the first civilian ski school. Cycling, equally a passion among males and females, had helped pry the door open for women in competition.

In 1899, already an experienced cyclist, Marie learned to drive an automobile and won her license. She was off! The list of her achievements began to grow as she took up tennis, golf, polo, jujitsu, boxing (she was photographed hitting a punching bag), and shooting (she was honored by the minister of war for her prize work). In 1905, she canoed from Nancy to Koblenz, traveling the Meurthe and Moselle Rivers. There was nothing she would not try and usually do well at. She loved to compete, she loved public recognition, and she was an excellent promoter.

In July 1906, fifteen professional swimmers took part in a swim in the Seine River around Paris, among them an Australian, Annette Kellermann, who placed third. Two weeks later, among a group of amateurs sponsored by a French society to encourage swimming, Marie swam the same course and placed fifth, with a time of four hours, eleven minutes, and twenty-three seconds, which beat Kellermann's record by one hour and ten minutes. She was hailed as France's best woman swimmer and secured that title the following year at Toulouse, where she won first prize, swimming twenty kilometers in the sea.

In between, she found time to ice-skate, ski, bobsled, and fence. Earlier, she had started mountain climbing, a sport usually pursued by men, which won her much attention. She was the first woman to scale the Dent du Géant, which only two men had done before her, and she followed up with ascents of Mont Blanc and Trélaporte. In 1908 she took part in the Tour de France, cycling 4,488 kilometers to finish the grueling course as 1 of the 36 athletes out of the 114 who started. It was the high point of her cycling career, but she made other trips—Paris to Strasbourg, Paris to Marseilles—and would continue to ride a bicycle even as a very old woman, when, a month shy of eighty-six, she bicycled to Paris from Nancy during January's cold weather and was hailed along the way for her performance. At dinnertime on that trip, she would pick the best restaurant in the area, wait to be recognized by the maître d'hôtel, then seat herself at a good table, where she held court to customers wanting her autograph. Naturally, there was no bill. Marie expected royal treatment, and she got it.

In 1907, an international ski competition at Chamonix did not have one woman; the next year, nine women, including Marie, finished a course of three kilometers. Two years later many ski competitions were open to women, due in part to Marie's efforts. Hailed in the French press as "queen of sports," her exploits kept her in the public eye and helped promote women's sports.

As early as 1901, Marie had turned her gaze skyward. Ballooning was a popular sport among the well to do, and where men had gone, women followed. In Nancy, Marie took up this new sport enthusiastically, traveling first with experienced ballooners to learn the ropes of spherical ballooning before she applied for a license. That same year she received license No. 145 to pilot a free balloon, and from then on appeared at balloon gatherings regularly.

Her most remarkable exploit was a balloon trip from Nancy across the North Sea to England. Early on the morning of October 26, 1909, the balloon *L'Étoile Filante ("Shooting Star")* was slowly filled with hydrogen while the necessary equipment to be carried was checked: statoscope, telescope, barometer, lantern, cushions, lunch, heavy cloaks, dragline, and ballast—bags of sand.

Traveling with her was Colonel Emile Garnier as passenger and assistant. When all was ready, the let go was given at 11:07 A.M. and the balloon rose rapidly in the morning air until it settled at about a thousand meters in a current heading north. Garnier held the map and called off the landmarks as the round bag sailed gracefully along, passing over the Krupp factories in Essen, where the wind shifted and carried the balloon northwest over Holland toward Amsterdam. "We were in the clouds most of the time, but we thought after we reached Amsterdam that the most dangerous part of the trip was over," recounted Marie as the North Sea loomed in the distance.

At 8:15 P.M., the *Shooting Star* floated over the sea, as the balloon began to lose altitude. By 9 P.M., the basket and instruments were beginning to ice up, then a snow squall covered the balloon with ice and snow, sending it rapidly downward, where high waves drenched the basket and its contents. Tossing a sack of sand overboard had no effect. More sand went over before the balloon rose to a safer altitude. Through the clouds Marie and Garnier could see the billowing waves that had lashed the basket, glad to be above them, then far ahead a light. At 1:30 A.M., Marie gave a cry of joy—England was just ahead. The cliffs loomed up, but an updraft carried the two travelers over the top.

Once over land, with the Southwold lighthouse to the right, Marie tried to valve the balloon to release air and bring it down. At first the rope, drenched by the elements, wouldn't budge. Finally, a great tug freed the valve, and the balloon dropped downward and settled in a tree with a sharp jar, tumbling Marie from the basket. She went for help, while her passenger stayed trapped with the bag. By four o'clock, all was in order. The local police had the balloon anchored and attended, and the two travelers were put up in a local hotel with dry clothes.

From there they went to London, where they were given a grand welcome by international journalists, who praised their accomplishments, particularly since it took place in the midst of a violent storm. Marie chalked up another first: first woman to pilot a balloon across the North Sea. The travelers had made the two hundred–kilometer trip in five hours, while the regular pack boats from Holland to England took eleven hours. Overall, the *Shooting Star* had traveled nearly a thousand kilometers in fourteen hours. There was great satisfaction in the accomplishment, which, in later years, Marie considered the most dramatic adventure of her life in the air.

She made two more prominent trips in a spherical balloon in 1910: the Grand Prix of the Aero Club of Paris, organized by the Stella Society, and a race organized by the Aero Club of the East at Nancy. In the first, Marie was the lone woman pilot; the Stella ladies went as passengers with male pilots. In the second, Marie won the Premier Grand Prix, traveling from Nancy to Neufchâteau, in Belgium, reportedly in fifteen hours, to beat one of her teachers, Georges Blanchet, three time winner of the Aero Club of France Grand Prix.

In 1912, Marie took part in the tenth running of the Paris–Sea of Ireland race, organized by the Aero Club of France. There were twenty-four participants, including Marie in her *Shooting Star,* with Quénardel de Warcy as passenger. It was an exhilarating experience; the wonder is that she was content to stop in Ireland.

Even when she turned to flying an aeroplane, ballooning remained a pleasurable experience for Marie. The uncertainty of where she might end up, the search for the right air current to carry her in a desired direction, at a desired speed, suited her adventuresome soul.

In 1908, Marie had visited the Voisin brother's factory at Châlons and decided the new sport had potential. When Roger Sommer took her up for a ride in September 1909, she was elated—and hooked. By the following year, she had signed up for lessons with Hubert Latham at Mourmelon to learn to fly his Antoinette, an elongated, graceful monoplane considered, by some, difficult to fly. The pilot sat well back from the wings because the weight of the machine was distributed among its parts, unlike the Blériot aeroplane, whose weight was centered in the front. Marie was the only woman pupil at Latham's school. Between early lessons, she made her historic balloon trip, and, on March 15, 1910, she was presented with the Médaille d'Or of the French Academy of Sports. Her activity was prodigious.

Aviation was a world of its own in those years. The enthusiasm and excitement that flying generated in the first decade of the twentieth century—the fever to explore the heavens—was shared by a small band, bound by camaraderie and the constant possibility of death. Marie did not dwell on the subject, nor did the others, but part of the attraction of flying was knowing the risk and overcoming it. She wrote about flying frequently, describing it as "intoxicating," stressing her belief that the true aviator's soul found the struggle with the atmosphere "a rich compensation for the risks." To fly like a bird was the ultimate romantic quest.

Early in her aviation training, on a flight with Latham, Marie was initiated into the rolling and pitching that typically buffeted an aeroplane maneuvering through gusty air currents. On landing, Latham, who seldom showed emotion, remarked that he had never been so violently shaken. Another time, flying with Charles Wachter at thirty meters high, their aeroplane almost collided with a biplane. Marie thought disaster was imminent, but at a few meters' distance, the biplane turned upside down, with no injury to the pilot, and Marie and Wachter flew on. Marie believed that the close calls she had with her teachers prepared her for whatever might come when flying alone. (Charles Wachter was less fortunate. He was killed when a wing collapsed while he was flying at Rheims in July 1910.)

In her 1910 article "The Intoxication of Flight," Marie described a close call that occurred on the morning of her license tests. As she began her second flight, a biplane flew off sixty meters from her. Instinctively, she left the course and rose to a height of eighty meters to avoid his wake and continued on her circle of the course without sighting the other machine. When she landed, Marie learned the two aeroplanes were within twenty meters of each other at one moment, but because of her machine's wing structure she was unaware of this. A change in the aeroplane's wing design would soon do away with this "inconvenience."

A first solo flight is always memorable. September 4, 1910, was just this for Marie, who called it "the most stirring." She had gained confidence from her training with Bernard Lafont, but she admitted a strange sensation—she rarely if ever had "nerves." The monoplane quickly rose to sixty meters, performing better than the one she usually flew in. On the first turn she was uneasy, but on the second that feeling "turned into joy unalloyed." Landing bothered her a bit, but it proved "quite normal," and on the ground, joy and relief mingled. It was done; she had soloed.

On November 8, after making figure eights, maintaining a certain altitude, and landing near a designated mark, Marie passed with flying colors, and was hailed as the third woman in France and the world to receive a pilot's license, No. 281, to join that unusual breed of *femmes-oiseaux*. Marie always insisted that she finished her training on the difficult Antoinette without *casser du bois* ("shattering wood"). Considering the fragility of early aeroplanes and the danger from capricious winds, that was a rare accomplishment.

Although she survived splintering a machine while learning, Marie had one notable accident as a licensed pilot. While flying her fragile Antoinette at a meeting at Sainte-Etienne, the motor stopped suddenly as the aeroplane flew over a large crowd that cheered lustily in ignorance of the danger overhead. Just beyond the crowd, a gust of wind caught the delicate machine and tossed it downward, where, fortunately, it landed in an acacia tree in the midst of a *boule* game. As was often the case with Marie, a camera captured her surprise landing, her wide smile, and the astounded *boule* players. The picture had a good play, and the press applauded her for her adroitness in avoiding a tragic accident.

Another time, flying a Deperdussin monoplane on a cold December morning, Marie capsized to the ground, headfirst into soft earth. Her head was bleeding, her mouth was full of dirt, but she was able to brush the dirt away and call for help, warning the men not to smoke, as she

Marie Marvingt crash-lands in a tree in the midst of a game of boules *after her motor stopped over Saint-Etienne, France.* MUSÉE DE L'AIR ET DE L'ESPACE, LE BOURGET

was drenched in gasoline. Incidents like this earned women fliers the same press recognition for bravery as men.

Two weeks after winning her license, Marie was practicing earnestly for the newly established Coupe Fémina. On November 27, she made a flight of forty-two kilometers in fifty-three minutes—at that time a record for distance and duration for women, which led to false reports that she won the Coupe. The record would be short-lived, as Hélène Dutrieu bettered it in December with her flight of 60.8 kilometers. By the following year, competition would be keen among a trio of women aviators: Dutrieu, Jeanne Herveux, and Marvingt, who competed each year but failed to win the prize. Not discouraged, she took part in meets around France and Turin, Italy, winning a reputation for flying, which she attributed to the joy she found in speed, the wind, and the view from above. She was a frequent contributor, as was Raymonde de Laroche, to journals that featured her flying experiences with those of prominent male aviators.

Before the First World War began, Marie had conceived an idea that would prove very beneficial in coming years—a flying medical service. *Aviation Sanitaire* became an important part of her life. Together with the engineer Louis Bechereau, she designed an air ambulance capable of carrying an injured person, on a litter slung under the chassis, from the battle scene to the nearest hospital. The service was not an immediate hit with the military, but the course of events would prove it extremely useful. A painting by Emile Friant, a well-known artist in Nancy, showing Marie with Georges Gille, a military doctor from Nancy, and a wounded soldier, was reproduced and shown everywhere to promote the service. Marie, often referred to as "the flying Florence Nightingale," spent forty years advancing the service, to which she was completely dedicated. In later years she was known affectionately as the "Godmother" of *Aviation Sanitaire,* which was a happy joining of her aviation skills and the medical skills she eventually developed.

With the outbreak of the First World War, Marie pursued a variety of careers. She spent several weeks in disguise as a foot soldier at the front, then wrote of her experience; she reported on the war on the Italian front; on skis, she helped carry food to troops in the Dolomites and assisted with evacuations; she trained as a nurse and assisted in surgery; and she served with the Red Cross. Reportedly, she took part in an aerial bombardment of a German base, which won her the Croix de Guerre after the war. The death of her father in 1916 slowed her briefly, but there was little time to consider her new life entirely alone in the midst of war. Felix had given her total encouragement and love; he was probably the only person who really knew her.

The years after the war were never short of causes. Marie attended conferences regularly—one estimate is an astronomical thirty- five hundred during her life—to confer nationally and internationally on her favorite topic, *Aviation Sanitaire*. In addition, she lectured on aviation matters and assisted with medical evacuations in Morroco and elsewhere in North Africa by *Aviation Sanitaire* during the French colonial wars, an experience that enabled her to learn the native languages. More than one commanding officer in the years between 1919 and 1925 owed his life to the swiftness with which he reached an operating table because of *Aviation Sanitaire*.

Among her other accomplishments, Marie, using her knowledge of winter skiing, invented metal skis for desert use. In February 1923 she drove across the Sahara, beating the speed record of Mrs. André Citroën, and entered In-Salah, a Berber stronghold in the Algerian mountains, reportedly the first European woman to do so, driving a Fiat 3549 with rubber tires. She spent three long periods in North Africa, 1922–27, 1932–35, and 1950–53. She worked on two documentary movies, *Saved by the Dove,* for which she did the narration, and *The Wings That Save,* filmed in 1934, in which she acted, and visited the United States twice before World War II to promote her *Aviation Sanitaire* and speak about aviation. On one visit, she met Amelia Earhart; both were recognized famous aviators. Marie was instrumental in founding a home for wounded airmen in 1939–40, and added to her credits the invention of a device used in surgical sutures; she received the first license issued as *secouriste de l'air* ("air rescuer").

Awards were many, a total of thirty-four medals and decorations. In 1935 she was made a Chevalier of the Legion of Honor with its red ribbon; in 1937 she was named Chevalier of l'Ordre de la Santé. On her third visit to the United States in 1948–49, at an international meeting in Los Angeles sponsored by the Women's Aeronautical Association, she received first prize for her autobiographical works *Fiancée of Danger,* a summary of her many careers, and "My Balloon Trip across the North

Sea." Her name was inscribed on a marble wall in Riverside, California, honoring pioneer aviators. The American press liked *Fiancée of Danger* and saluted Marie accordingly. No copies of that work survived, but her long life is well documented.

In 1954 at the Sorbonne she received la Victoire de Samothrace, a grand prize, presented by Henri Deutsch de la Meurthe, an oil magnate and early aviation supporter, in recognition of Marie's pioneering work for *Aviation Sanitaire* and the *services de secours* ("rescue services"). In 1957 she received a Gold Medal in recognition of her work for Physical Education and a Silver Medal from the *Service de Santé de l'Air.* Two years earlier, on her eightieth birthday, she was treated to a flight over Nancy in an F-101 at twelve hundred kilometers per hour by an American officer from the base at Toul-Rosieres—an extraordinary experience for a veteran of bamboo and fabric machines.

Hailed as "the most extraordinary woman since Joan of Arc" by the American press, Marie more than earned that tribute. Blessed with a long life, she enjoyed the recognition that came to her through the years. She collected many mementos, but they did not buy food or heating in her later years, when she was forced to live very frugally. Older inhabitants of Nancy remembered their famous octogenarian neighbor, who still rode *Zepherine,* her ancient bicycle, around the city streets, but a younger generation had to be reminded of her history on special occasions. Her famous bicycle trip to Paris from Nancy at almost eighty-six was one. Ensconced at the Ritz Hotel, she visited an air base outside Paris and climbed into a French helicopter for a flyover of Paris that made all the city newspapers. (Her private pilot's license was renewed three years before, at age eighty-three; her last pilot's physical examination was dated August 2, 1956, when she was eighty-one. For the authorities, it was a way of honoring this exceptional woman. They knew she would never fly again.)

Marie's recipe for good health stipulated four or five hours of sleep and eating half-a-dozen snacks a day, like mountaineers—no big meals. For her, a healthy diet included tender red meat and plenty of chocolate, sugar, and fruit, but no spicy food, bread (it wasn't made well anymore), boiled beef, or alcohol. It was a regimen that served her well for almost ninety years. Interviewed in Nancy on her birthday in 1958, she announced proudly with a big smile, "I'm eighty-three years old, and I have all my teeth!"

After all the headlines, decorations, and accolades, Marie died in poverty in 1963 in a nursing home run by the sisters of Sainte Charles in Nancy. Her obituaries were glowing; she would have loved them. Her funeral was dignified and well attended by representatives from the aviation and civilian ranks who knew her legendary record. As one of that special group of women aviation pioneers, her place in history is assured, not just because of the publicity surrounding her countless exploits but because of the steadfastness of character she demonstrated, her concern for those in need, her humor, and her warmth. Asked once why she did so many unusual things, tackled so many risks and challenges, her answer was that of the mountain climber attempting Everest: "Because it is there." In doing these unusual things, she believed she learned about nature and herself. There was a prayerful side to Marie that many people never saw, but her firm religious belief certainly contributed to her supreme confidence.

Two years before she died, an interview with Gordon Ackerman for *Sports Illustrated* revealed she had lost none of her sense of humor. She told him with amusement of the city's plan to build a museum to hold her trophies. When she was ill some years before, the city fathers decided her time had come, and they visited her to tell her their plans to honor her. Said Marie: "So every few days since then somebody has come to look in and see if Marvingt is still around, and if they can start work on the museum. This has been going on for a long time. They are starting to lose interest." Then she flashed her famous smile, radiant still in old age.

3
Vive les Femmes!

THE FRENCH SKIES continually beckoned women to discover for themselves what the excitement was all about and gain a measure of liberation doing what only men had done. Marthe Niel—even before Hélène Dutrieu and Marie Marvingt had received their brevets— became a licensed pilot, encouraged by her husband, Albert, to take to the air. She was issued No. 226 on August 29, 1910, after passing her tests on a Koechlin aeroplane. Jean Paul Koechlin was a successful builder of monoplanes and biplanes, but his name is not as well known as that of some of his contemporaries. He had flying schools at Mourmelon and Issy-les-Moulineaux, near Paris. We can't be sure at which one Marthe was trained.

She was born December 29, 1880, in Paimpont, Brittany. Little is known about her early years, only that she was swept up in the excitement of flying and was trained at a Koechlin school in a matter of weeks. She apparently had a healthy amount of confidence and determination, for, reportedly, she once said that "flying for a woman is not a book with seven seals."

There are few references to Marthe. Probably she was content to fly for her own satisfaction and had little interest in competitions. This was not unusual. Women proved they could meet the requirements of the official licensing body, then flew for their own pleasure.

The fourth woman to earn a pilot's license before the end of 1910 was Jeanne Herveux (sometimes spelled "Herveu"). Her first name is anglicized to "Jane" in many references. Born in Paris, December 10, 1885, she had taken up the automobile like other modern young women before progressing to the aeroplane. Her daring exploits "looping the loop" with an automobile took her to the Crystal Palace in London, where, dressed in yellow silk, she was paid twenty pounds a show and performed four times a day. After she returned to France, her family begged her to give up the "loop." Jeanne took up a Wernert eight-horsepower motorcycle for a while as a safer course, but soon she was back in an auto and racing the courses at Deauville, Château-Thierry, Gaillon, and Laffrey. Like Dutrieu, she had boundless energy. Doing seven-hour races did not faze her.

One day, she received a message: Someone needed an auto to do some hauling. The someone was Louis Blériot, who needed to move his glider. Jeanne accepted delightedly; it was her first contact with an aviator. That chance meeting led her to turn her eyes skyward.

In her twenty-fourth year, she enrolled in the Blériot school at Mourmelon, where she made swift progress with her training on the monoplane considered the best for speed. Blériot's successful Channel flight in 1909 won him not only the plaudits of France and all of Europe, but numerous young enthusiasts eager to learn to fly and explore the skies. Jeanne succeeded better than some others. One student bought a Blériot aeroplane, as was required by the school, but his lack of skill and heavy-handedness on the machine required regular, costly repairs by the company staff. Landing was this student's bête noire. Repeatedly, he dropped too fast, at too sharp an angle; he walked away from the machine, but each time the undercarriage had to be rebuilt. This would-be pilot paid the cost happily—it was his ticket to association with the aviation world. Fortunately, he was never licensed.

Jeanne, on the other hand, successfully passed her tests and was issued license No. 318 on December 7, three days before her twenty-fifth birthday. She was still too much a novice to think about the Coupe Fémina and its two thousand–franc prize, but the following year would see her actively flying in appearances around the country and competing for the Coupe.

In the spring of 1911, Jeanne signed a contract with La Société de l'École Nationale d'Aviation in Lyons for appearances there from May 28

France's Jeanne Herveux, an accomplished automobile stunt driver and racer, became the fourth woman to earn a pilot's license. MUSÉE DE L'AIR ET DE L'ESPACE, LE BOURGET

to June 8. The contract was typical for that time—the main difference from pilot to pilot was that the amount paid reflected his or her stature in the aviation world. The pilot's first-class train ticket between Paris and Lyons with return was paid by the company; Jeanne received thirty francs a day, May 26 to June 9 inclusive, to cover her expenses at a hotel; her mechanic traveled second class both ways and received ten francs a day for expenses for the same number of days. Oil and gasoline were furnished by the company; Jeanne's aeroplane would be housed in the hangars of the society free.

The aviatrix was guaranteed three thousand francs in addition to any prizes she might win—five hundred francs to be paid on her arrival in Lyons, machine and mechanic ready, no later than the afternoon of May 26; one thousand francs on June 5; and the balance on her departure. For this sum, Jeanne agreed to fly at least two exhibitions, morning and afternoon, in good weather (she would make that determination), and more if the company thought it worthwhile or if the public demanded it. However, she would not be asked to make more than six flights in the same day. The requirements were not unlike the auto race courses where she had appeared, except at the moment aviation exhibitions were number-one entertainment.

By August, Jeanne was preparing for the Coupe Fémina. On the 19th, she flew her Blériot with Gnome motor for one hour forty-five minutes, covering 101 kilometers at 600 meters altitude. That wouldn't do it. Hélène Dutrieu flew more than 260 kilometers to retain the Coupe and its prize money. Jeanne wasn't discouraged. She continued to compete, but the Coupe always eluded her. There was no award in 1912, and Raymonde de Laroche won in 1913.

Toward the end of 1911, Jeanne planned to open a flying school for women only, to be taught by women. Announcements appeared in French, English, and American newspapers, aimed at women who until now were put off by the male aviation environment. Unfortunately, Jeanne's timing was poor. There were numerous flying schools in existence by 1912, and the separation of the sexes failed to have its expected appeal.

At this point Jeanne Herveux vanished from the public eye. A 1922 French newspaper article, lamenting the disappearance of the country's famous aviatrixes, reported that she had married an American the previous year and was living in the United States, where she was running a flourishing fashion business. (Another source had her living in London.) In either case, aviation was a thing of the past. It was aviation's loss.

In the years between 1911 and the beginning of the First World War, the Aero Club of France issued pilot's licenses to nine more women. They were a varied group—native French, English, Indonesian, Rumanian; they flew a variety of aeroplanes: Astra, Blériot, Sommer, Breguet, Deperdussin, and Caudron.

In addition, there were several women who practiced flying with varying success but never earned a license. Mlle. Aboukaia, a diminutive Japanese woman, was especially active, appearing in exhibitions in 1910 and 1911, flying the difficult Demoiselle. She had been a successful bicycle racer in England and France on the enclosed circuit tracks popular at the height of the cycle craze. She made the switch to aeroplanes easily.

Mathilde Frank, a French citizen who became Mrs. Edwarson with her marriage to an English newspaperman, had studied at the Farman camp and planned a Channel flight in 1910. Bad weather prevented a takeoff, and she then went to England, where she had a tragic crash at Sunderland. A boy on the ground was killed when Frank's aeroplane caught a flagstaff and flipped over onto the ground. The motor fell on the boy, several spectators were injured by other parts of the machine, and Mathilde suffered a broken leg and internal injuries. Her flying career ended with this mishap.

Other women were mentioned as flying during the same period, including Lottie Brandon, Mme. Beroul, Mme. Copin, Mlle. Dindineau, and Mme. Dorival. None earned a license, but their presence showed that women could do the unusual in France without the hassle sometimes encountered elsewhere.

Two young women had almost finished their training when they were killed in a crash: Denise Moore, at age thirty-five, and Suzanne Bernard, at age nineteen. Their deaths plunged aviation circles into mourning. There was much soul-searching in the press at the loss of such young lives, and there was equal condemnation of parents who permitted their daughters to pursue such dangerous activity. Actually, Moore, born in Algeria of English parents, according to French and German sources (others claim her as American), did not use her real name, Jane Wright, because she wanted to keep her parents ignorant of her flying. Her death in July 1911 was headlined as "Aviation's first female sacrifice." Many men had preceded her, but the death of a woman was viewed as more tragic than that of a man, because it was outside the normal expectation.

Marie-Louise Martin Driancourt was born December 1887 in Lyons, a center of propriety, good food, and bourgeois attitudes. As a young woman she went to Paris, married into the Parisian bourgeoisie, and became Mme. Driancourt and mother of three children when she was bitten by the flying bug. Her husband, also an ardent aviation enthusiast, encouraged her. In 1910 she trained at the Blériot school at Chartres, but by the next summer she had moved to Crotoy near Paris to work at the Caudron School, where she won pilot's license No. 525, dated June 15, 1911. The Caudron biplane was known for stability and speed. Driancourt made exhibition flights at the airfields around France and was a great success at the aviation meet at Crotoy in September, which was followed by a meet in Pamplona, Spain, where she was congratulated by Alphonse XIII for her achievements in duration, altitude, and virtuosity.

Her career was not without accident, due on one occasion to unsuspecting spectators who blocked her landing site. Rather than injure them, she glided into some trees, smashing her biplane and fracturing two ribs. The death of her husband in a car accident early in 1912 caused second thoughts about continuing her aviation career with family responsibilities. She appeared one more time at Juvisy in April 1912, with many of the greats of that period, but then retired to care for her children. Shortly after, illness claimed her, probably tuberculosis, and she died at the end of 1914 at L'Hay les Roses.

Mme. Béatrice Deryck (or de Ryk), an Indonesian national, was flying at the same time as Driancourt. She won license No. 652, dated October 10, 1911, with remarkable ease, flying a Hanriot monoplane. She was an enthusiastic sportswoman, a member of Stella, the aeronautical society, and combined ballooning and aviation. A journalist writing in *L'Aérophile* was impressed by her bravery and coolheadedness—both "would be the envy of the uglier sex." Described as a lover of new experiences and emotions, Béatrice was last mentioned when she stepped into a balloon November 12, 1911, with Mme. Gustave Goldschmidt and disappeared from public notice. She was not interested in competition; she flew for her own enjoyment.

Jeanne Pallier took up flying at forty-eight years of age, the oldest of the French aviatrixes, and won license No. 1012, dated September 6, 1912. She passed her tests on August 2 and astonished the aviation world by flying over Paris at a height of seven hundred meters for her distance test, a flight described by one journal as "particularly brilliant."

Mme. Pallier trained on an Astra biplane, a large machine with three seats arranged behind one another in the covered fuselage, the last two occupied by student and teacher with separate controls. Pallier won respect for her ability to handle such a large aeroplane. However, when she soloed and took her test flights, she used a smaller biplane. The Stella ladies welcomed Pallier as an associate member in recognition of her achievement.

Once she had her brevet, Pallier made a series of cross-country flights from Villacoublay to Chartres, with a stop at Étampes. The next day she flew to the forest of Rambouillet, over Menviller, before returning to Chartres. The following day, she returned to Villacoublay, flying between five hundred and nine hundred meters high. Today such flights are nothing, but at that time, without compass or landmarks, they were remarkable. As one writer said, she had the instincts of a bird, and a lot of luck. Mme. Duchange was a passenger on the flights, permitting Jeanne to credit herself as "first" to carry a passenger cross-country. (Hélène Dutrieu flew successfully with her mechanic in Belgium in 1910, but Pallier obviously didn't know that.)

Jeanne competed unsuccessfully for the Coupe Fémina against Marie Marvingt and Raymonde de Laroche in 1913. Undetered, she flew at the Vienna air meet in June 1914, one of the last meets before the war, competing with men to win third place in duration and a prize of a thousand kronen.

During the war, Jeanne raised money to organize a squad of ambulances driven by women to transport the wounded. A *New York Times* article in February 1916 noted that her service was gratefully accepted by the government. As president of the Club Féminin Automobile, Jeanne had encouraged that group to establish the service. Now she hoped to involve the American public: "I hope our large-hearted American cousins will show their interest and collaborate with us in this enterprise." Contributions could be sent to an address in Boston.

After the war one newspaper reported that Jeanne was doing sculpting and had given up aviation. She devoted herself to social work at the Renault factory, and she established the Coupe Jeanne Pallier to encourage young women in competitive sports. She died March 6, 1939, in the Couvent des Perpétual-Secours at Villeneuve-sur-Yonne, where her daughter was a nun.

Hélène de Plagino and Marthe Richer were issued their brevets on the same day, June 4, 1913. They had similar qualities: They were good at sports, as much at ease on a horse as in an automobile, and artful in their skill flying a machine. Plagino was the daughter of a diplomat stationed in Bucharest. Before she achieved her brevet, she accompanied the aviator Edmond Perreyon when he broke the altitude record. The Aero Club officials present at her tests were impressed by her mastery and ease in the maneuvers. She received brevet No. 1399.

Marthe Betenfeld Richer was one of the more enigmatic of the French aviatrixes. Born on April 15, 1889, at Blamont in Meurthe-et-Moselle, she was well aware of the German presence in the skies of Lorraine. She married Henri Richer, a wealthy attorney, when she was twenty-two. Newly brevetted (No. 1369 on June 4, 1913), she was eager to put her aerial talents to use for France. She approached General Hirschauer, who headed government aviation concerns, to recommend the formation of a feminine squadron. Hirschauer's response was a firm no; the proposal was "contrary to the Convention of the Hague." Exposing a woman to the dangers of combat was unthinkable. Marthe would have to find some other use for her patriotism.

When her husband was killed at Verdun, Marthe adopted a pseudonym (Richard) and set about using her many talents for France. With the assistance of Captain Ladoux, who was responsible for intelligence, she was posted to Spain as agent S.R. 32 Alouette. Her youthfulness and wide blue eyes captivated Baron von Krohn, a German naval attaché and a nephew of German general Erich Ludendorff who, if he was as ugly as he has been described, must have pinched himself daily on his good fortune in winning such a lovely treasure. Loving lips are careless ones. The baron passed along military information on naval operations unwittingly to the compliant young woman, and in exchange he received unimportant, ridiculous bits of misinformation to report back to Germany.

Writers question whether patriotism inspired Marthe or pure enjoyment of adventure and sensual pleasure. Marthe never told, but the French government was sufficiently impressed with her work to award her the red ribbon of the Legion of Honor in 1933, which, according to one writer, created "the loveliest effect on her Chanel suit."

Richer was married before World War II to Thomas Crampton, a Briton and the director of the Rockefeller Foundation, who left her a widow within a few years. When France was conquered by Germany, Marthe returned to espionage work with the Résistance. She loved the life and found it an adequate replacement for the excitement of flying, reportedly her first love, yet she never resumed flying after World War I.

When World War II ended, Marthe was elected to the Paris municipal council and worked to pass a law to close the brothels regulated by the police, earning her the sobriquet Madame la Vertu in the press. Very quickly, despite her concern for the women workers, she realized she had made a mistake; unregulated prostitution, without any health controls, flourished in broad daylight. Until she died in 1982, Marthe regretted her misplaced morality. Closemouthed to the end, she never revealed the secrets of her other life in intelligence. A 1937 movie, starring Edwige Feuillère, hinted at the talents of this unusual aviatrix-turned-spy, but Richer herself died with her secrets. She remains a fascinating mystery.

Carmen Damedoz won license No. 1449, dated September 5, 1913, flying a Sommer biplane. Her tests were not uneventful. On her first try flying figure eights on an old machine, the twenty-five-horsepower motor lost speed and the aeroplane slipped to the ground. Carmen fractured two ribs. When she was ready again, she flew a Sommer with a fifty-horsepower Gnome motor and passed her tests "brilliantly," according to *Flight,* the aviation journal. Sometime later she won the prized gold medal for altitude for women pilots, offered by Senator Reymond, for reaching 1,020 meters. *L'Aérophile* in 1913 described her as one of the most visible women fliers; her energy and tenacity were "exceptional." Carmen was a member of the Stella society (she also made balloon trips); the organization's social and political clout rose even higher when Mme. Raymond Poincaré, wife of the French president, became a member.

Before the thunder of guns began, two more women won their brevets in 1914 from Aero Club of France: Hélène Caragiani, No. 1591

(February 6), and Gaétane Picard, No. 1653 (July 10). About Hélène, reportedly Romanian, little is known. Gaétane, a resident of Buc, trained at the Blériot school there, where her rapid progress was reported regularly in the aviation journals. When she soloed for the first time, she volplaned down with her motor off and had a perfect landing. Her right turns, often tricky for aviators because early rotary motors revolved right to left and their weight, coupled with thrust, could overturn the lightweight aeroplanes, were well executed. Gaétane had trained with a group of male fliers who brought out the best performance from their machines. They tested and delivered aeroplanes to the military as the buildup for war accelerated. Gaétane was a small woman, but she handled the Blériot machine expertly. On July 2, the Ministry of Public Works had issued her brevet No. 76 for aeroplanes and hydro-aeroplanes, a separate category from civil pilots, signed at Versailles by the local prefect. She was unquestionably a talented flier.

Within a month, the war began; dreams of flying achievements ended. Gaétane did as the women of France did; she volunteered to fill a man's place and drove ambulances and trucks as needed. The Army of the North and North-East commended her for courage and devotion during the perilous period from March 21 to April 2, 1918, when, under continual bombardment, she assisted in the evacuation of the wounded from the front to a place of greater safety. Unfortunately, Gaétane did not resume flying after the war.

A Florencia Madera is listed in Bernard Marck's book *Les Aviatrices* as winning license No. 1421 on September 5, 1913, but the staff at the Musée de l'Air et l'Espace is unfamiliar with her.

Four long years took their toll. The cost of retraining on new machines, or beginning new lives with new responsibilities, all made climbing into an aeroplane again a difficult prospect. Raymonde de Laroche was the only aviatrix aside from Marie Marvingt, who worked tirelessly for the air-rescue service, to renew her aviation career. The first and in some ways the most exceptional of the group, Raymonde proved that flying was natural for women because it did not require physical strength as much as mental coordination. A new generation of French women would testify to that in the 1920s and 1930s.

4

den Tragödien unseres Berufes

IF EVER SOMEONE lived by Polonius's advice "To thine own self be true," it was Melli Beese, Germany's first woman aeroplane pilot. Some inner voice propelled her on a course from which there was no turning back. Destiny, a particularly German obsession, shadowed an aviation career that began with great promise. Melli herself would have said that some people are born under a lucky star, others are not. Talent, ability, worth have nothing to do with what happens. The star is the determinant.

Amélie Hedwig Beese was born on September 13, 1886, the second daughter of an architect, Friedrich Karl Richard Beese, who lived at 84 Hauptstrasse (today Ostereicher Strasse) in a suburb of Dresden. Besides her sister, Hertha, and an older brother, Kurt, the children of Richard's first marriage, Melli had a younger brother, Edgar. Their mother, Alma Wilhelmine Hedwig Beese, was a traditional woman of her day—a good housewife, an excellent manager of family affairs. The family was solidly middle class—the father a gifted stone artist as well as an architect, two professions that influenced Melli's future career. The family address was in an area where financially secure government workers and officers lived; the family was comfortable, if not well to do. (A German family's address is still an accurate gauge of the family's financial and social status.)

Melli, as she was known all her life, was a precocious child. Reportedly she was using her father's materials to make creditable drawings at three; at six, she was playing the violin and later the piano, among other instruments. She had a talent for languages and spoke several, including Swedish. No doubt, her parents worried about her future when Melli began to have her own ideas about life.

Properly brought up young girls of Melli's time did not work—that was the unhappy fortune of poor girls. They married, had a family, and prided themselves on managing a household with efficiency and being a good mother. Attendance at a girls' school for the daughters of upper-class families reinforced these ideas. Finding a husband who would be a good provider was a consuming preoccupation for most young girls, but not for Melli, whose interests were totally different from those of her peers. Marriage wasn't a consideration for her at that time. As a result, the bright, talented young girl had few close friends of her own age. She was too atypical for her time.

In the early 1900s, women were beginning to question a society that limited their activities, to demand rights they were denied. Why shouldn't women receive higher education? Why not pursue a career and have the right to vote? Above all, why should marriage limit these rights?

These ideas undoubtedly had some influence on Melli, who decided to become a sculptor. From her early years, she had been drawn to art, and her ability with her father's tools confirmed a talent with her hands. The decision was easier made than finding a school for training. In the years before World War I, not one woman student had been accepted to study sculpture at the academies of Dresden and Berlin. Luckily, Sweden was more progressive—women were accepted at the Royal Academy of Free Art—and in the fall of 1906, Melli went off to Stockholm to study.

Stockholm opened the door for Melli in many ways. She enjoyed working with other young women and men, and the freer environment in Sweden. She made good friends, among them Allen Egnell, a painter. A bronze bust of him is among remaining pieces of her work. Classes in model studio, monument sculpting, and figure study opened new ways of viewing subjects, which influenced her work. She did a group sculpture of soccer players in clay and plaster; a full-size nude in plaster; and a bust of John Forsell, later head of the Royal Opera, also in plaster. Her group sculpture, *The Soccer Players,* won a prize in 1908 from the academy and praise in the press, following the customary display of work by upper-class students for the newer students.

The open seas beckoned, and Melli discovered the joy of sailing—of skimming across water under a sail more like a large wing than part of a boat, of ice sailing, when the wind drove sailboats across the ice at enormous speed. A stray thought came to her. If she had wings, she could . . . But the thought remained unfinished, a restless, teasing idea that would reoccur.

In 1908, news of Wilbur Wright's flights in France caught Melli's attention; the new ideas and technology springing up everywhere intrigued her. She read the stories in the press avidly, and, inevitably, art had less appeal—the world of technology beckoned.

By the summer of 1909, Melli had finished her course, said farewell to Sweden and her friends, and returned to her parents in Germany, who were now living in a new house designed by her father in Blasewitz, close to Dresden. The house was a large villa with a garden and numerous trees behind. For Melli, despite the studio her father had built for her, the house was gloomy. Richard Beese understood his daughter without asking a lot of questions. He spent time with Melli discussing matters of interest to her; occasionally this would include flying, which was just then beginning to make an impression on the German public consciousness.

On July 25, 1909, the French flier Louis Blériot flew across the English Channel from Calais to Dover, a flight that fired imaginations everywhere and changed the way people viewed the world. English newspapers hailed his achievement, observing at the same time that England was no longer an island and the time had come for England to awaken to the military and commercial realities of aviation. The aeroplane was no longer a toy.

Melli was so moved by the news of Blériot's success that she determined she would learn to fly. It was new, part of the changing world of invention, and she longed to be part of it. Her parents were less enthusiastic; this new sport was not as genteel as art. The Beeses played for time. The news that French women were taking part in aviation, as the new sport was called, did not make the idea acceptable in Germany. French women through history were known for doing the unusual.

Richard Beese persuaded Melli to attend the polytechnic school in Dresden, arguing that it was the right step in preparation for becoming an aviator, with the hope that she would soon tire of the idea. Melli spent less than a year on technical studies before she convinced her father of the seriousness of her intentions. He knew he had lost and, being a supportive parent, he gave Melli a sizable check to cover studies and living expenses at a flying school near Berlin.

Johannisthal, outside of Berlin, was then the center for German aviation activity, such as it was. In 1910, the airfield was primitive—a wide, flat space with a distant stand of pine trees to the north and east, which hid the village behind. A high wall that looked like a dark string from the air enclosed the field, its wide expanse pockmarked here and there by rabbit holes, which were a constant threat to the chassis of any vehicle, auto or aeroplane, lest it end up as kindling. At the south end stood a few wooden hangars where aeroplanes were being built; alongside was a grandstand left over from automobile racing.

Hans Grade, inventor and early aviation pioneer, had flown his own construction in October of 1909—a graceful one-winged machine resting on bicycle wheels that looked too fragile to endure a strong wind— signaling the arrival of aviation in Germany. Grade, Karl Jatho, and Hermann Dorner, a talented trio, were the earliest German aeroplane builders of inexpensive sport machines, flimsy creations of bamboo and wire with little to recommend them in the way of security, but they carried men aloft. By 1910 the aeroplane was a marvelous new plaything for those who could afford one. Those who lacked the necessary wherewithal did the same as enthusiasts elsewhere in Europe and America— they built their own.

In addition to building aeroplanes, Grade was known for training ninety-nine civilian pilots before the First World War, using principles he had learned from experience. After an introductory flight, students followed a sequential training routine. First, they learned to clean and repair a motor; then, they proceeded to "dry training," learning which levers to use while seated in the aeroplane, followed next by practice with the motor running. Rolling over the ground taught students to increase and regulate gas while steering; making short starts, or hops, gave them practice in getting up a little, then down again. Finally, students used all the exercises to take off and fly straight within the enclosure of the flying field. Flying a circuit was the ultimate step, but it depended upon a machine with the proper equipment. The Wright machine would turn, and, in France, once Henry Farman flew a closed circuit, aeroplanes quickly developed maneuverable wings for turning. Grade's step-by-step training approach was highly successful, and safe.

November 1910 was gray and cold when Melli arrived at Johannisthal, but there was activity at the field in spite of the weather. The grandstand and wine restaurant were boarded up, but on the side where a row of hangars stood, men were at work at the Albatros site, the Rumpler Works, and the building where the German flying ship *Deutschland* was under construction. Hermann Dorner was busy building a new monoplane with the help of young Bruno Hanuschke, and the Wright Brothers' enterprise was active. In each hangar, construction of aeroplanes and training of young would-be pilots went on side by side. Official aviation schools were yet to come. If you were male and enthusiastic, the chances were good you would be taken on for training, but you did your turn working in the shop.

Georg von Tschudi had taken over the management of the airfield. His encouragement brought enthusiasts from Denmark, Norway, Austria, and France to take part in the exciting projects under way. It was an eclectic group—all male—that spent countless hours talking technical shop at the Café Senftleben. Melli, like the other students, soon had a special table where, gradually, a group of young men joined her. The coffees, beers, and schnapps were many, the air thick with smoke, as dedicated young people—"crazy" was the townspeople's description—talked the night away.

During that year several aeroplane builders offered instruction at Johannisthal on their particular type of machine, monoplane or biplane. The cost of lessons was about three thousand marks, plus another thousand for breakage, a sum that most would-be pilots did not have. Consequently, they built their own machines, cadging parts and advice wherever they could, and as soon as a machine was judged finished, it was tested by the builder with varied results. Hopping over the ground and touching down without crashing was considered success. This was repeated for a certain length, then the machine was turned around by hand—the pilot had yet to master the turn—and the hopping return was begun. A crash on the first hop meant more months of work.

The cost of machines was prohibitive for most students. A Wright biplane cost thirty thousand marks; an Albatros, twenty-five thousand marks; a Grade monoplane, twelve thousand marks. Melli did not have that kind of money. Her father's check allowed for training, and monthly payments covered living expenses. She resolved to build her own aeroplane as soon as she earned a pilot's license.

Preoccupied with her own plans, she had forgotten one thing. There were no women in the flying world of Johannisthal. Käthchen Paulus had earned a reputation as a balloon pilot and parachute jumper some years before. Dressed in boots and bloomers, she and her fiancé performed dangerous leaps that thrilled the crowds. Then one day her fiancé was killed when his parachute failed to open. Reportedly, Paulus continued to jump. She also trained to fly for a time with Paul Engelhard, the chief pilot for the Wright Company, but did not try for a pilot's license, which prejudiced Engelhard against women flying.

Melli quickly discovered that women were not welcome, an attitude fostered by the Wright Company and Engelhard, who considered women unsuited for flying. (Later the Wrights agreed to instruct women in Dayton, Ohio, but that was two years in the future—and in America.) However, women as passengers was acceptable; Orville Wright signaled approval when he took Frau Hauptmann Hildebrandt as a passenger at Tempelhof airport. The Wright establishment set the tone at Johannisthal, and Melli's attempts to sign a training contract with first Albatros, then the Wright Company, failed. Both establishments had the same answer: *nein*. An invisible wall seemed to shield the male world of aviation from assertive women.

Fortunately for Melli, a group of aviation pioneers had pooled talents to form a company—Ad Astra ("To the Stars"), financed by Rudolf Kiepert, a wealthy businessman—to build aeroplanes. The group included two Frenchmen—Gabriel Poulain, famous as a bicyclist, and Charles Boutard—and a Norwegian, Robert Thelen, who was chief of construction, as well as a pilot and teacher. Thelen agreed to take Melli on as a student when he found time. In the meantime, she could make herself useful around the shop; there would be no special treatment, which was fine with Melli. She was used to working with her hands, but her dream of flying had a rude comedown in grease and oil.

Melli described Thelen years later as a dark, very reserved man, famous for opening his mouth only to smoke a cigarette. He tested his own aeroplanes with optimism and unfailing courage. Like most of the pioneers, he sacrificed his health and his belongings to advance aviation knowledge. Writing about the early years of aviation, Melli described him as the foremost promoter of German aviation in its infancy.

While Melli waited impatiently for training to begin, she learned a thing or two about aeroplanes in the shop by observing and by helping when asked. Adolf Ludwig, who would become her trusted mechanic, took a shine to Melli the moment she demonstrated she was used to handling tools. He assured her that Thelen was a great pilot; he would teach her to fly. When was another matter.

One December day Thelen gestured to a machine—was it ready?—and with a wave of his hand to Melli, the door of the hangar was opened, and the Wright model biplane rolled out to the takeoff site. Pilot and student climbed up, Melli seated beside Thelen, where she could observe his handling of the levers that operated the machine. The moment she had waited for had come.

The motor coughed, throbbed unevenly, then steadied as the number of explosions per minute increased until its rhythm was smooth and regular as a heartbeat. The mechanics released the wings, and the biplane dashed across the field for takeoff. It was bumpier than Melli expected. Then she was caught up in wonder as the machine lifted into the air and raced toward the horizon.

Below to the side was the hangar, ahead was the widening gray sky, as Thelen maneuvered the levers without speaking. Train tracks appeared below, making small designs on the earth; the wind was strong and cold. Melli shivered in her leather jacket, but her spirits soared. She wished the flight would never end. The long waiting was forgotten; soon she would fly completely alone.

Thelen circled the field twice, his hands working the levers expertly on the turns that brought the ground closer before the wings straightened. As Melli watched his sure, skillful maneuvering, it seemed to her that man and machine had fused. The air, pushing against their bodies, held them in place on the small wooden seats—seat belts were yet to come. Then Thelen nodded toward the ground, and the giant bird started down. The motor was cut as the machine glided toward the ground, before leveling itself to hop again along the surface before coming to a stop.

Ludwig, waiting near the Ad Astra hangar, hurried to the plane as pilot and student climbed down. Melli's face beamed as she told him, "It was fantastically beautiful." On slightly unsteady feet, she turned to speak to Thelen, but he was already on his way to the hangar. Still floating from the experience, Melli helped Ludwig push the aeroplane into the hangar.

The days were routine: Melli arrived at the field before sunrise, warmed by a cup of coffee at the café, to wait for a free hour with Thelen. His lessons, a series of explanations by doing, took Melli through the steps of flying an aeroplane, making turns and landing, insisting that she feel the movements with him, until she did them instinctively. On the ground, Ludwig showed Melli the mechanical side of keeping a machine running. Gasoline and oil became perfume to Melli as her small, capable hands learned to dismantle and reassemble a motor.

On December 12, Thelen and Melli prepared to fly, watched by Melli's curious sister, Hertha von Grienberger, who had come expressly to watch her sister fly. The big bird rose in the sky; the flight seemed routine. Suddenly there was a loud bang. Thelen's hands moved automatically on the control levers as he shouted to Melli to hold fast, a chain was loose. The aeroplane lost power and slid sideways, dropped toward earth, and hit the ground. Melli's leg was pushed into her stomach; the sound of splintering wood filled the air. Thelen got out first and assured Melli that things were okay; their heads were still in place. Field hands arrived quickly with a wagon, and Melli realized a throbbing foot made walking impossible. Leaning on the shoulders of two men, she hobbled into the hangar, where her anxious sister waited.

Hertha spoke out immediately: Flying was much more dangerous than she was led to believe; Melli must give it up. In need of a doctor (Johannisthal had no doctor on duty at that time), Hertha bundled her sister into a taxi for the trip to Charlottenburg, in the western part of Berlin. As they left, the Ad Astra group waved good-bye, reminding Melli that if she returned, she belonged to them.

The doctor, when he saw Melli that night, was adamant: The foot must wear a plaster cast for four or five weeks; rest was essential—there were five broken bones, sore ribs, and a bruised nose. Realizing she couldn't keep the accident a secret from her parents, she wrote that night to tell them and keep them from worrying.

At this juncture, Richard Beese died suddenly of a heart attack. Melli was devastated. Filled with guilt, she blamed herself for distressing her father, for not bringing him more happiness. Against doctor's orders, she traveled to Dresden to gaze once more on his face, and, as the shovels of dirt fell on his casket, the door closed on her youth.

Melli tried to be a dutiful daughter to her mother, to content herself with life in Dresden, but it was no use. The foot was feeling better, and Melli, despite her mother's and sister's efforts to keep her there, argued to pursue her goal. Frau Beese agreed reluctantly; every person must follow his or her own path. Hardly thrilled by her daughter's choice of profession, she nevertheless was a sympathetic listener to Melli's plans and expectations.

In the middle of January of the new year, Melli returned to Johannisthal, limping with two canes, more determined than ever to learn to fly. Her father's inheritance allowed her to pursue flying without worry. But this time things were different.

Although Thelen never mentioned the crash, he went out of his way to avoid her. Melli wondered whether superstition or fear of her falling again prompted his behavior. She tried to wait patiently, her pride turning to obstinacy, but she was unable to find the right words to correct the situation. Unburdening herself to Ludwig, she insisted she would fly. That's why she came back.

In the long hours of waiting for something to happen, the Café Senftleben was a refuge for the students and workers who waited on the weather or an available machine. Days, sometimes a week, were spent waiting for the colored ball that signaled flying weather: Black meant no flying; white, maybe; red was go! At Melli's table, a group of other young aviators, Bruno Hanuschke, Hans Bockemüller, Benno König, and Georg Schendel, all from different aeroplane hangars, talked shop seriously, and continuously. Schendel, in particular, had a thorough knowledge of technical matters, which he explained to Melli in terms she could understand, with drawings to illustrate a point. The smoke-filled café was a warm haven in the lingering German winter, but an impatient Melli began to think she must break with Thelen completely. He flew to demonstrate technical and flying knowledge, yet never with her. It was as if she didn't exist.

On the field one day, a new aeroplane was rolled out—a monoplane, light and sleek, the creation of the Frenchman Poulain. The talk was lively as the crowd questioned the machine's ability to fly. Rumor was, the

Argus motor had one hundred horsepower. Unheard of! The pilot was Charles Boutard, who had helped build the new machine but was not yet a licensed pilot. Melli had seen him coming and going on the field, always intent on his work. Seated in the pilot's seat, he removed his cap to signal the two mechanics for takeoff. Boutard went up quickly, steadied over the field, and headed toward an area where road repairs were being made. Would he make the turn? The spectators below waited expectantly, as the speedy machine shot over the fence and headed for the stand of pines beyond. "Kindling" was the laconic comment when, in the next instant, sounds of a crash reached the onlookers.

Boutard was lucky. Writing years later, Melli described how the machine splintered trees before it came to a halt; it was a "miracle" that Boutard survived. The motor hung suspended above him, which prevented him from being crushed to death. He was bruised, a leg was broken, and his nerves were severely shaken, but he would be back at work in a matter of weeks. Melli spoke to the unhappy pilot in French—she spoke it better than his German. She praised Boutard for his courage, and in the next weeks she didn't forget him while he recuperated in the clinic.

By May, tired of waiting for lessons, Melli decided to cancel her contract with the Ad Astra company, knowing that Robert Thelen was not sorry to see her leave. Thanks to the intercession of Ellery von Gorrissen, an Aero Club observer, she was directed to Robert von Mossner; an old Africa hand and a student of Engelhard, he was working in Weimar. Melli would get lessons, and Ludwig would be going along to work on Mossner's machine. It seemed a good solution.

Melli went to Weimar with high hopes, but Mossner was primarily interested in finding experienced workers with mechanical talent. He did not own his machine, a Wright biplane, but he hoped to compete in the Sachsenflug, which was about to begin in Saxony, and improve his shaky financial status. Melli's fee would help, and she would serve as passenger for the flight. Unlike Thelen, Mossner was a friendly person, and pilot and student got on well.

Their first flight together was hardly auspicious. As Melli described it years later, the two were lost in thick rain clouds on the way to Dresden for the Sachsenflug, which made reading a map impossible as darkness approached. Seated on the lower wing, exposed to the rain, both fliers were thoroughly drenched by the time they landed—and discovered, to their dismay, that they were back where they had started. They gave up any idea of the competition and made their way to Weimar.

Melli had several lessons on Mossner's aging Wright. On her third flight, she took over working the control levers and experienced the thrill of the machine's quick response to her movements. For the first time, she held life and death in her hands, something no other sport could offer. To her delight, the merest touch on the levers brought a response. Recalling that flight years later, she wrote: *Die Wright Machine folgt ja so herrlich leight auf den kleinsten Steuerdruck.* ("The Wright machine flies so gloriously light with the slightest touch of the steering lever.")

However, as the weeks passed, Melli realized her hopes had led her down the wrong path. Too many days were spent with Ludwig trying to make rusted valves useful again on a worn-out motor. Mossner did not own his machine and had to relinquish two motors to the owner for use in a competition, leaving the two mechanics with a discouraging repair task. In the meantime, Mossner departed to the south, leaving Melli and Ludwig alone for three long weeks.

At this point, news of her friend Georg Schendel's death at Johannisthal reached Melli. He had crashed attempting a new altitude record during the Spring Fly Week. His death hit Melli hard, despite her awareness that death was always present and waiting. Such a good person deserved better, but his star was unlucky. Realizing how much she missed her comrades at Johannisthal, she packed her bag and departed. Ludwig would follow shortly.

Melli returned to Berlin to find the situation at Johannisthal had changed in her absence. The once primitive field was now enlarged with grander seating—the most expensive placed near the train station—a restaurant, a promenade, and new office space for the field management and the Aero Club representatives. The field area, so essential for takeoff and landing, was extended to 2,100 meters by 1,240 meters, the whole enclosed by a high wooden fence with entrances at intervals around the enclosure. The roof of the clubhouse held a beacon light to provide orientation for the aviators. New hangars indicated a steady growth in aviation activity, and there was still room for further expansion. Competitions were planned for the 1911 summer and fall in anticipation of many more aviation fans.

The military establishment, newly awakened to French progress in aviation and the dangers that entailed, realized Germany must take steps to catch up. The Rumpler Works, already turning out machines in increasing numbers, was positioned to catch the attention of the government, while smaller builders, like the pioneer Dorner, who worked on a shoestring, had little chance of winning the military contracts that would keep them afloat. Ad Astra had already gone under, its workers scattered to other companies. The next two years would see growing military activity at Johannisthal, with the larger establishments increasingly busy.

Georg von Tschudi, who was planning ever bigger flying competitions at Johannisthal, took Melli under his wing and persuaded Edmund Rumpler to take her on as a student. Tschudi saw her as a magnet to draw the crowds that would make the field a financial success. Rumpler, involved with building a new, fast monoplane, the Taube, had a clever idea for promotion: A woman pilot would demonstrate the machine to show the government how easy it was to fly. Melli's appearance was timely. She would have lessons, promote his aeroplane, and his company would make millions. Melli, oblivious of these designs, was thrilled at the prospect of flying again.

Rumpler's chief pilot was Hellmuth Hirth, one of the stars of early German aviation, who later spent eighteen years in aviation in the United States. Handsome, egotistical, he believed firmly that women were unsuited for flying. They might be useful for entertaining the public, but they lacked the physical ability to fly; besides, their presence detracted from the stature of the male pilots. The rumor that a woman was about to enter the school under his instruction had the field agog. His attitude was well known.

Hirth assigned numbers to his students and called them for instruction from either the first or the last, a system that kept the students in high expectation. Who would be first? Melli was number four. Dressed in a white shirt with a black tie, she sat waiting at a table for the drawing that established the order. As numbers were called, it was soon apparent there was no number four. The male attitude was "the woman after us." When questioned, Hirth was defensive; he promised she would have her turn in good weather. The café crowd waited with some amusement.

When Melli finally took her seat in front of Hirth in the Taube, a two-seater monoplane, she found the arrangement far less satisfactory for instruction than it was on the old Wright biplane. Not only were the structure and the steering apparatus different, the entire feel of the monoplane was different. Contact with each other was difficult. The motor below her, at twelve hundred revolutions per minute, hummed smoothly; then, with surprising speed, they were off. Turning to the side, she saw the large wingspan that provided the machine's lift. Straight ahead, the horizon beckoned as Melli absorbed the machine's power and speed. Under Hirth's direction, she discovered the slightest finger pressure maneuvered the aeroplane. It was faster, more powerful than the Wright, but in the turn it took more strength to steer. It seemed to Melli the Taube was flying her as if she lacked the power to control it, unlike the Wright, which was easy to maneuver. Hirth warned her before landing, "Be careful or you'll drill a hole in the grass."

Very quickly the turn was reached; pushing with her right foot, Melli gracefully curved the machine to the right—the ease was wonderful. Mindful of Hirth's warning, Melli worried as landing neared. As the machine touched down, the uneven ground caused the Taube to swing from side to side as it slowed. But they were down, and Melli was in love with the Taube. The curious onlookers decided that a woman might do after all.

Eager to advance, Melli asked when she could take the aeroplane up alone. Hirth was not enthusiastic. She needed more knowledge, he explained, but Melli was quick to recognize an excuse. When pressed, he leveled: "But, you're a woman." Hirth pleaded responsibility and concern for her; Melli would have none of it. After endless protests, Hirth agreed she might solo in a week's time.

On July 27, Melli flew for the first time alone, climbing to one hundred meters before making two circuits of the field. When it was time to land, she dropped down lower to test the gliding speed, then landed without bouncing near the Wright hangar. The Berlin press noted that for the first time on the airfield at Johannisthal a woman, Miss Böse, demonstrated her flying skill by flying two times around the field without her teacher and landing "without smashing the machine." Melli appreciated the recognition of her achievement, but the misspelled name was a bit of a put-down.

Hirth's resistance was just one obstacle to be overcome. The men around the flying field had watched Melli's progress with interest. Some played tricks on her, convinced by their own importance that she was there only to catch a man. Taking their cue from Hirth, others considered her presence strictly as amusement for the public. Melli put up with these attitudes but learned to check her gas tank before each flight, after one experience with an empty tank caused an emergency landing. That time, she came down so suddenly that the delicate machine was a tangle of wires. Another time, Melli was less fortunate. Unequal cable lengths, upsetting the machine's balance, brought her machine down and she received a broken nose. Early fliers knew only too well that emergency landings seldom enjoyed the luxury of level or clear ground, but an emergency was more upsetting when suspicion pointed to a malicious prank.

In September 1911, before observers of the German Aero Club, Ellery von Gorrissen and Cornelius Hintner, Melli became the 115th licensed German aeroplane pilot, the lone woman of the group. Melli had picked her test day to coincide with Hirth's absence because of a flying competition; Gorrissen and Hintner, both teachers at Johannisthal, had no connection with the Rumpler company or its chief pilot. Melli was taking no chances. The *New York Tribune* in a Berlin dateline of September 8 announced that Melli was Germany's first woman pilot. September 13, her twenty-fifth birthday, the date commonly given, is the date the certificate was issued by the German Aero Club. Observers at the time described her glide, the last requirement for the test, as a downward spiral of fifty meters that ended in a faultless landing. The journal *Flugsport* wrote that her eights and loops in the Taube showed "outstanding knowledge." It was a triumphal day for Melli and her friends, Josef Suvelak and Alfred Pietschker, who toasted her with champagne that night at the café. Pietschker, following on Melli's heels, earned license No. 116.

Within two weeks the Autumn Fly Week was to begin at Johannisthal. It was an ever-expanding event since the first Fly Week in 1909. Now, a more sophisticated and knowledgeable public was expected, lured by ballyhoo in the press, to watch Germany's best fliers perform. Women came in larger numbers, hoping to see their favorite airmen, the public's newest heroes, at close range; prizes, world records, and national fame were the attractions for the fliers. Melli entered the competition (she would fly an older Taube with a seventy-horsepower motor loaned by Rumpler) along with twenty-three other entrants—all men.

In the flying before the exhibition began, Melli found herself ostracized by the men on the field; no one trusted her enough to go up with her. Charles Boutard was her savior. He went up with Melli and returned safely to the ground, followed by Alfred Pietschker. As soon as the spectators saw she was proficient, "the ice was broken," said Melli. She had more takers than she could handle. Although the Rumpler pilots—Hirth, Suvelack, and Hans Vollmoeler—at first threatened not to compete with a woman, the meet was too important, the prizes too attractive, to miss. They changed their minds.

Opening day, September 26, was not favorable. Gray clouds covered the sky, fog hovered near the ground, but the wind was calm, always a flier's delight. Berliners stayed at home despite the chance to see the "Flying Girl, Melli Beese." The expensive seats in the grandstand were largely vacant, but the cheaper standing area was packed with die-hard fans. Melli looked forward to a keen, friendly competition with her fellow pilots, undisturbed, if she knew of it, by the Rumpler pilots' reluctance to compete with her.

The first competition, beginning at noon, was the endurance flight, with a prize for the aviator who stayed in the air the longest carrying a passenger. Melli had a full tank of gasoline, but pressure from the Rumpler group kept her from finding a willing passenger. Thanks to a young Swiss, Robert Gsell, a Dorner pilot who volunteered, she was able to enter the event. Gsell wrote his impression years later: Melli could *really* fly; she wasn't on the field just for publicity photographs. Waving to the fans with a small flag, she took the Taube up and was lost to sight in the fog and clouds. Two hours and nine minutes later she landed, one minute less than the best duration flight of the day and a world record for women. The field crowd was impressed. Gsell, recalling that day, joked that he enjoyed brief fame as an "accessory."

The next day, a sunny flier's day, seventeen machines were in the air at the starting gun, with Melli's soon among them. In spite of the weather, attendance was still below expectations. Round and round the machines raced, competing for endurance. Melli missed her old Wright biplane on the turns. Gustav Witte was flying one with remarkable success. It was easier to maneuver than the Taube, but then the joy of racing in the air crowded out all thoughts. Pietschker in his Albatros played tag with Melli, cutting under the Taube when turning toward the field, to delight

A smiling Melli Beese, Germany's first woman pilot, lands after setting a women's flight endurance record with Robert Gsell as her passenger, 1911.
FLUGSPORT

the viewers below. At the day's end, Pietschker and Witte were in the lead; Suvelack, third; Melli, fourth; and Karl Caspar, fifth. Considering that Melli lost fifteen minutes tinkering with her motor at the start, it wasn't a bad day.

One exciting moment, captured by the photographers, made the international press. As Melli was flying the course, the *Parcival,* a German dirigible, one of the week's attractions, loomed up ahead of her on its way to its base. She could see activity in the gondola and the maze of ropes suspended from it, a dangerous threat to the delicate Taube. Melli made a quick decision and flew under the airship, giving the spellbound spectators below a thrill. The picture, snapped at that moment, was spectacular.

On Tuesday, reports of the preceding activities at the field finally brought out the crowds. Tschudi rejoiced as the cashier's box overflowed. Machines rolled out to the starting line, motors clattering, as excited spectators looked for their favorite aviators. Melli came in for much attention, as much for her fur costume with pants as for her record. Women in pants were as novel as a rare specimen at the zoo. There were cheers and applause all around as the mechanics finished their checks, pilots mounted their machines, passengers climbed aboard, and one by one the big birds took to the sky.

Again Pietschker played tag with Melli. She tried to shake him off by going up as they flew around the course, but at eight hundred meters her machine was slow responding to the stick. In the sky, more spring-like than fall, the Taube climbed slowly upward while the crowds below watched the machines' gyrations with open mouths. The Albatros and the Taube disappeared from sight as they climbed upward and outward. Were they lost, in danger? When the cannon signaled the end of the day, aeroplanes gradually returned to earth, until all were down except the Albatros and one Taube. At the last moment, they appeared. The Albatros landed in front of its hangar; the Taube, at almost the same moment, stopped at the starting line.

The cheering and noise were thunderous. Melli, mystified by the crowd's roar, was helped out of the machine by Ludwig, who shouted in her ear: "A world altitude record, Miss Beese!" Reaching 825 meters with a passenger, Melli had broken the women's record set by Hélène Dutrieu's 450 meters and established a new endurance record by extending her first record by eleven minutes. Pietschker's barograph registered 1,280 meters, but Melli's older Taube was unable to push any higher. Melli was speechless. She was presented with flowers to mark her achievement and made a brief statement, expressing the hope that many more women would follow. On this third day of the Fly Week, Melli was in third place behind Pietschker and Suvelack.

Just two years before, Orville Wright, flying with Paul Engelhard at Tempelhof Field, had reached a world altitude record of 172 meters. The year after Melli's flight, Lyubov Golanchikova, a Russian pilot flying in Russia and Germany in the early years, would topple Melli's record, reaching twenty-two hundred meters. Almost three times Melli's record, this 1912 flight indicated how rapidly motors and aeroplanes were improving. Lyubov's machine was a Fokker; unlike Melli, she flew alone, without the weight of a passenger.

Captain Paul Engelhard, chief pilot of the Wright Company, one of the bright stars of German flying and a witness of the Wright 1909 record, drove onto the field in his automobile to offer Melli his congratulations. For a year and a half, he had insisted that women lacked the ability to fly—the very idea was unthinkable. Now, here he was, with something like a smile, congratulating a woman. His gesture, which did not go unnoticed by the field crowd, was the ultimate accolade, far better than a medal from the kaiser.

The Berlin press reported on Melli's records: She was the "Sensation of the Week"; "a little woman has accomplished what her professional men colleagues would be proud to achieve." In the Rumpler hangar, male vanity was seriously wounded; Germany's first woman pilot was in striking range for first place.

September 28 was poor for flying. Gusts of wind and rain swept the field. The sky was dull gray. Hellmuth Hirth, smarting at the possibility that his student might win first place, had just the opportunity he needed. He announced to the pilots that Melli would not fly; as chief pilot for Rumpler, he could not be responsible for the machine she had on loan. Hirth insisted he had received orders; it was not his fault. Melli saw the ban for what it was, an obvious effort to keep her out of first place.

Hirth, perhaps conscience stricken, offered to carry her as a passenger and credit her with the time, but strong winds limited flying time for even the seasoned pilots. According to the *Berliner Tageblatt,* Melli went up as Hirth's passenger, but the flight lasted a bare ten minutes before valve trouble brought the aeroplane down. At the day's end, Melli, with a total record of eight hours, fifty-three minutes, was in third place behind Pietschker (ten hours, fourteen minutes) and Suvelak (nine hours, forty-one minutes).

The day's showing had not been impressive. The Wright biplane seemed to do better in the wind than the monoplanes. The next day the press needled Melli, referring to her as a "sunshine pilot," and angering even the chauvinists who had joked about her ability. They made it a point to say something encouraging to her, saving their ire for the journalists who wrote such ignorant stuff.

Charles Boutard, one of the flying comrades, sensing Melli's disappointment and anger at the turn of events, tried to distract her with thoughts about the future. In the warm comfort of the café, they discussed plans for a flying school, for building aeroplanes, goals that meant more to Melli than competing for money. She had proved she could compete with the best of the men; now, she should do what her heart wanted, urged Boutard. His concern was comforting.

The next day was again gray and windswept, but Paul Engelhard, nicknamed the "Captain" from his naval days, known as a fearless flier in bad weather, would test the sky. His performance up to this point in the meet had been disappointing. Forty-five minutes later, while making a turn in the distance, his new "Baby" Wright disappeared behind a small wooded hill, followed by the sounds of shattering wood, and then all was still. Ground crews and spectators rushed to the scene and found a splintered aeroplane, a dying pilot, and an unconscious passenger. Engelhard died almost immediately; his passenger, Gerhard Sedlmayr, a student, was injured, but not fatally.

Writing later of the accident, Sedlmayr raged at the chaotic conditions resulting from the behavior of the spectators after the crash. A valuable tiepin belonging to Engelhard was taken from his body; Sedlmayr had his cap and glasses stolen; any souvenir was fair game as defenseless pilots lay on the ground, behavior that was most evident in Germany and America. Sedlmayr, speaking for the pilots, resented being entertainment for a thrill-seeking public. Even Tschudi lost his temper when excited spectators, women among them, climbed over the guard rail and surged onto the airfield, oblivious of the danger to themselves, to get closer to the action. After one meet, a more sophisticated spectator complained to him: "Today was boring; there were many flights, but no accident." This mentality was typical among many spectators.

Across the Atlantic, the *New York Times* noted Engelhard's death, his association with the Wright Brothers—Orville had taught him to fly—and his reputation as Germany's foremost aviation authority. At Johannisthal, the pilots were devastated. They knew death was possible for anyone anytime, but not the "Captain." Anthony Fokker noted years afterward: "Every flying field I have known is soaked with the blood of my friends and brother pilots. . . . My memory is one long obituary list."

The pilots in the meet wanted to cancel activity the next day in Engelhard's honor, but management said it was not possible to notify the public in time. The weather, as if in mourning, continued to be poor for flying. To show respect for their fallen hero, aeroplane wings were draped with black bands, flags were lowered to half-mast, and a cannon salute marked his passing. The pilots sat in their hangars, depressed and cold as the starting hour came and went. Finally, a Taube was pushed to the starting place, and Melli, red-faced from the wind and cold, tried repeatedly to start the motor, but failed. She was willing, but the motor was not. One reporter commented the next day that the idea of a woman showing the men up was intolerable. Vanity forced the male pilots to roll out their machines, especially with Prince Joachim of Prussia present. Suvelak charmed the anxious crowds, half anticipating another fatality, with a splendid performance in his Taube. For once, the critical reporter found himself lost in the beauty of the graceful aeroplane's maneuvers.

The final results of the Fly Week were not sensational. Pietschker led the total flying record (thirteen hours, fifty-six minutes, to win 3,716.71 marks), with Melli in fifth place (nine hours, twenty-two minutes to win 2,498.56 marks). Pietschker won the aeroplane competition for altitude, which paid 5,390.07 marks; Suvelak was second, winning 4,609.03 marks. The altitude and duration records with one or more passengers were acceptable in Germany, but elsewhere pilots were achieving better records. *Le Matin,* the French newspaper, rated the results "zero," pointing out that lengthening flights from Paris to Madrid, or Rome, and back to Paris demonstrated a steady progress in aviation not present in the week just ended. By the end of the year, records for altitude, speed, distance, and duration were all held by the French, a situation that did not sit well with the German government, nor did the expressed French determination to maintain their advantage in the air. The German military establishment got the message.

The following year, with the support of Crown Prince Heinrich of Prussia, the German government called for establishment of a National Flying Donation to raise money by contributions for the improvement of German aviation, aware at last that an aeroplane was a useful weapon. The country was seized with patriotic fervor, its goal to make Germany number one in the air. The defense aspect of the fund for protection against unnamed enemies was played down. Within six months, 7,647,950 marks and 48 pfennigs were raised from contributions nationwide. Many, like Melli and Boutard, contributed for the national good. In addition, taxes were levied on aeroplane production, and the bailiff became a familiar sight at Johannisthal, checking to see that each machine bore a stamp showing it had paid its share. For the smaller builders, the contributions, or taxes, were barely affordable, which meant that the individual designers and builders would end up squeezed out of business by the Flying Donation's demands. The old days of experimental aeroplane construction with parts collected from wherever were gone. Aviation was becoming a commercial enterprise; the idealists and dreamers were disappearing, their place taken by a production line capable of turning out large numbers of the same model.

With two colleagues, Melli took part in two exhibition flights in Hanover and Detmold, but her experience there cured her of making appearances. Male students resented her appearance and played tricks, resulting in an emergency landing on one occasion. At Detmold, excited crowds broke though fences and flooded the field, making it impossible to take off. For Melli this was the last straw.

In the weeks following the meet, Melli planned to establish a flying school of her own. Even before her experience during the Fly Week, she had spent hours discussing ideas with her friends at the field. Alfred Pietschker, Werner von Siemen's grandson—comparable to being a Rockefeller—was especially helpful. Reportedly, he proposed a romantic and technical merger between them, but, for Melli, he remained just a good friend. Her life would have been very different in years to come if she had accepted his proposal, but Charles Boutard's blue eyes had charmed her. She valued Pietschker's friendship, enjoyed talking about God, life, and flying, as young people do, and his death testing a new monoplane of his own design in November, barely a month after his Fly Week victory, was a tragic loss. Melli and Ludwig had pleaded with him for more work on the machine, but Pietschker wouldn't listen. One source hints that Melli's refusal of marriage led him to fly his machine devil may care, without first checking its readiness.

In January of the new year, the Melli Beese Flying School opened with Charles Boutard and Hermann Reichelt, from Dresden, as partners. Melli's mother and Karl A. Lingner, an important Dresden businessman, were financial backers. Boutard and Reichelt each brought a monoplane of their own construction, and Melli bought a used Rumpler Taube from another flier—these three were the school machines. Adolf Ludwig, whom Melli met her first day at Johannisthal, agreed to be the mechanic at the salary of two hundred marks a month, plus 1 percent for each student. Two hangars on the old starting place housed the school. Boutard practiced for his test, earned his license on April 4, and helped teach.

Melli had definite ideas about a school, based on her experiences at three. She was determined that students learn the theoretical and technical side of aeroplanes when not actually flying rather than the all-too-familiar aimless wait of days or weeks for an available machine or teacher, or appropriate weather. Training would proceed on a regular routine; students would be limited to a manageable number. She proposed to have three teachers and three machines available. When students failed to materialize in sufficient numbers, reluctantly, she let Reichelt go. She and Boutard would teach and begin building a machine of their own design. Money was short, but Melli believed a new machine would improve the school's financial situation. She also believed the government's Flying Donation would encourage technical development among smaller builders.

There were never many students; the school hardly paid its way, but its record was enviable: no deaths; not one serious accident; no severe breaks, only four minor ones. (Tora Sjöborg, a young Swedish student, was responsible for these. More interested in the pilots than their machines, she later married Bruno Hanuschke and gave up flying.) The school fell behind when the Flying Donation began to pay for training military pilots. Army officers could not come to Melli for training because her partner, Boutard, was French. Moreover, her civilian students were forbidden to compete in national meets. The old international spirit at Johannisthal was disappearing. Although the flying school had established quality in flying training, the changed national scene in aviation led Melli and Boutard to place their hope for the future in construction.

In early 1913 the first Melli Beese machine, the Melli Beese-Taube, was rolled out onto the field by Boutard, who collaborated on its construction. It was an amalgam of the Rumpler monoplane with French improvements and with original parts designed by Melli, which improved on the original design. Igo Etrich, the Austrian designer of the first Taube, visited frequently while the machine was being built and approved the work in progress—it was clean, technical work. The light machine, named for Melli's deceased friend Georg Schendel, performed perfectly at its debut at Johannisthal, showing speed and maneuverability. Its stronger motor allowed it to carry three passengers as easily as one; only one part of the chassis was original. The machine was used for training students when—despite a patent for an original part and its lower price (twelve thousand marks compared with the Rumpler Taube's twenty thousand marks)—there were no buyers. The military came and looked, agreed the machine was clean work, first-class material, didn't say no and didn't say yes. Undeterred, Melli and Boutard

Melli and her husband, Charles Boutard, at the unveiling of their first plane, a Beese-Taube, in 1913. Despite turning out innovative, first-rate flying machines, their enterprise was soon squeezed out of business. DEUTSCHES MUSEUM, MUNICH

continued with plans for more building, confident that part of the national aviation moneys would be given to small builders like themselves who were improving German aviation.

Sadly, they were wrong. Money for exceptional German design performance, and similar advances, was dropped; funds went to train pilots for the military, with the large manufacturers—Rumpler, Albatros, Aviatik, and later Fokker—winning the pot for construction. Their machines were avidly sought after, to the detriment of innovative German designers. And always there was the unspoken reality about a Beese machine: the builder was a woman. When Melli and Boutard married in January 1913, their situation became even more difficult. According to German law, Melli became a French citizen when she married Boutard. One stipulation for receiving government funds required that aeroplanes be German made; as a foreigner, Boutard had been eliminated from benefiting. Now, Melli was excluded.

Despite financial concerns, Melli wrote that the period between January 1912 and August 1914 was the happiest of her life. Work was nonstop—no time for sleep, only work, with every ounce of energy. Such dedication "needs great love for the cause and even more energy." Yet she was happy.

The couple busied themselves with plans for a flying-boat, the dream Melli had held since her days in Sweden. If a fast monoplane was not in the German picture, surely a flying-boat would capture public attention. Hope carried them a long way, and there were still a few civilian students to be taught.

Hermann Dorner, one of the three great early German aeroplane builders, returned to Johannisthal at this juncture to be greeted joyfully by Melli and Boutard. Dorner, like Melli, was an idealist whose enthusiasm lay in construction, but now reality forced him to compete to earn money, since his own business had closed. He had worked for a while with another company where he could do some scientific work, but this didn't satisfy him.

Could Melli lend him an aeroplane? She was only too happy to do so, because, as she explained to him, her marriage had made her a foreigner and barred her from competition. Now part of her would be in the contest. With the borrowed Melli Beese-Taube, Dorner won a Flying

Donation prize of a thousand marks, which would keep him afloat for a while.

According to one source, Melli promptly asked him to join her in the flying-boat project, for among his many talents, Dorner was a whiz at computing construction figures. Other sources leave open the question of how much he had to do with the flying boat. Melli claimed she had worked on it for four years (this seems an exaggeration), but it is possible Dorner helped compute costs of the construction, after first analyzing every aspect of the boat to judge its feasibility. His genius in construction combined with Melli's technical ability was security that the flying boat would establish her as Germany's first woman aeroplane builder.

The flying-boat design was advanced for its time. Again, Melli obtained a patent for an original part (No. 290072), which after the war was used internationally. The fuselage of the machine, narrow and pointed like a boat at each end, with a fairly broad keel that curved inward as it rose to counter rough water, was composed of two parts, an outer shell and an inner section. They were joined in such a way that the outer part would absorb the movement of the water and cushion the interior section, which would house the motor, gas tanks, steering equipment, and people. A lining of cedar bark, pliable and water resistant, would shield the inner section, reduce vibration, and keep the compartment dry. The unique construction was intended to create stability in the water without sacrificing speed and safety. The fuselage would be built by the Oertz Yacht Works in Hamburg.

Above the main body, two wings separated by metal struts would provide lift and maneuverability; the upper wing, greater in length than the lower, had curved fins at each end for maneuvering. In the rear, the rudder rose elegantly from the fanned-out surface atop the boat. Wing surface measured 36.5 square meters; there was a six-cylinder, one hundred–horsepower Mercedes motor for lift and speed; and the boat had a distance radius of two thousand kilometers. The machine would not be inexpensive, but Melli was determined to go ahead. If necessary, she would give up everything she had to raise the money. The flying-boat and the Beese-Boutard monoplane, still in construction, carried the couple's hopes for the future. Their single-mindedness blinded them to outside events and the shadow of approaching war.

Johannisthal was no longer a compatible workplace. The Beese-Boutard endeavors were not viewed favorably by the military establishment now firmly entrenched, as nationalistic fervor swept the country. Symptomatic of the changed atmosphere, Georg von Tschudi was criticized frequently in the press for encouraging Russian, Rumanian, and Swedish fliers to work at the field. His position as manager would be taken over by the military when war broke out. In this changed climate, Melli and Boutard no longer felt welcome at the field, and, once construction began, they found the old hangar too small and moved their enterprise to Neukölln, outside of Berlin.

The second Beese-Boutard machine was finished in the fall of 1913 and named for Alfred Pietschker. Its debut met all expectations. It was elegant, light, speedy—a combination of the best aspects of three monoplane designs: Morane, Hanuschke, and Boutard. Boutard's work was of the highest quality, down to the finest point; he had great technical skill. A knowing eye could detect the differences from the Rumpler look; its performance was unquestionably different. The motor, a French air-cooled model, was three times more powerful, allowing for quick ascent or descent. It was perfect for stunt flying and would make a good observation machine. German military observers came to inspect it, suspicious of the French test pilot, and found it inconceivable that a woman had helped build it. German pilots never had a chance to see the machine, much less fly it. The fast one-seater monoplane, which incorporated the best of aeroplane design at the time and influenced the design of Fokker's popular machine in World War I, ended on the trash heap, Melli wrote later, because of "patriotic fanaticism."

Earlier, in the fall of 1912, when the purpose of the Flying Donation became evident, Melli had written an article for the newspapers pointing out the government's mistake in cutting out experimentation in aviation construction and settling for mass production of established models. She insisted that technical improvement in German aviation would come only through healthy competition in experimentation in design and construction that included smaller, individual companies. Her comments—an emergency call from small builders—were ignored in the rush to expand wings for Germany.

The first German air parade, held in September 1912 at Tempelhof Field, had shown all too clearly that aviation had become big business.

Excited spectators craned their necks to watch as trumpets heralded the overhead flight of Rumplers, Albatroses, and other machines with military approval, flown by ever-increasing numbers of German pilots. It was a spectacle designed to fan patriotic fervor, to warn neighbors to the west that Germany was prepared, and to show the Flying Donation was being put to good use. By the time war was declared, Germany had some eight hundred trained pilots and an impressive number of aeroplanes.

As the work at Neukölln neared completion in the spring of 1914, Melli and Charles prepared to move to Warnemünde, near the water, for the first tests of the flying boat. The Northern Flying Competition was scheduled for August, and there was still work to be done. Two competitors were already on hand: an AFG and a Rumpler, which boasted pontoons amid a tangle of wires. There would be twenty-six boats at the start. Studying the boats, Melli was convinced they didn't offer real competition. Her beautiful boat with its sleek line and delicate appearance hid unbelievable strength in the inner structure of the wings, every inch of which had been carefully crafted.

The first of August was filled with summer delight, the kind of day that sent Germans to the seashore. The sea, capped with white foam, extended a challenge to all comers, but the competition would never be. The marine administration sealed the port on orders from Berlin, the competition between some of the country's foremost aeroplane builders was canceled, and later that day Melli and Charles were arrested as enemy aliens as rumors of imminent conflict rippled across the country. Melli was released, but Boutard was imprisoned in Holzminden, where inhumane treatment soon put him in the hospital. The authorities seized and destroyed everything the couple owned—workshop, tools, materials, aeroplanes, the automobile, even their home. Dreams and hope collapsed; a long, dark period of suffering began.

Melli returned to Johannisthal briefly, but it was closed to her. Old companions like Thelen couldn't or wouldn't help. Embarrassed by orders to clear the field, he explained, "It's the war," which was the excuse for everything that happened. The Albatros Works had tried to hire her to make parts for them, but an official government inspector forbade it. Melli's only help was the little her mother could provide. Even then, patriotic neighbors regarded Melli as one of the enemy. While Charles was hospitalized, he urged her to divorce him and improve her situation, but she refused to hear of it.

On his release, the couple was confined at Prignitz, far enough away to be no threat, where they had to find their own housing and food. It was pure hell, according to Melli's memoir written in 1921. They found a room with the widow of a minister whose daughter had tuberculosis. The inevitable happened; Boutard contracted tuberculosis in both lungs. Despite a doctor's certificate, nothing was done to remove them; there was no place for them to go. It was a time when, as Melli later wrote, "we were pressed to be self-sufficient," living on greens from the garden, buying secretly from farmers at extravagant prices until their money ran out, enduring their changed lives in a cold, damp room. Illness was a daily companion. Relief came in the form of political upheaval.

The November revolution of 1918 brought freedom, and, with the end of war, the Beese-Boutard couple returned to Berlin and Johannisthal. Physically and mentally, they were human wrecks, but hope was the tonic that could restore them. The familiar flying field was a disheartening scene. Used military aeroplanes were everywhere. The old hangar was a skeleton, as most of it had been burned in the harsh winter of 1917–18, but Melli cleared a place on the old starting field, struggled to restore the hangar, and tried to start anew. The rent was forgiven until she could pay in the future. There were few familiar faces.

Melli sought out a lawyer, laid before him the facts on the seizure of her school and flying machines, and started the legal process to gain compensation for her loss. She planned to buy a used aeroplane and fly exhibitions to make money with her share, or open a flying school; Boutard, more of a realist, planned to buy an automobile and drive a taxi in Berlin.

The news that two Englishmen, Alcock and Brown, had flown the North Atlantic in an old bomber fired Melli with another idea: a round-the-world flight. Businessmen, newspapers, and film companies were approached; the idea excited interest, particularly the fact that a woman would attempt the flight. According to one source, she made a deal with Rumpler for two aeroplanes, with the understanding that if she failed to meet payments in a year, she would lose the machines and the down payment. People in the know questioned whether she was physically and mentally capable of flying—reportedly, morphine was now a part of her life.

Luck was against her. The world flight failed to gain the necessary financial support, and Melli's attempts to adjust to newer machines, more advanced than the prewar models she knew, failed. Rumpler reclaimed the aeroplanes; the world flight was dead. One relic from this period is a short film clip of Melli and Charles in an aeroplane that was used by Walter Jerven in a 1940 documentary, *Himmelstürmer,* based on archival material.

Little is known of Melli's last years. She worked demonstrating motor-cycles for twenty marks a day. It paid for food while she waited for compensation from the government. Her old friends at Johannisthal were scattered, or dead. The once busy airfield was but a memory, as aviation activity moved to Tempelhof. The change was disheartening for Melli, who could not bear that the pioneers who had done so much for the advancement of flying be forgotten. She approached publishers with the idea of a memoir of Johannisthal but ran into a familiar attitude about women. A man should write such a work!

Undeterred, in 1921 she wrote a remarkable memoir of the Johannisthal flying field that was published in the German magazine *Motor.* It is a valuable source on the pioneer days of German aviation. Covering the years 1910–13, the memoir is unalloyed Melli—idealistic, passionate, at times poetic, but unswerving in her opinions. She was determined that the early heroes of German aviation be acknowledged. Men who had sacrificed all, even their life's blood, who had challenged God in their zeal to conquer the air, deserved the thanks of their country every time an aeroplane passed in the German sky.

The emotion in Melli's memoir was partly triggered by medication and the increasing strain in the couple's marriage. They separated. Boutard is said to have gone to France alone in hopes of better job prospects there, but he found himself arrested as soon as he crossed the border. He was brought before a war court and questioned about his activities during the war. Many weeks later the court found him not guilty, and he was free once again. The experience dampened his plans, and he returned to Germany, a disillusioned man.

Finally, the long-awaited government compensation was received. The lawyer took his share for his work and the credit he had extended to them, and inflation absorbed much of the remainder, which was divided between Melli and Charles. Melli may have invested in an automobile venture that failed, leaving her with a small pittance for living. Charles bought an automobile and earned enough as a taxi driver to get by.

The stress and deprivation of the past years took their toll. Melli was never strong after the suffering of the war years, and her life, so involved with flying, was now hardly worth living. She resided in a rooming house in the city, enveloped by depression much of the time. If she had any hope of flying, she had to renew her license, which was seized when the war began, an undertaking now more of a threat than a challenge for her tired spirit.

At the end of a flight on a gray October day in 1925, she shattered the aeroplane, a wartime Fokker, on landing, by either accident or design. It was the period to her flying career.

Two months later, on December 22, 1925, the gloom of her life ever deeper, Melli went to her bedroom and shot herself with a revolver. It was an unusual act for a woman, but then Melli had been unconventional all of her life. Without a dream, her life ceased to have meaning.

In 1986 a plaque was raised at her birthplace near Dresden to commemorate the one hundredth anniversary of her birth. It was a small tribute from a nation that failed to appreciate her achievements while she was alive. An exhibition in 1992 at the Heimatmuseum Treptow, Berlin, brought Melli a measure of the recognition she deserved.

In a period that witnessed the stirring of feminism, Melli had no interest in the movement nor in political parties. Totally involved in flying and building aeroplanes, her life was one eloquent statement of the capabilities of women and their ability to compete with men on equal terms. Many men admired her; many others disliked her for forcing her way into a man's world and winning a place there with success.

Other women were flying in Germany in the years when Melli was at Johannisthal. Bozena Láglerová, a Czech, and the first woman student of Hans Grade, was the second woman to receive a pilot's license in Germany, No. 125, issued October 19, 1911. Earlier, on October 10, she was issued Austrian license No. 37, the first woman pilot recognized by the Austrian Aero Club.

Bozena began her training in the spring of 1911. A crash in July that demolished the aeroplane seemed at first to have injured her only slightly. When internal injuries were discovered, she went home to Prague to recuperate. Toward the end of that period of rest, she started flying again and won her Austrian license. This success encouraged her to return to Germany to finish her training contract with Grade, resulting in her winning a German license.

With her new professional rank, she returned to her homeland. On October 22, while flying fifteen hundred meters high at Kladno-

Krocehlavy, near Prague, she crashed. Fortunately, she had only slight injuries, and the aeroplane was later repaired. In the next two years she flew extensively in Europe, making appearances at Leipzig, Hamburg, Johannisthal, and Friedrichshafen.

The second German woman to earn a pilot's license, the third issued to a woman, was Charlotte Möhring, from Pankow near Berlin, who studied with Grade at Gelsenkirchen. Flying a Grade monoplane, she won license No. 285, issued on September 7, 1912, despite an earlier landing smash. She was shaken up but without serious injury, and the machine's right wing was soon rebuilt. Early in 1913, she was manager and teacher at a small flying school at Mainz-Gonsenheim, founded by Curt von Stoephasius. Stoephasius occasionally delivered aeroplanes to new owners.

On one such trip to deliver a Rumpler Taube from Johannisthal to Döberitz, Charlotte was listed as passenger. She described the trip later for a journal—her total delight with views from a thousand meters, then twenty-three hundred meters, and "Mother Earth" spread out below. The one hundred-horsepower Mercedes motor made the forty-five-kilometer trip to Döberitz in eighteen minutes, ending in a long, slow glide downward from twenty-three hundred meters in marvelous turns and eights with the wires humming. For Charlotte, the sound offered complete contentment.

About this time, Charlotte met Georg Mürau, also a Grade student, from Bork, who had started a small flying school at Gelsenkirchen. The two married and in 1914 were running a flying school in Crefeld with Charlotte acting as manager and teacher. She and her husband made flights and exhibited in twenty-one German cities, as well as foreign countries, in an aviation career that lasted until the First World War began. Writing in 1953, Charlotte never lost her enthusiasm and interest for the "beautiful flying sport." Apparently, she did not resume her career after the war.

Martha Behrbohm, the third German woman pilot, earned license No. 427, issued on June 4, 1913, after first studying at Johannisthal under Paul Schwandt, an early student of Grade, then with Hans Grade himself at Bork. Like Melli, she was the daughter of an artist, who was an enthusiastic supporter of aviation. Through flying, Martha met Hanns Georgi, who obtained his training at Leipzig-Lindenthal from Oswald Kahnt, another Grade student, before going to Bork for his license tests. Their mutual interest led to marriage, and the two were known as "the flying couple" in exhibitions. Actually, Germany had three flying couples at this time: Beese-Boutard, Möhring-Mürau, and Behrbohm-Georgi all of whom operated flying schools.

Early one Sunday morning, Martha and Hanns set off from the Bork flying field on a short flight to Johannisthal to take part in the Round Berlin Flight. Aviation was still such a primitive science that what should have been a short flight took most of the day. Shortly after takeoff, the Grade *eindecker* ("one-wing," or "monoplane") became lost in early morning fog. Martha had a self-made map of basting pins fastened to one leg of her trousers to indicate the direction of flight, but in the encircling gloom, it was useless. The aeroplane made an emergency landing, hoping to orient the pilot, and in doing so broke one axle of the underchassis and half of the propeller. A telegraph was sent to Bork for the necessary repair equipment, and the two fliers settled down to wait.

An hour later a car from the Grade factory arrived with Mr. Grade himself and two mechanics, who promptly went to work to install the replacement parts. Martha and Hanns waited at a nearby restaurant, to the delight of the owner, who was thrilled with the visitors, who had literally dropped from the heavens. On the ground, curious country people appeared as if by magic and watched every move of the mechanics. It was their first introduction to the technical advances in the world beyond their farms.

Hours later, the repairs were finished, but the propeller was now smaller by six centimeters and too weak to carry the weight of two passengers. Martha got out, and Hanns continued alone to Johannisthal, a six-minute flight after all day spent on the ground.

Years later, remembering the flight, Martha enjoyed telling people about the "kindergarten" days of German aviation, when pilots were at the mercy of wind, rain, and fickle weather, when pilots made emergency landings using their legs as brakes and passengers held on for dear life to the brace rails of the chassis. In those days fliers could not imagine the enormous development in aviation, and the speed of it, that would occur after 1913.

Behrbohm-Georgi bought two Grade monoplanes and opened a flying school in August 1913 at the new flying field at Leipzig-Mockau.

They had great plans and much confidence, but their timing was poor. There were many flying schools, and, coupled with the public's general disinterest in aviation technology, their plans did not succeed. The public wanted stunt flying; tumbling in the sky was what attracted spectators. The couple exhibited and the school limped along until the war ended civilian activity.

It is worth mentioning that Hans Grade, an important personality in German aviation, trained more women pilots than all the other German flying schools together. In this regard he was a man out of the German mold; Grade's view was why shouldn't women fly? An officer student of that period recalled that women students were subjected to severe verbal ridicule—double-entendre references to women's anatomy were popular—that he likened to running a gauntlet. The only defense was to ignore the shouted comments and laughter.

The last woman pilot licensed in Germany before World War I was Else Haugk, who earned license No. 785 on June 6, 1914. (Her name is sometimes mistakenly written as "Haugh.") Else was Swiss but went to Germany because there was more aviation opportunity there. She received her training in Hamburg at the Hansa Flying Works under Karl Caspar's direction. Like Melli, she learned to fly on a Rumpler Taube named Hansa Taube by Caspar, which was actually a copy of the successful monoplane from Johannisthal. Weeks after Else passed her tests, the coming military conflict ended all civilian flying.

During World War I there was no civilian aviation, and for several years after the war Germans were forbidden to fly. Judging from Melli's case and the silence of her compatriots, when aviation revived, the first women fliers were left behind by the tremendous advances in technology in the intervening years. A new generation of women would have to pick up where the pioneers left off.

Two other women deserve mention, Lilly Steinschneider and Rosina Ferrario. Lilly, Hungarian by birth and a student of Karl Illner, won license No. 4 from the Hungarian Aero Club early in 1912. Notably, she competed with men in 1913 in competition at Vienna, one of two women—Jeanne Pallier from France was the other. The women won a creditable third and fourth place in a duration contest. Lilly was flying an Etrich Taube with an Austrian Daimler sixty-five-horsepower engine, Pallier an Astra biplane with a Renault eighty-horsepower engine. Both women were scheduled to compete for altitude a day later. Unfortunately, Lilly crashed in a cornfield in an emergency landing when her motor stopped, ending her competition. According to an account in the *Arbeiter-Zeitung,* Lilly, who emerged unscathed, was glad to be rid of the machine; it was old. One writer commented that Lilly, an accomplished horsewoman, drove her aeroplane like a Lipizzan—the performance was precise, regal.

Rosina, born in Milan on July 28, 1888, received license No. 203 on January 3, 1913, from the Italian Aero Club. Flying a monoplane, she debuted at Como in the Circuit of the Lakes, and from there she appeared at Naples, Rome, and the better meets in Italy. She was the only Italian woman to win wings before the war.

5

The Imperial Eagle Sprouts New Wings

FAR TO THE EAST, a succession of exhibitions by French and German fliers brought aviation to the attention of the Russian public. Raymonde de Laroche showed Russian women that flying was not just for men. The following year, Lydia Zvereva, the first Russian woman to earn a pilot's license, received certificate No. 31, on August 22, 1911, at the Russian Aviation Association Flying School at Gatchina, flying a Farman.

Born into a military family in St. Petersburg in 1890, and educated at the Czar Nicholas I Institute for Girls, she proved herself equally as capable in an aeroplane as on the ground with a wrench. Once, when there was a problem with the motor of the school Farman before a flight, her instructor told her to wait while he fetched a mechanic. She waited, but when no one came, she took a look at the motor, discovered what was wrong, and repaired it. When her instructor returned with the mechanic in tow, the motor started and ran perfectly.

All was not uneventful, however. As in Germany, Lydia discovered some men were not thrilled by her presence: The Aero Club demanded such a high security deposit for a contest at Tsarskoe Selo that she had to bow out; at Gatchina airfield, a competitor put iron filings in the motor of her Farman. Lydia was amazed: "I do not know who could get such an outrageous idea; could I really be competing with somebody?" Of course, and, obviously, she was a threat. A fellow student said of her flying: "Zvereva carried out flights in a bold, decisive manner. I remember everybody was paying attention to her masterful piloting, including the high-altitude flights."

Such episodes and the rigor of exhibitions in places as diverse as Baku, Tiflis, and Latvia—for a while she teamed with E. Spitzberg, sportsman and pilot—led her to consider other aviation work. Marriage to her flight instructor, Vladimir V. Slyusarenko, a sports flier and teacher, led, with the help of Fjodor Gerogievich Kalep, well known in the world of motors, to Lydia and her husband's establishing an aeroplane manufacturing plant. Originally, a repair and flying school in Riga, the operation expanded, building ten Farmans under government contract by the summer of 1914, before moving to St. Petersburg, where Farmans and Moranes were manufactured. Lydia helped in the factories at Riga and St. Petersburg; she flew infrequently, mainly to try new models.

In May of 1914 it was announced in Riga that Lydia would perform a flight on the 19th in a Morane monoplane. The hippodrome was standing room only, with more crowds along the fence. At the appointed time, 8 P.M., Lydia climbed into the monoplane, checked the motor, and took off, climbing for several minutes to some eight hundred meters. At that point she switched off the motor and pointed the Morane into a dive. As the seconds ticked off and the crowd tensed, the motor roared again, and the machine turned upward and completed a loop. Leveling off, Lydia proceeded to spiral downward to the field. No more than ten minutes, the astonished spectators could hardly believe what they had witnessed: the first woman pilot to loop an aeroplane. Male aviators, Peter Nesteroff and Aldophe Pégoud, had performed this feat before her, and other women would follow her in the next two years, but Lydia did it first.

When war came in 1914, Zvereva and Slyusarenko concentrated their construction at St. Petersburg, where output in 1916 totaled about eighty Farmans and Moranes, both French models—the work of some four hundred workers and "eight office employees and specialists, an enviable proportion even today."

Unfortunately, Lydia caught typhoid fever in April 1916 and died on May 1 at the age of twenty-six. She was buried in Alexander Nevski Monastery while an aerial formation flew over the cemetery in her honor.

Lydia was unusually outspoken about wanting to win equality with men in the air: "Thus, by opening the path to aviation for Russian women, I am inviting them to follow me to score a victory in the air by women, in this respect to have equality with men." The majority of the women pioneers may have felt this same sense of purpose, but, more conscious of social attitudes, they didn't state it so boldly.

The second Russian woman to win a pilot's license was Eudocie V. Anatra, who, on October 3, 1911, won certificate No. 54 at Gatchina airfield. Together with the flier Naumov she opened a flying school in 1912. One of their best-known students was Eugenie Shakhovskaya, who began her training with them before going to Germany. Little is known about the rest of Anatra's career. She did not make headlines, as some of her contemporaries did.

Eugenie Shakhovskaya, a titled princess, born in St. Petersburg in 1889, reportedly a cousin of the czar, began training at Gatchina, the third Russian woman to take to the air, following Raymonde de Laroche's lead. Flying was now acceptable for women, and more exciting than driving an automobile.

Eugenie, whose aristocratic birth freed her from worry about respectability, flew with Vladimir Lebedev in Russia, where she started her training before following Wssewolod Abramovitch, chief pilot of the Wright Company, to Germany. Abramovitch, with Karl Hackstetter as navigator, had made a long-distance flight slowed by technical difficulties from Berlin to St. Petersburg, arriving on August 6, 1912, twenty-four days after takeoff. The two had traveled sixteen hundred kilometers; the actual flying time was nineteen and a half hours. Ten days after his arrival in St. Petersburg, Abramovitch returned to Germany, possibly with Eugenie. An eager student on the Wright aeroplane after beginning lessons on a Farman, she would win her license within days.

On August 16, 1912, Eugenie received German license No. 274 having successfully passed her tests at Johannisthal airfield near Berlin. When war broke out in September between Italy and Turkey, she reportedly offered her services to the Italian government but was turned down. We do know she returned to St. Petersburg as a licensed pilot to demonstrate the Wright biplane to the military. At this time the Russians relied largely on foreign-designed aeroplanes, particularly Wrights and Farmans; Russian models were slow to appear, though factories turned out foreign models on a lease arrangement.

The press reported that Shakhovskaya made flights for the young women at a girls' high school in addition to flights for the military. Eugenie quickly gained a reputation for fearless flying; a strong wind did not faze her from going up with a passenger. On one such flight, the gas tank burst and the motor stopped, but Eugenie had the presence of mind to glide down, and landed safely. Shortly after this incident, she returned to Johannisthal.

The Fürstin, as she was known in Germany, spent much of her time with her countryman, Abramovitch, who was also known as a daring stunt flier and an excellent teacher. Apparently, Eugenie was content to fly and to teach students on the Wright biplane; competition did not interest her. Eugenie was greatly loved by Abramovitch, a feeling she reciprocated—the two fliers were a familiar sight, flying together frequently.

Early one April morning in 1913, the two went for a ride in a Wright biplane, possibly a new model, with Eugenie as pilot. As the aeroplane gained altitude, it suddenly lost power—vibrating like a stricken animal—side slipped, and, despite the pilot's efforts, dropped heavily to the

Russian pilots Eugenie Shakhovskaya and Wssewolod Abramovitch seated in a Wright biplane. In April 1913, Abramovitch died in a crash when the plane that Shakhovskaya was piloting lost power and plummeted to the ground. Shakhovskaya survived her injuries. LIBRARY OF CONGRESS

ground. (*Flugsport* reported the Wright was caught in the backwash of a Taube flying ahead, but there is no mention of this from any other source.) The crash shattered the aeroplane. Abramovitch, with a concussion and internal injuries, died the following day; Eugenie suffered a broken nose and chest and lung injuries, but she survived.

It was an unfortunate day. Fifteen minutes later, the Russian aviator Elia Dunetz died at Johannisthal when he glided down from a great height in a Schneider monoplane. Pressure folded the wings back, the machine plummeted to the ground—the motor still running—and the pilot was crushed beneath the aeroplane. The scene was all too familiar when pilots pushed fragile machines too far.

Little is known of Eugenie in the years after, other than her grief over Abramovitch's death, but rumors swirled around her. According to one sourced (probably apocryphal), she gave up flying, married a German officer in 1918, left him, and ended her years in a poorhouse in the south of France in the 1930s.

Other historians place her flying in Russia for the forces of Nicholas II as an ensign assigned to the First Field Air Squadron performing artillery spotting and reconnaissance. She did not fly combat missions, but some historians describe her as "the world's first woman combat pilot."

According to these sources, there is much speculation about her activities while on military duty: She was involved in "numerous liaisons" with officers in her unit; she squandered her wealth on pleasures and shared her bed with "countless officers." Charged with giving information to the enemy and attempting to flee to enemy lines, she was convicted of treason and sentenced to die by firing squad. Nicholas II commuted her sentence to life imprisonment in a convent—she was pregnant—from which the Russian Revolution freed her.

When next we hear of her, she had joined the Red forces and, reportedly, was chief executioner in Kiev for General Tcheka, dispatching captive officers with her Mauser pistol. The same sources claim she had become a drug addict (morphine was the standard treatment for pain) and, while drugged, shot an assistant for no reason. In return, Eugenie was killed by her fellow revolutionaries. No dates are given for any of this information, which reads like a romance novel.

There is no question that Eugenie could fly an aeroplane and she flew at Johannisthal; the rest needs more confirmation. We do know that she and her fellow countrywoman, Lyubov Golanchikova, were strong personalities, unconventional, thrived on adventure, and, like other women, took to the air for the sheer joy of it. Possibly Russian history has painted Eugenie more vividly than she actually was. If so, future historians may discover the truth about her life after Abramovitch.

Lyubov Golanchikova, another intriguing Russian—who was also a former dancer-singer known as Molly Moret with a small-time vaudeville company—was the object of wild enthusiasm after breaking Melli Beese's altitude record at Johannisthal in 1912. The third woman after Zvereva and Anatra to win a license in Russia (Eugenie won hers in Germany in August 1912), she received license No. 56, issued December 29, 1911, flying a Farman biplane at Gatchina. Like Eugenie, she had watched Raymonde de Laroche fly in April 1910, and her budding interest increased after a flight with Michel Efimoff, who won his license at Châlons, during the 1911 summer meets. She was hooked.

In the fall of 1911, Luba, as she was known in later years, took instruction in the early morning and performed on the stage at night, determined to get a license regardless of the effort. One source says her lessons were paid for by an admirer who found the idea of Luba flying intoxicating. Certainly for Luba, flying was passionately exciting. She described herself and fellow fliers as "aerial wanderers; eternity took us under its wing as a free child of ether." ("Ether" was often used back in those days as a synonym for air.)

Luba soon discovered that despite a license in hand, the expected door of opportunity was closed. She signed up with an exhibition company to make appearances, but it was not the career she had imagined. In April 1912, while flying at a meet in Riga, Luba crashed on landing when bystanders threw sticks at her machine. She lost control of the Farman, hit a fence, and was hospitalized with minor injuries. It was a rude baptism to exhibiting in the countryside.

Michael Gregor described the hazardous conditions in exhibition flying at that time. Barnstorming around Russia, he planned a flight at Rovno in Russian Poland. The first site was far too open; spectators didn't have to pay to see the action. A second site, a racetrack in the middle of thick woods, was ideal, except for the trees and capricious wind conditions. On his first attempt to ascend, he failed to clear the trees. On the second, he blew a tire. Each time, repairs delayed the show until the excited crowd became impatient and started calling "fake." Nervous police canceled the exhibition without consulting Gregor, and when the aviator tried to leave, the angry crowd followed him to heckle. Finally, when he drew his revolver and threatened to shoot, the crowd gradually melted away. Gregor said most pilots carried guns, claiming they were for protection in the air against birds flying into the propeller. Luba didn't have that assurance.

When Anthony Herman Fokker came to St. Petersburg in May 1912 to demonstrate his aeroplane to the military, he met Luba. Advised by his friend C. MacKenzie Kennedy to hire a woman pilot to demonstrate his aeroplane, he persuaded Luba to join his company in Germany and fly Fokker machines. That she was glamorous as well as a capable pilot was a bonus. The switch from biplane to monoplane was easily done, Luba was billed as the "Flying Girl," and her warm camera presence helped make Fokker's advertising campaign a success. They saw much of each other at this time.

On November 21, 1912, flying a Fokker eindecker with a one-hundred–horsepower Argus motor, Luba established a women's world record for altitude, with a flight of twenty-two hundred meters, and became an overnight sensation. The newspapers hailed her flight, pointing out it was almost three times greater than Melli Beese's record the previous year. Actually, any comparison between the two records is useless. The machines were too different, as was the weight carried, but both records were remarkable for their time. One result of the flight was the military took a second look at Fokker's aeroplanes, which became stalwarts of German aviation in the First World War.

When in July 1913 the French aviator Léon Letort flew nonstop from Paris to Berlin in a Morane monoplane, Luba was among the welcomers. On the return trip to Paris, Luba left with him, leaving some Germans to wonder, was it love of adventure, or espionage? (Germany already exhibited signs of paranoia regarding the French.) If there had been a romantic relationship with Fokker, it had cooled. He admitted years later, after a failed marriage, that he spent too much time thinking about aeroplanes.

When Letort met Luba, he learned there was a ten thousand–mark prize still unclaimed for the first flight from Berlin to Paris, by a pilot of either nationality, to be made in one day. Flying time could begin one

Russia's Lyubov Golanchikova in the Fokker monoplane that she used to achieve the women's altitude record in November 1912. However, in the early days of flight, records were short-lived because of rapid advancement in aviation technology. HEIMATMUSEUM TREPTOW, BERLIN

hour before sunrise and end one hour after sunset. The prize attracted Letort, and on July 23, he and Luba departed in his Morane at 4:30 in the morning. Weather soon dampened any hope of winning the prize, as heavy storms grounded them. Four days later the dispirited pair landed in Paris, where the enthusiasm of the French did much to allay their disappointment.

Letort died in a crash near Bordeaux a few months later, when his machine overturned and he was crushed by the motor. According to the Russian writer Boris Tageev, Luba remained in France for some time, flying Nieuport and Morane monoplanes, before returning to Russia, where she signed a year's contract to test aeroplanes for Fedor F. Terechenko. Terechenko had set up an aeroplane factory on his estate south of Kiev, in the Ukraine, and was producing aeroplanes of his own design before the war.

Sometime before the Russian Revolution, Luba married Boris Philipoff, known as the "bread king of Russia," who may have financed her lessons. When the revolution began in 1917, Luba was reported flying for the Red Air Fleet and training much-needed pilots. Historian Christine

White writes that she flew several missions for the revolutionary forces during the civil war. Details are scanty.

We do know that Luba and her husband settled in New York City in 1923, using Philipps, an Americanized version of their name. In June 1927, Luba was in the news, trying for an altitude record over New York City. The aeroplane, a trimotor Fokker capable of carrying ten passengers, was the same model that Commander Richard E. Byrd planned to use for a transatlantic-flight attempt. The Fokker took off from Roosevelt Field on Long Island with Lieutenant W. L. Stultz at the controls, who then handed them to Luba. The flight, with seven newspapermen as unofficial observers, lasted about an hour. When Lieutenant Stultz landed the aeroplane, the altimeter registered eleven thousand feet, which Luba claimed as an altitude record for women.

In August of that year, the *New York Times* printed a story on Luba. Citing her sixteen years as a pilot, the article noted that she was planning an Atlantic flight simply "for the glory of it and to show that what man can do woman can." She had signed a contract for one year with Oliver Morosco, a theatrical producer; there were two backers for the venture who preferred to remain anonymous. Luba had sole responsibility for all technical arrangements, including the type of aeroplane. She favored a single-engine Fokker, since she was familiar with that model. While the venture was strictly noncommercial, the contract was specific about picture rights.

Luba's plans failed to materialize. Finances and time were both factors, and Lindbergh's success made another flight less newsworthy, even if a woman made it. Luba's aviation career ended.

When next in the news, she was a beauty-parlor specialist at the Hotel Ansonia in New York City. In 1930 she made headlines with a suit against Vladimir Rachevsky, a fellow Russian émigré, who allegedly owed her money from years before in St. Petersburg. The suit's result is unknown, but the defendant was connected to former Russian nobility and married to the daughter of a prominent American hotel owner. At the time of her death in 1959, the *New York Times* reported that Luba had been a taxi driver since 1942. Possibly, the legal suit did not end well.

Luba apparently never looked back on her early flying career, which earned her an international reputation as a knowledgeable flier and a charmer.

Helena P. Samsonova was the fourth woman to receive a Russian pilot's license, No. 167, dated August 25, 1913, which she obtained at the Imperial Moscow Aviation Association Flying School. Born in 1890, Helena was interested in sports and raced automobiles, winning third place in a speed race sponsored by the Moscow Automobile Club, before switching to aeroplanes. Her teacher, Lev Uspensky, noted that her training was quick; already, after a few flights, Helena had control of the Farman biplane.

When World War I began, she was studying at medical school, but volunteered for service as a nurse in a military hospital. Stationed in Warsaw, she changed to chauffeuring for a general at Ninth Army headquarters. From there she won a transfer to an aviation unit, the Fifth Corps Air Detachment, as a reconnaissance pilot. Her stay was brief; her commander found her flying ability less than satisfactory, and she was removed.

When Alexander Kerensky, head of the Provisional Government following the revolution, permitted women to join the army, Helena enlisted in the Twenty-sixth Corps Air Detachment. Her duties were that of observer for artillery spotting and reconnaissance. At the end of the civil war, Helena became a sports and physical-culture teacher. She died in 1958.

Two more early Russian women fliers are worthy of mention: Sophie A. Dolgorukaya, who claimed the title "Princess," and Nadeshda Degtereva for whom the claim "combat pilot" is made. Sophie started training in France with Léon Delagrange but received her pilot's license in Russia, No. 234, dated June 5, 1914. In the late stages of the First World War, Sophie served as a pilot, then, like Helena, she joined the revolutionary army as a pilot and/or an observer with the Twenty-sixth Corps Air Squadron. Little is known of that service or of her life after the civil war.

Nadeshda, the daughter of a wealthy merchant, was from Kiev. At seventeen years of age, she joined the air service. Although there is no record of her receiving a pilot's certificate, she apparently was successful in hiding her sex and in qualifying as a combat pilot.

Posted to the Galician front, she flew active combat missions as the pilot of reconnaissance aeroplanes. On one mission in 1915, her machine crossed enemy lines and was attacked by Austrian fighters. The pilot and observer defended themselves valiantly and, although wounded, the aeroplane and its crew made it back to base safely. When Nadeshda was hospitalized, her true sex was revealed. Her valor won a promotion to the rank of sergeant and the Cross of Saint George, Fourth Class.

When she fully recovered, Nadeshda was transferred to the Caucasus front, where her story ends. Nothing more is known about her, but she had won fame of a sort: "the first woman pilot wounded in combat."

D. I. Kuznetsova, like women elsewhere, learned to fly but never earned a pilot's certificate. She flew frequently with her husband, Pavel A. Kuznetsov, a well-known Russian aviator, and was recognized as a talented pilot who flew solely for her own enjoyment. There were probably others like her, but more research is needed on the subject.

When the turmoil of the First World War and Russian civil war subsided, women would find a place in Russian aviation just as they did in professions previously thought to belong to men. The first women who responded to Kerensky's call for military service in the air proved aviation was not exclusively a male activity.

When the need for pilots arose in World War II, the Soviet government organized three women air regiments for combat in 1942. Unlike the American WASPs, who did not fight, these pilots flew bombing missions at night and earned a reputation for deadly accuracy that won them the name "Night Witches." Theirs was the distinction of being the only women to fly in combat in World War II.

6
The English Catch the Bug

HILDA HEWLETT

IN 1864, ENGLAND was firmly settled in the formality of Victorian behavior. Among the accepted tenets guiding the activities of proper women was that a woman's place was in the home, under the benevolent instruction of her husband. The queen herself took pains to follow that rule; loyal citizenry could do no less. But in 1864, a girl was born to the Reverend George W. Herbert and his wife, Louisa, who would prove to be a remarkable individual, one who pursued her own interests in total disregard of conventional female behavior and pointed the way for the new woman emerging in the twentieth century.

Hilda Beatrice Herbert was born on February 17, the second child in a family of six daughters and one son. The family was unusual for its time in its active concern for the poor and working-class families filling up the area of south London that was formerly the Vauxhall Pleasure Gardens. Reverend Herbert had considerable wealth, thanks to his father, who had come to London and established a successful building and carpentry firm, and he used some of that money to build a modern church, St. Peter's Vauxhall, that became part of a complex to help the poor of the neighborhood. There was a school, an orphanage, and a training center for the young people, who would then work in the Royal Doulton works on the South Bank in Lambeth. Both parents were involved in parish life, and their children were expected to assist in the office or surgery. Good Christians could do no less. Louisa Herbert used her connections with wealthy women to foster the work at the center and help with adoptions, much to Hilda's annoyance, who considered time spent on social activity with snobbish people a waste. However, her strong-willed parents created a haven for the needy in the squalid South Bank area. When Reverend Herbert died, the streets were lined with local people who gave him a rousing send-off to his last resting place.

Hilda showed unusual talents early; she was imaginative, mischievous to the point of troublemaker, confident, and very practical—her small, clever hands could make anything. She was probably a trial to the Herbert family because she did what she wanted, when she wanted, much to the dismay of the governess in charge of the children. She was especially fond of her brother, George, with whom she played all kinds of wonderful games, which were much more fun than doing lessons and memorizing French verbs. As a young lady, she attended the South Kensington Art School, where she did wood carving, metalwork, and sewing, and designed and made tiles. Anything that interested her, she could turn her hand to and do well. She trained as a nurse in Berlin for a year. She was a free spirit in a very conventional age.

On her return to England, she met and married Maurice Henry Hewlett, a young lawyer working in his family firm, who longed to write—a man the complete opposite of Hilda: a lover of nature, artistic, a dreamer in the world of romantic literature who cared little for money or position. Perhaps it was their differences he found intriguing. The couple first met at a Shakespeare reading, which Hilda's daughter always thought highly unlikely of Hilda. However, James Knowles, publisher of *The 19th Century,* was a friend of both the Herberts and the Hewletts, and the young people, invited to a literary gathering at Knowles's home in Clapham, a common form of entertaining, apparently liked what they saw in each other.

Maurice courted Hilda with eloquent letters when legal business kept him from seeing her. In his own way, he was as unusual a personality as Hilda. He assured her in one letter that he did not see why "obedience" should follow "loving and honouring in the Marriage Service at all." St. Paul's dictum to wives to submit to their husbands was not part of his belief. This understanding was the solid basis for what was apparently a happy, if unorthodox, marriage. In 1888, when Hilda was twenty-four and Maurice was twenty-seven, the two were married. Two years later, Maurice succeeded his father as His Majesty's Keeper of Land Revenue Records, which entailed a good bit of traveling about the country.

When the cycling craze hit England, the young Hewletts took it up and whirled around London and far afield enthusiastically. By 1900 they had moved to 7 Northwick Terrace, London, which had ample room for their growing family. Next, Hilda took up motoring and drove about the city and the surrounding countryside during "the red flag" era, a time when motorists were responsible for hiring a man to walk before the automobile with a red flag to prevent collisions with another vehicle or wagon on narrow dirt tracks. Not only was Hilda adept at driving, she also could repair a motor, from watching the family chauffeur at work. In 1906 she accompanied Miss Hind, the only woman entrant in the grueling Land's End to John O'Groats Trial, as passenger and mechanic. Driving a Singer Tricar, they made the trek successfully, a remarkable achievement considering there were few roads in existence. Hilda attended meetings and rallies all over the country. Two children had not slowed her down a bit. Maurice, in the meantime, was writing full-time and was widely known as a romantic novelist. His success paid for a country retreat, where Maurice wrote and Hilda busied herself with grapevines, one of Maurice's hobbies.

Years later, Mrs. W. K. Clifford, writing in the *Saturday Review of Literature,* recalled her first impressions of Hilda: "She was as clever as she could stick, and as unconventional as himself [Maurice]; she decorated their beautiful rooms in Moorish fashion; there were few things of this sort she could not do." Mrs. Clifford had not met the Hewletts until one day Hilda appeared at the door and explained they had read one of her books, her husband wrote poetry, they were neighbors—and "would we know them?" It was typical of Hilda to waste no time on the usual social pleasantries.

In 1909, at one of the motor meetings, she met a talented Frenchman, Gustave Blondeau, a qualified engineer who had designed bridges, sugar-beet factories, and other plants, besides inventing a two-stroke engine to power a bicycle used for racing. He had worked with the Farman brothers, helped in early trials with aeroplane propellers, and believed firmly in the future of aviation. His enthusiasm rubbed off on Hilda, with whom he shared flying magazines and reports, which increased her interest. Throughout the years of their association, Hilda always spoke French to Blondeau.

Shortly after they met, the two motored to Blackpool for the October aviation meeting. Despite dreadful weather, they were impressed by the work of Hubert Latham, whose courageous flight on his Antoinette monoplane, battling wind gusts that brought him almost to a standstill in the air, was a revelation. Critics said he was showing off in a foolhardy flight. To Hilda, the sight of Latham's machine lifting from the ground as the space under it widened was so exciting that she "wanted to cry or else to shout." She felt in her bones that Latham and his machine stood for a new power and a great discovery. The image of the big white bird stayed with her; she would find a way to take part in aviation.

Her friends and relatives thought it was Hilda's newest high jinks, not realizing her seriousness. A few months later, she met Blondeau again and learned he had given up his other interests to devote himself to aviation. There was one problem: money. At that time there were no flying schools in England or France; there were only builders of aeroplanes, who gave instruction on their machines in order to sell them. The price of an aeroplane had to be paid up front. The two wrote to builders in France and received only vague answers about building or flying an aeroplane. The price was even more depressing. (The reported price of an aeroplane in the American press was fifty-six hundred dollars; the course of flying, five hundred dollars. The course ended when the pupil could fly ten kilometers alone.) The two enthusiasts agreed to become partners. Hilda would put up the thousand pounds to buy a machine, Blondeau would learn to fly it and then teach her to fly.

Hilda spent the next three months thinking of ways to raise money until she had scraped together the needed sum. How she did it was best left a mystery, she once said. The next question was: What machine to buy? Hilda dreamed of a graceful Antoinette flying in the wind, but Blondeau, who was in Paris making inquiries, wrote that the Farman machine was considered the safest and most dependable. That decided it. The partners would buy a Farman and go to the Camp de Châlons at Mourmelon to learn all they could about aeroplanes. So as not to embarrass her husband, now a prominent name in literary circles, Hilda called herself Mrs. Grace Bird.

Châlons, a vast military training camp that stretched for miles to the horizon, was ideal for flying. Farman's original 1908 shed along the western perimeter of the field was now a factory with numerous buildings, where he was building machines and teaching would-be pilots to fly them. Other aeroplane builders followed his lead, so that a line of hangars marked the western end of the plain. The Antoinette monoplane company was there, as were the Voisin brothers, and the Blériot school had opened a branch along with Roger Sommer and MM. Koechlin and Saulnier. The local authorities in Mourmelon blessed the name of Farman, who had attracted hundreds of residents to the village and rich men from everywhere.

The Farman brothers were impressed by Hilda's enthusiasm, her familiarity with the working parts of a motor, and her ability with French, and permitted her to work in the shops along with Blondeau and the mechanics on occasion. They talked and breathed aviation, despite the dispiriting cold and dampness. Hilda admitted she wanted to cry many times from cold feet while standing about on the windswept plain waiting for something to happen. She soon learned to wear warm "gouties" and sabots, like the natives, which helped her feet. Clothing, never of importance to Hilda, was a practical thick jerkin, bloomers that reached well below her knees, a woolen balaclava helmet, and cat-skin gauntlets over fingerless mitts. There was no escape from the waiting, but Hilda came to believe that it served a purpose. Watching repairs being made on a broken machine, aeroplanes in flight, or attempting to fly all provided insight into the new science; demonstrations by students and builders allowed the spectators to judge the faults or virtues of each machine, leading to much discussion around the dinner table.

Students at the various camps tended to congregate in one of two hotels, according to their type of machine, biplane or monoplane. Rivalry was keen between the two groups. The Farman gang was housed at the Hotel de l'Europe along with the Voisin biplaners. The Antoinette monoplane students stayed at the Hotel Marillier with fellow monoplane enthusiasts. Dinner at the Farman hotel was often a spirited meal with discussion led by Henry, who pointed out the failings of various aeroplanes and explained their shortcomings. Farman learned Esperanto to communicate with foreign students, notably the Russian Efimoff. English, French, German, and Italian were commonplace at the table, including a patois that used the evolving aviation terminology.

During the day, if a student was lucky to be chosen from a crowd, and the weather agreeable, he or she climbed up behind either Maurice Herbster or M. Van den Born on a tired Farman with an old motor to pick up flying skills. There was some explanation, but students learned by watching the instructor handle the controls. According to Hilda, Blondeau had three lessons in as many months before he flew alone. She admitted she could never learn that way.

In May the long-awaited Farman was ready, a two-winged contraption with long, fabric-covered wings separated by wooden struts, the whole tied together with piano wire. The pilot sat on a bucket seat fastened to a ladder on the lower wing, with feet placed on the rudder bar and the control stick between the legs. The only instrument was an oil pulsator, which was timed on the ground for a minute or two to be sure the engine was making full revolutions. A student sat behind the pilot on the ladder and reached over the pilot's shoulder to hold the stick.

Blondeau practiced on the new machine with its Gnome motor, then took his license test and received his certificate from the Aero Club of France on June 10, 1910. In July the partners packed their treasure, named *The Blue Bird* at the suggestion of Maurice Maeterlinck, a friend of Maurice's, and brought it to Brooklands in England, where they set up shop. Maurice had stopped at Mourmelon on his way from Italy to see how the partners were doing. During his visit, he had a ride on the Farman and bought shares in the fledgling Hewlett-Blondeau Flying School, which was being organized.

It took ten days to assemble and tune *The Blue Bird,* watched all the while by skeptical locals at Brooklands, where within the raceway a few ditches had been filled in and some leveling done to provide a large broad area for motorcar or aeroplane, making training and testing of aeroplanes fairly safe and easy. From this unlikely location, three quarters of British aviation would emerge. When the new machine was wheeled from its hangar, a small crowd gathered, full of gloomy predictions: "Brooklands is a death-trap for flying, what with the river and the sewage farm"; "The Gnome engine is not the one for here, it hates the

Hilda Hewlett was a talented aviator, flight instructor, and airplane builder. In 1910, she and Gustave Blondeau started Great Britain's first aviation school at Brooklands. Here she poses in front of one of the Hewlett-Blondeau airplanes they designed and built. BROOKLANDS MUSEUM damp air"; "Look, the machine does not look right, no one knows how to tune up a Farman, it's a secret." They were dumbfounded, therefore, when the Gnome started on the first pull of the propeller, and the Farman glided smoothly away and rose steadily into the air to circle the field before making a perfect landing close to its starting point. The crowd was impressed. So was T.O.M. Sopwith, who was curious about aviation and signed up for a flight around Brooklands with Blondeau for a "fiver." Two circuits of the track and he had caught "the bug." From that beginning, Sopwith would make aviation history.

Following Blondeau's demonstration, life was easier at Brooklands, where an active aviation village was growing inside the motor raceway, which opened in 1907. The partners were no longer considered oddballs but serious aviation workers. Blondeau gained a reputation as a Gnome motor expert and pilot, and advertisements in the aviation journals soon had people coming to him for passenger flights and flying lessons. In September, Hewlett and Blondeau opened a flying school in shed No. 32—tuition was seventy-five pounds, which included breakage—but the demands on the one machine for flights, lessons, and prize competitions meant that Hilda had little time to practice for her pilot's license. The two decided to build another machine and saved every penny to buy a Gnome motor.

The school, the first in England to graduate a full-fledged pilot and the first to graduate an army-officer pilot, flourished with pupils who were devoted to Hilda Hewlett and Gustave Blondeau. An advertisement in the aviation journals touted the school's record—"Has never had a smash nor damaged an aeroplane"—and Blondeau's reputation: "a good teacher means safety and rapidity." Holidays and spare time were spent at the school, doing any job whatever, sharing primitive meals and washing up. In summer, the pupils swam in the river Wey; otherwise there was a minimum of washing. Pupils slept in the hangars or in the large packing cases outside, enjoying a strange communal life with endless aviation shoptalk day and night, not unlike the Farman school at Châlons. (Gertrude Bacon, a journalist and aviation enthusiast, writing of the early days of aviation, observed in one book that Hilda Hewlett slept in a hangar with her aeroplane, which Bacon probably considered bizarre. Bacon wrote enthusiastically about various male pilots but had nothing more to say about Hilda, although one would expect an active member of the Women's Aerial League to promote women in aviation.)

By the summer of 1911, the Hewlett-Blondeau School was in full swing, with some half-dozen pupils, which continued to limit the time Hilda could practice for her license. Nervousness about her first solo flight was intensified by fear, lest she damage the school's only machine. Blondeau told her that whatever she did, "don't go near those lumps where the house was pulled down, nor to the sewage farm." Hilda started off fine, gathered speed, and headed straight into the piles of old bricks, where she stuck. Fortunately, the machine was not seriously damaged, and she proceeded to make a successful flight, preserving the school's reputation.

On August 18, 1911, at forty-seven years of age, Hilda Hewlett passed her tests to become the first English woman to obtain a pilot's license, No. 122, issued on August 29. Representatives from the Royal Aero Club, down from London, were curious observers when she took her tests. As the first woman to try, they were rooting for her. She took off, did the required turns, the altitude and landing tests, and became an entry in the record books. The press noted her achievement, identifying her as "wife of Maurice Hewlett, the novelist," but she was never featured, as Raymonde was in the French press, probably because aviation was still a limited sport in England and primarily for men. But for a short time, Hilda was showered with telegrams, letters, and gifts; the scoffers took back their comments—she was almost a celebrity.

The difference between the acceptance of women in aviation in France and England was considerable. French numbers alone indicate that women, who endured the sometimes grueling training, were treated with respect as members of the flying community. In England there was mistrust and even open hostility. Claude Grahame-White, the leading English aviator, had served notice: there was "no place in the air for women." According to Grahame-White, the only reason women had escaped serious accidents was because they were flying exclusively in aerodrome flights, which were very different from cross-country work and the hazardous achievements undertaken by men. In spite of these critical comments, the Grahame-White schools did offer training to a few women, but only one received a license, Mrs. Stocks. Lily Irvine, when she married American James V. Martin, went to the United States without a license. Aviation in England was very much a male pursuit.

Two days before Hilda's successful tests, the British Army staff gained a certified pilot, one of the first, Brigadier General David Henderson, chief

staff officer to Sir John French, who studied under the name of Henry
Davidson at the Bristol Company's school at Brooklands. (The first army
officer to earn a pilot's license was Snowdon Smith, a Hewlett-Blondeau
graduate in 1910.) A diary of Henderson's course showed that in seven
days he made seven passenger flights, some long and some short, and
practiced rolling on the ground for a total time of a half hour. On the
sixth day, he flew as passenger again, then flew three flights alone for a
total of thirty-five minutes, at an average height of 60 feet, rising to 150
feet at one point. Reportedly, he flew no straight flights but took off and
flew circuits. The next day he successfully passed all tests for his license.
Aviation circles cheered his achievement, believing that it would be helpful to have such a high-ranking officer at the War Office qualify as an
aviator and that aviation would receive needed government attention.

Three months later another Hewlett joined the ranks of licensed
pilots, when naval Sub-Lieutenant Francis E. T. Hewlett, taught by his
mother, received license No. 156, issued November 14. According to the
family, young Hewlett learned to fly over a weekend, in forty-eight
hours. By the end of the year, the Hewlett-Blondeau School had taught
eleven pupils to fly without breaking wood. Two more pilots were certified before the school closed early in 1912 to do full-time construction.
Hilda never flew again once the school closed.

The school's first graduate was Maurice Ducrocq. Hilda described
Blondeau's method of training him for the *Daily Mail*. First, the student
makes one or two long passenger flights with the instructor to get used
to the sensation of speed and the noise of the motor. Next, the student
takes partial control of the machine in flight so that gradually he or she
is ready to make brief "hops" without the instructor. This gradual approach, Hilda believed, made all the difference between success and failure when the crucial time came to actually take control of the machine.

Ducrocq, a Frenchman living in England, wrote an appreciation of the
Hewlett-Blondeau School in which he stated that no school in France
or England could have served him better. Ducrocq had investigated
so-called schools in England and found them wanting. Then he heard of
Blondeau's debut using a Gnome and, after more inquiries, he went to
Brooklands and arranged for lessons. His teacher, Blondeau, was a very
quiet man who never lost his head or his temper. On the first lesson,
Ducrocq was treated to a cross-country flight at a considerable height to

allow him to enjoy the thrill of flying, sense its possibilities, and lose any fear he might have. After that, the student went round the course at a lower altitude for several days to observe how the machine was run before being allowed to touch the lever and feel his hands on the machine. After eleven lessons, he began to fly in straight lines forward and back along the ground, then leaving it for short hops until the aeroplane was finally in the air. Twenty-one lessons later, Ducrocq was licensed by the Royal Aero Club of England.

Following her licensing, Hilda was invited to address a meeting of the Women's Aerial League in October. She used the occasion to warn that England was two years behind France in aeronautics. Ever a realist, she pointed out the best way to change this situation was not to ignore it but to admit the nation's shortcomings. She was especially concerned by the practice of copying French aeroplanes and advertising them as original designs: "This was unworthy and mean." She proposed that England buy the licenses from French firms with the best machines and build aeroplanes in England from those designs. This way English firms would have current models—aeroplanes change rapidly—and England would benefit with every improvement, the same as France. As it was, French builders hid their new designs and inventions until a race was to take place, to keep competitors from winning the prizes on copied French designs. On a less sober note, Hilda said that women were capable of piloting their own machines just as well as men, but not in races, like Beaumont and Védrines (two successful French long-distance racers who, for a week, wearing the same clothes, slept on the ground at night, their wings the only cover), whose nerves were strained almost to the breaking point. As students of the science, women were as capable as men, and they didn't have to give up society, as she had done, to take part. Most important, women could help form public opinion so England wasn't left behind in aviation.

Construction on the new aeroplane progressed slowly, but Blondeau's success at tuning the motor, tightening wires, and making repairs on the school machine caught the attention of would-be purchasers, who approached the partners with orders for new machines. Among the buyers was the Vickers school, which ordered three Farman-type aeroplanes. Space became an immediate problem; in addition, there was no water, light, or power. Writing in later years, Hilda observed: "It was difficult to

exist on makeshift, construction had become an engineering propo-
sition." Early in 1912, Blondeau was offered the position of constructor
of the Hanriot aeroplane in England. The partners decided they would
move to where they had needed space and services, and Blondeau accepted. They formed a limited company, Hewlett and Blondeau, to manufacture aeroplanes and leased the former Mulliner factory, which built
specialty aeroplanes, at 2-16 Vardens Road, Battersea, under their new
name "Omnia Works." It was a tremendous undertaking that would prove
important for them personally and the nation. Maurice undoubtedly
helped with some of the financing.

The partners, who had invested their entire capital in the new venture, soon found themselves embroiled in labor problems. The workers
obtained through the local labor exchange were a mixed lot. Hilda's
assessment was: two were really good, two were passable carpenters, and
"the others were simply rotters." The partners set wages according to the
men's industry and ability, influenced perhaps by the English Socialists,
but the local union organizers would have none of this. They insisted
that all should receive the same pay, an idea Hilda thought ridiculous
and told them so, adding that she wished to keep the good ones and dismiss the others. This was contrary to union rules and, said the organizers, if she did not comply, not a man would work for her. This was
serious. Hilda later wrote that "too late, we learned that Battersea was a
hotbed of unions, and no other labour could be got there."

The partners placed an advertisement in the *South Western Star* in July
and August: "Wanted, a few intelligent boys as apprentices; also improvers
for aeronautical engineering—Omnia Works, Vardens Road." Similar
advertisements placed in northern and Scottish papers brought immediate
replies by letter, even telegram. Within ten days the partners had obtained
a suitable workforce, much to the chagrin of the union organizers lurk-
ing outside.

The union campaign ended on a Saturday, when Hilda, on leaving
work, told the representatives outside: "Good-bye, it's Saturday so you'll
get off early." They replied grudgingly that she had won with a lot of
dirty foreigners, but Hilda corrected them, pointing out they had more
men from the north than foreigners. The union men declared they were
"a stupid lot," but again Hilda had the last word. She told them she
believed in the future of flying, she had taken a great deal of trouble to
learn, and she would do her best to overcome any obstacle that got in

her way. She congratulated them on being such sporting opponents and asked to shake hands. Then "we shook hands and left in peace."

Inside the plant, things were still unsettled. A newspaper article dated August 2, 1912, reported that a joiner, Alfred Knight, was charged with assaulting an engineer, John Moncrieff, at the Omnia Works. The joiner had been given notice, whereupon he deliberately struck the engineer on the chin with a plane. The joiner spoke up and insisted he hit the engineer with his fist, that had he used a plane it would have broken his jaw. The Honorable John de Gray, judge of the Police Court, countered: "That depends on how hard you hit him. You had no business to hit him like that. Pay ten shillings." Once the new force was assembled and trained, work at 2-16 Vardens Road proceeded more smoothly.

The partners had spent most of their capital to equip the works, which meant there was no money for an office staff. Bookkeeping and most of the administrative tasks were done by Hilda, who was also running her home in north London, an hour's travel time each way. Commuting across the city proved impossible; Hilda rented a flat at 34 Park Mansions, Prince of Wales Road, Battersea, a short distance from the Omnia Works. The firm's reputation grew in the next two years, not only as builders of aeroplanes but as suppliers of aeroplane fittings, turnbuckles, wire strainers, oxyacetylene equipment, and a stranded cable, of which they were the lone manufacturers in England. Hewlett and Blondeau advertisements appeared regularly in *Flight,* the journal of the Royal Aero Club; their products were shown at aero shows and received glowing praise for their workmanship.

By November 1912, the firm was making news for its manufacture and sale of two Hanriot single-seaters and one two-seater to the French and Russian governments. *Flight* questioned why machines of English material and workmanship should be sent out of Great Britain to be used for defense in other countries when England needed fast, good aeroplanes for the Army and Navy. The Hanriot had performed well in the 1912 Military Trials in France; it was designed to maintain supremacy in the air.

Later that same month, a *Flight* editorial discussed the improvement in English aviation, due to the ability of certain companies to mass-produce their aeroplane design. Hewlett and Blondeau were mentioned as missing an opportunity to build their own aeroplane instead of the Hanriot. The editorial argued that a good model would win them

Hewlett helps cover the fuselage of a BE2C, a small military reconnaissance plane, being built at her Omnia Works in Leagrave, England. MICHAEL GOODALL

business in quantity, whereas seeing a Hanriot built by Hewlett and Blondeau does nothing for the firm. The writer stressed that the government needed to spend more money on aviation because as a world power it lacked an aeronautical establishment in keeping with its position. Pointing to the Bristol Company, which reported earnings of seventy thousand pounds for the past twelve months, the editor urged other competitors to join the aviation "game" in designing and building machines. The more, the merrier was his attitude, which showed complete ignorance of the efforts of independent aircraft manufacturers to stay afloat.

Omnia Works was becoming well known despite its lack of an aeroplane model bearing its name. A long article in *Flight,* dated December 7, 1912, described the physical structure of the company, its management, and the administrative concerns of running an aeroplane factory, and, in particular, the construction of the Hanriot machines. Except for one part—a type of wire strainer that was French—the machines were entirely British built. The firm aimed to build machines on a large scale at low cost, to the designs of their clients. Each worker had a number, and when he performed a task, or picked up material, that number was noted with the length of time of the operation, so the cost of the material and labor could be figured, down to the penny. To these costs were added rent, rates, lighting, etc., until the finished product was tallied and placed in the stockroom, or the machine was assembled, which was accounted for down to the last nut. Hilda's strong practical sense was apparent in the shop's management. The shop's motto showed serious purpose: "Remember you have a man's life depending on how you do your work."

In 1912 the firm was awarded an order for BE2cs, small biplanes designed by the Royal Aircraft Factory for reconnaissance work. A number of these, including an AD Scout, were built at Vardens Road. A seventy- or seventy-five-horsepower Renault motor powered the machines. Anticipating more orders from the British government, the partners decided to look for larger work space, as there was little room for expansion in Battersea. In 1914, Omnia Works moved to the Leagrave countryside, near Luton, in Bedfordshire, where it had needed room and an available workforce that expanded to seven hundred during the war years. When war came in August 1914, Omnia was in a better position to aid the aviation effort as the listing below indicates.

Year	Type	Serial Nos.	Total
1915	Dyot Fighter	3867, 3868	2
1916	BE2c	9410–8433	24
1916	Armstrong-Whitworth F.K.3	A1461–1510	50
1916	A.W.F.K.3	A8091–8140	50
1917	A.W.F.K.3	B9501–9800	300
1918	Avro 504J/K	D7051–7200	150
1918	Avro 504K	F9746–9845	100
1918	Avro 504K	H7413–7562	150
1918	Avro 504K	J3992–4051	Canceled

Hilda was especially proud of the training school the company established at Leagrave to train young girls and women who, for the duration, performed work normally done by men, including welding. Hilda had firsthand experience, a generation before Rosie the Riveter.

Early in 1914, Hilda wrote a letter to *Flight* regarding relations between the Royal Air Force and Omnia Works in answer to complaints about the RAF elsewhere. Omnia had always found the military fair and helpful in the work done for them. Hilda argued that the time had come for the aviation manufacturers to stop fighting each other and to join together to build the best machines possible at a fair price; complaints against the RAF would vanish, and the various aviation builders would have a return for what they had spent, with time and money left over for new experiments. She pointed to the urgent War Office need for machines in the next two months, which had the RAF working day and night shifts to meet demand, a demand that independent manufacturers could have filled had they not been so occupied "killing each other." The female half of the partnership had a keen mind; her observations, sharp and to the point, went to the crux of a problem; and she was not afraid to speak up.

Sometime in 1916–17, Hilda found time to write a short booklet entitled "Our Flying Men," inspired in part by her son's wartime experience. Early in the war, now Flight Commander Hewlett took part in an aerial raid on the German fleet at Cuxhaven, off Heligoland, on Christmas Day, 1914. German gunners and aeroplanes were partially effective in deflecting the English bombing attempts, although zeppelin sheds were reported damaged; six English seaplanes returned safely to their ships, except for Hewlett's machine, which went down. Declared missing for six days, Hewlett landed safely in Ymuiden, Holland, on December 31. He had been picked up by a Dutch fishing trawler that returned to port only when it had a full catch. Within a few days, young Hewlett arrived home to a hero's welcome and a joyful reunion with his parents.

Hilda was very aware of the danger in aerial combat, and her booklet praised the young men serving in aviation. She did not try to tell personal stories, but she wanted the public to understand what was behind the bald statements seen in the press: "Our aircraft was very active and proved of assistance to our artillery," or "Ten of our machines bombarded a station of great importance; five failed to return." In very clear language she described the logistics and importance of the work done by aviators. She stressed the newness of aviation as a science and its development almost daily in the war, advances that could never be made in peacetime because "no civilised people would have tolerated the risk of life to attain such proportions for the furtherance of a science."Thanks to the war, aviation "came into her own as the fourth arm of the war machine." Ever practical, Hilda gave a lively account of the capture of a Fokker, then compared its technical qualities with the English and French machines in use, pointing out the worthwhile improvements on the German machine. She knew her subject.

Once the war ended, the downturn in the aviation industry claimed another victim when Omnia Works, unable to convert to peacetime production profitably, went into liquidation on October 27, 1920. Seven years later the property was sold to Electrolux, and for the first time, Hilda and Blondeau benefited from their investment and years of hard work. By that time, Hilda's husband had died, and when her daughter, Pia, moved with her family to New Zealand, Hilda went along. She had visited there in 1919 and found it an appealing place.

At that time, as Hilda passed through San Francisco to catch a ship going west, the *San Francisco Chronicle* printed an article filled with inaccuracies—Hilda had won a Brooklands-to-Brighton race, beating ten male competitors; she plans a lecture tour of America shortly; she will establish a flying school in New Zealand—but there was a charming close-up picture in her good leather flying costume. (Actually, Hilda won one competition, a quick start. It was a fun activity organized when students and teachers from several schools at Brooklands had time on their hands. Hilda proved swift on her feet as she ran to the machine, started the motor, and took off in shorter time than the men. It was a onetime event. She had no interest in competing.)

England's first licensed woman pilot never lost her enthusiasm for aviation. In 1929 or 1930 she bought an interest with H. T. Morris in Southern Cross Airways Ltd., a New Zealand company formed in February 1929, which boasted a single Blackburn Blue Bird III. Despite the new management, the company folded, apparently, without doing any flying, and the Blue Bird was sold.

Hilda scored another flying first in 1932 as the first through passenger to fly from London to Batavia (now Jakarta, Indonesia) en route to New Zealand. The trip took eleven days in the KLM airliner *Oolevaar* (Stork), a Fokker FVIIb/3m, with frequent stops for fuel, a cigarette, and a stretch. Hilda loved meeting people of different cultures, the insights glimpsed along the way; having tea served while flying at one hundred miles per hour was absolutely marvelous. The view of earth from seven thousand, sometimes ten thousand, feet, delighted her. The technical aspects of the trip held her attention, particularly as the aeroplane neared Batavia. There were no landmarks as the aeroplane, flying lower now, passed over endless forest; the pilot flew on compass while the wireless operator constantly checked the drift through the trapdoor in the floor. He saw a tiger once, which kept Hilda glued to the window; she saw birds but no tiger. Her son, a retired group captain, thought traveling as a passenger dull; there was nothing to do but look out the window. His mother saw the possibilities of global travel and applauded.

In New Zealand, as president of the Tauranga Aero Club in the early 1930s, Hilda was involved in finding a permanent airfield to replace the one on the tidal flats of the Waikareao Estuary, where flying time was limited to an hour on either side of low tide. When her son retired to New Zealand, he continued the search, which took a good six years before a suitable site was found at Whareroa. The airfield, linking Tauranga to the commercial air traffic on the east coast of New Zealand, opened January 14, 1939, with both Hewletts present.

Commenting on women in aviation after the war, Hilda observed that there were very few women pilots in the early days of aviation because the difficulties to be overcome were "many and great." She knew several women "who tried very hard and made great sacrifices—they certainly lacked neither nerve nor courage—yet they were forced to give up the idea." Comparing the number of motorcars driven by women before the war with the numbers driven by women during the war, Hilda was encouraged by what women had done and "can do in the mechanical line when they want to, or when they have to." Will women become pilots? Her reply was: "I never could see the reason why they should not, there is no physical reason that I know of; they have ears, hands, nerves, and courage. What more do they want?"

In her later years Hilda was an enthusiastic gardener, loved camping, fly-fishing and deep-sea fishing, all of which she enjoyed in New Zealand. Her grandchildren remember that, almost blinded by glaucoma, she still made up the most wonderful games to play. She became more eccentric with the years, and her patience did not improve. When she could not find something in her purse, she would sit down where she was and turn it upside down to find what she wanted. Another time, she chopped up a lovely piece of furniture to make it fit in a smaller place where she fancied it.

England's first woman pilot died on August 21, 1943, at age seventy-nine, in Tauranga, New Zealand. She was found dead in bed by her housekeeper, with a note: "Dump me in the sea." Forgotten were her days at Brooklands, but aviation hands remembered and respected her as an able and determined person who knew what she wanted to do and did it. "The Old Bird," the family's affectionate name for her, had freed herself from Victorian constraints.

The *Bay of Plenty Times,* New Zealand, observed May 8, 1999: "It was typical of this eminently different woman that she should have an unusual burial. After a funeral service held at 1.20 pm on 23 August at the Railway Wharf, this woman of the air, also a keen game fisherwoman, was buried at sea." It seemed just right.

CHERIDAH DE BEAUVOIR STOCKS

The second English woman to win a pilot's license, Cheridah de Beauvoir Stocks, was social, charming, and considerably younger than Hilda Hewlett. Born in 1887 in the Somerset countryside, with a rosebud face, she belonged to the country gentry who amused themselves with endless social gatherings. Cheridah decided to take up flying, it was the in thing among the young men she knew, and at twenty-four years of age she earned license No. 153 from the Royal Aero Club, on November 7, 1911. She had trained at the Grahame-White school at Hendon (despite G.W.'s negative public comments on women in aviation), where *Flight* photographed her seated on a Farman biplane, the machine she used for her tests.

By the summer of 1912, she had changed to a Blériot monoplane with a thirty-five-horsepower Anzani motor. Apparently, she was a regular at Hendon meetings, where her circuits—"a finished performance," according to the journal writers—were cheered by the public. Hendon airfield had planned to organize a Ladies' Day in July under the auspices of the Women's Aerial League, with Hilda Hewlett, Hélène Dutrieu, and Jeanne Herveux mentioned as possible starters, but, reportedly, the French women wanted high financial guarantees, which were not forthcoming.

Since Hilda was not interested in competing, the field was left to Cheridah, the lone woman flier. Unfortunately, a tricky wind that day was judged too risky for a lady pilot, and the cross-country passenger handicap and the ladies' speed race were postponed. Cheridah continued to appear at meets, winning occasional prizes for women, but without any competition. She was an enthusiastic spectator as well as a performer, and she enjoyed being a passenger in the speed races favored at the meets.

On September 20, 1913, at Hendon aerodrome near London, Cheridah asked to go along with Sydney Pickles, another popular pilot, who was about to take a short flight on a 110-horsepower Anzani-powered Champel biplane, an interesting new model. It was a pusher type, with the outrigger behind and seats in front, similar to the Farman machine. Dusk was drawing in, but there was still light for a short trip to top off the successful second Aerial Derby Day. As soon as Pickles and Cheridah were seated, the machine started off and rose quickly to about 250 feet, to the other side of the aerodrome, and proceeded around the course usually used for races. The lights of London were visible in the distance. Pickles turned to comment to Cheridah on their beauty, then decided it was time to come down. The ensuing flight was described vividly by Pickles in *Flight* some eight months later.

Continuing toward the No. 1 pylon, he planned a sharp left turn to glide across the aerodrome toward the pylon at the opposite end before turning back to land. He throttled the motor down and started his turn. The turn completed, he discovered the rudder bar, which brings the rudder straight again, refused to budge. The aeroplane made a complete circle, banking wide as Pickles tried to work the lateral control to reduce the bank, but the machine kept spinning and side-slipping.

At this point, Pickles remembered the fate of Paul Beck, who had crashed in America. At the time, one critic said that if Beck had turned his motor on, he might have saved himself. Pickles felt he had nothing to lose and quickly reached for the throttle lever, and with the throttle opened wide, he pulled the elevator lever back, hoping to get the nose up. After another complete circle with no improvement, Pickles closed the throttle, realizing that the machine's position was desperate. He reached forward and turned the motor switch off, thinking that at least there wouldn't be a fire after the inevitable crash. In the next instant, the green megaphone stand flashed past and Pickles realized the machine was coming down in the enclosure, where shortly before people and cars had stood, instead of over the field. The only explanation he could give was the machine had drifted as it spiraled down and opening the throttle increased this. In the next moment there was a loud crash as the aeroplane hit the ground.

Pickles and Cheridah, who through the crisis had not made a sound, were seriously injured. Both were taken to Central London Sick Asylum, Hendon, where Pickles underwent surgery for a compound leg fracture and Cheridah remained unconscious for several days, with a concussion and back injuries. Recovery was a long affair for both unfortunate fliers. Cheridah gave up flying, but Pickles continued to fly "as an amateur"— strictly for pleasure. His analysis months later blamed the accident on his heel becoming wedged between the rudder bar and the flooring of the fuselage so that the machine kept turning. Opening the throttle only aggravated the situation.

Two years later, Cheridah was well enough to visit Hendon, where she was warmly greeted by the old-timers, to watch flying activities. Still paralyzed on the right side, she had learned to write with her left hand and kept in touch with aviation activities through *Flight,* which passed along information about her to its readers. An ardent supporter of Flying Services Fund, which helped aviators in the service and their dependents, Cheridah donated a litter of three Pekingese puppies in 1915 to be sold for the benefit of the fund. *Flight* published her letter with two photographs of Cheridah, stylishly dressed as usual, and her favorite dog, Peter. Even before the war, she was active in raising money to purchase a hydro-aeroplane for the British Navy as a gift of Somerset County. Like Hilda Hewlett, she believed that aviation was the wave of the future, and, although she never flew again, she remained an interested supporter of aerial progress.

WINNIE BULLER

An English citizen, Winnie Buller won her license at the Bréguet School at Douai, France—No. 848, dated May 3, 1912, flying one of the school's machines. Although she was born in Bacton, Norfolk, England, aviation historians in that country regard her as French; the French, as English. Winnie first flew in an aeroplane in England in 1910 with the Comte de

Montalent, who was demonstrating the Bréguet. Much taken with the machine, she determined to learn to fly. When business required her husband to travel for a long period, Winnie closed her house, packed up her two small sons and their nurse, and drove to Douai, eighteen miles south of Lille, for aviation training.

As was the practice at French flying schools, Winnie spent time in the workshop, where she learned to weld, solder, and make any fitting needed on a machine. The first lessons consisted of example and explanation. On her third lesson she was told to do "straights" back and forth across the field, but Winnie found she could turn easily and, before she knew it, she had lifted into the air, where she remained circling the town of Douai for an hour, to the dismay of her instructors and fellow pupils. In no time she was making cross-country flights, one as long as one hundred kilometers, from Douai to Arras and back. Shortly after, she passed her tests and made cross-country flights carrying a passenger.

The English journal *Aeronautics* hailed her arrival on the flying scene with an article headed "Men of Note in Aeronautics—Mrs. Winnie Buller." The editor wrote: "No apology, after all, is needed for the contradiction implied in the title, since Mrs. Buller has, by sheer force of merit, won for herself a place among the first rank of pilots, and merit knows no distinction of rank or sex." Her try for the Coup Fémina in the fall was mentioned in particular. Winnie had been flying for more than two hours in a severe wind when the oil pump failed and the motor froze and stopped with the propeller vertical in the air. Without hesitation, the quick-thinking pilot turned the machine downward and volplaned to a perfect landing. At the time, Winnie said that students at Douai have such confidence in the stability of their machines in the air, and the protection offered by the aeroplane's design, that they fly in any weather. Seated behind the engine in an enclosed body gave a secure feeling. How secure, she found out for herself, when her machine flew into the wash of another aeroplane and came down with "a nasty bump"—without injury to herself.

Aeronautics looked forward to seeing Winnie perform in England to uphold national pride, because by the end of 1912, English skies were empty of women pilots. By early 1913, Winnie was waiting at Shoreham, England, for her own aeroplane to arrive. In July, the Bréguet arrived, to her delight, with M. Brégi, who would assist in assembling it. She did not compete in England, since competitions and competitors for women were nonexistent there. Viewed as less able pilots—after all, women were fragile and prone to fainting—women could not compete with men under regulations set by the Royal Aero Club, which controlled exhibition flying. It is small wonder that the number of licensed English women was no more than two.

In May 1914, Winnie was at the Caudron School at Hendon, learning to handle a new aeroplane of French design. She found it quite different from the Bréguet because of the footwork required to fly it, but she was soon making exhibition flights on the Caudron to demonstrate its maneuverability for the British Caudron School. Unquestionably, she was a competent, versatile flier.

When the war came, Winnie went on active service with a volunteer motor ambulance corps in northern France. Before she left England, the aviatrix admitted she was not much of a nurse, but she could see that the ambulance engines ran properly—no small matter, considering the corps's problems with sluggish, overworked vehicles. There is no record of Winnie's return to flying after the war.

LILIAN E. BLAND

Even before Hilda Hewlett and Cheridah de Beauvoir Stocks, a young woman in Northern Ireland had succumbed to aerial fever. Showing great imagination and engineering skill, she designed and built an aeroplane from scratch, and flew it in Carnmoney, Belfast, in the years between 1909 and 1911.

Lilian E. Bland, a young woman who was anything but bland, was one of the more colorful personalities of the early aviation period. She smoked, took prizewinning photographs, and wrote sports articles for London papers, all activities considered not quite proper in Belfast, especially for the granddaughter of the Episcopal dean of Belfast. Her early interest in photographing birds, watching as they soared overhead in flight, kindled a wish to do the same. The news of the Wright brothers' achievement led Lilian to read everything she could find about their invention and, curious to see how it worked, she built a model biplane, which she flew as a kite. Fortunately for Lilian, her late uncle General

Smythe, had left a well-equipped workshop in her aunt's house, where she and her father lived. After she fashioned the kite model, she resolved to build an aeroplane.

Being a handy young woman, with patience and skill, she drew designs, assembled materials, and went to work. In a December 1910 issue of *Flight,* Lilian described the slow process of building first a glider that evolved into an aeroplane. Using a variety of woods, she built wings of ash, the ends steamed to bend, like those on the gulls she had studied. The ribs and stanchions were spruce; the skids, ash; the outriggers, bamboo; and the engine bed, American elm. The engine bed sat on the lower wing, the whole of it fastened by wires to the upper and lower wings so the engine could not shift unless the whole machine were wrecked. This wiring added extra strength to the wings. The wings were covered with a strong material coated with photographic solution to make them waterproof. The chassis carried the gas tank and the pilot's seat, which was enclosed on all sides, so falling out was impossible. The whole chassis was removable in one piece, with or without the engine, which was held in place by four bolts.

The controls consisted of a bicycle handlebar, which rocked and turned. Turning to the right raised the right elevator and depressed the left—the connecting wires being crossed. The elevators were connected to the horizontal tail planes, which worked in the opposite direction to the elevators. All controls were double-wire and strong waterproofed whipcord. The balancing planes hinged to the rear stanchions were controlled by the back of the seat. Leaning to the right pulled down the right hand balancer, and vice versa. The vertical rudder worked by pedals. The engine controls were a butterfly valve, to regulate the gasoline supply; an air throttle; and a lever to the magneto, one cylinder of which was cut when starting. The controls sounded complicated, but Lilian assured readers that in practice they were "quite simple to work." Built in sections, the machine gradually outgrew the house and was finished in the coach house. By early 1910, the glider, spanning twenty-seven feet, seven inches, was ready for testing. During its construction, Lilian corresponded with *Flight* to apprise its editors of her progress, with drawings to illustrate each step. *Flight* was always ready to print her reports.

Christened the *Mayfly,* a joining of two words showing there was some doubt about its ability in the air, the structure minus an engine

Lilian Bland, a member of one of Belfast's most prominent families, about to take off in the Mayfly. PUBLIC RECORD OFFICE OF NORTHERN IRELAND

was carried to the top of Carnmoney Hill to test its gliding ability. The glider soared well in the wind, but breakage and repairs were necessary as weak spots developed. To test the weight-lifting ability of the glider, four six-foot members of the Royal Irish Constabulary were enlisted to hold on to the wings together with Joe Blain, the garden boy who acted as Lilian's assistant. With this load aboard, the *Mayfly* rose into the air, to the surprise of the policemen who let go at once and dropped off, leaving Joe to hang on and bring the glider out of the wind. Lilian estimated that, if five men could be lifted, the glider would carry an engine.

She wrote to Alliott V. Roe in England to ask if he could produce a light engine. His reply was positive; he could make a two-stroke air-cooled unit, which Lilian accepted at once. There were delays, however, and it was sometime in June before the engine was ready and Lilian crossed to England. At the first demonstration of the twenty-horsepower Avro engine, with Lilian an excited spectator, the connected propeller shattered into bits on the first roar of the motor. Luckily no one was hurt. A new six-foot, 6-inch adjustable-pitch Avro propeller was supplied, and early in July Lilian returned to Ireland with the treasured engine, resting beside her in the railway compartment in her bag.

On arrival in Belfast, Lilian couldn't wait; the engine, seated on a strong wooden stand behind the pilot's canvas seat, was tested that night in a pouring rain. The gas tank was not ready yet, but, ever resourceful, Lilian substituted a whiskey bottle and used her aunt's ear trumpet to feed the engine. It worked! As soon as the gas tank was in place, testing began in earnest. The motor was not easy to start and, when it was running, vibration snapped most of the wires between the struts and loosened most of the nuts on their bolts. There were more adjustments—all the fastenings were strengthened, heavier wheels and tires were fitted—before the *Mayfly* was deemed ready to fly.

Lord O'Neill loaned his park at Randalstown, eight hundred acres of open space with but one drawback—a loose bull and cattle. On good-weather days, Lilian and Joe Blain bicycled twelve miles to the field to see if the machine would go up under its own power. It did, but continuous storms for the next five weeks forced the builders to postpone any flying attempts. Finally in September, Lilian Bland was flying Ireland's first powered aeroplane, taking off about thirty feet for its first hops before sailing slowly along in the air. "I have flown!" the ecstatic pilot wrote to *Flight*. She could hardly believe she was off the ground and ran back each time to see where the wheel tracks stopped in the grass. The hops lengthened until the *Mayfly* was sailing along for short distances, bobbing up and down like a boat, despite the curious cattle. Lilian's pride was evident: "I am naturally awfully pleased, having made and designed her myself. It is a very small, but promising start anyway."

Modifications continued, particularly preventing rust on the wires in the dampness of Northern Ireland. Lilian found that paint corrected the problem, a good black enamel; the woodwork was varnished with copal to protect it. The gas tank and carburetor float were placed crosswise to keep the fore and aft tilt from interfering with the gas supply when the tank was near empty. Lilian thought that starting on one cylinder let the motor pick up slowly, causing less strain.

Lilian did not claim any expertise for her flying ability, admitting she was not yet a good-enough pilot "to give much advice." She believed much could be learned from watching good pilots, although there were none in Ireland in 1910. She was fortunate to have seen Farman, Louis Paulhan, and Latham fly, whom she considered "masters of the art."

Would she do it again? Certainly. Her enthusiasm remained intact; aviation was the "finest sport in the world." Her experiment had been hard work, requiring time and money, said Lilian, not only for the initial construction but for the inevitable repairs. The *Mayfly* had been practically rebuilt with two propellers, several pairs of skids, three different tails, countless nuts and bolts, and yards of unbleached calico.

Lilian offered to fill orders either for gliders or full-size machines using her own designs; she guaranteed they would glide or fly and the work and quality would be of the best. She stipulated that the engine and propeller must be reasonably efficient, otherwise "it is only waste of time." She knew from her experience that a strong engine was essential for successful flight, that her fragile machine was too delicate to hold together with a stronger motor, that her machine was really more of a grasshopper than an aeroplane that could fly anywhere.

This realization and the lack of offers to buy one of her machines convinced her to give up flying to please her father, who, worried by his daughter's dangerous hobby, offered her a motorcar in exchange. Lilian accepted gracefully. She had made her point—a woman could build and fly an aeroplane—and silenced the scoffers. Lilian advertised in *Flight* for people interested in acquiring the *Mayfly*. Eventually the motor was sold and ended up at the Science Museum in London, and the biplane frame was presented to the Dublin Flying Club.

Aeroplanes played no further role in Lilian's life. She taught herself to drive and was soon running a Ford agency in Belfast. When she received a proposal of marriage from a Canadian gentleman who admired her spunk, she accepted and went to British Columbia in 1912, where she and her husband farmed on Galiano Island near Vancouver. She returned to Britain in 1935 and retired eventually in Cornwall, where she lived into old age, an original among a collection of unusual women.

There were other Britons mentioned in the journals of the early years: Dorothy Prentice, whose brother started an aero club in Surrey, was learning to fly at Hendon; Lily Irvine was taught by her husband, James V. Martin, at Hendon, but before she earned a license, she returned with him to the United States, where both Martins flew exhibitions. According to *Flight,* the day she sailed for America, Lily circled the Hendon Aerodrome twelve times on the school Farman. A Mrs. Palmer was mentioned as

training on a Martin Handasyde, and Miss Edith Meeze was studying at
the Valkyrie school. None of these women earned a license, but their
mention indicates that more English women were becoming interested in
aviation despite the barriers.

An article in the *New York Evening World* of May 20, 1911, said that a
Mrs. Gavin could rightfully claim to be the first English woman to fly, a
claim open to debate. Mrs. Gavin, also an excellent golfer, attended the
Charles Lane Gliding School at Brooklands, the first school at the raceway in the spring of 1910. The biplane glider, similar to a Farman, took
off from a starting rail lane installed on the hillside below the grandstand. By July 1910, Mrs. Gavin was making solo glider flights, an experience that led her to cross to France, where she was reported flying on a
powered machine at Issy-les-Moulineaux. According to the newspaper
article, she made flights of forty-five minutes' duration, but there is no
record of her earning a pilot's license.

Two other women received regular mentions in the journals, but only
as passengers. The ubiquitous Eleanor Trehawke Davies bought two Blériot
machines and picked good pilots to fly her about, notably Gustav Hamel,
a leading winner in English meets; B. C. Hucks; and James Valentine. On
one such jaunt, she went along with Hamel when he crossed the Channel to Paris. Harriet Quimby, the American aviatrix who was readying
her Channel flight on the south coast, thought it unsporting of Hamel
to steal her thunder by taking Eleanor along, because Miss Trehawke
Davies then qualified as "the first woman to cross the Channel in an
aeroplane." (Eleanor enjoyed collecting labels.) Another flight took her as
far as Germany.

When looping the loop became popular, Eleanor decided she must be
the first woman to experience a loop. When Hamel did a loop on Boxing Day in his Morane Saulnier, a determined Eleanor climbed out of
her sickbed against doctor's orders and went to Hendon on January 2.
Hamel and Eleanor took off as dusk gathered, climbed to one thousand
feet, and looped the loop, followed by a half roll, the aeroplane on its
back, before diving out to return to normal flight. Dallas Brett's *History
of British Aviation* describes a satisfied Eleanor as "the first passenger of
either sex to loop with an English pilot" and "the first woman in the
world to loop-the-loop." She returned to bed contentedly and "underwent a minor operation." One can only wonder what a woman of such

unusual spirit and determination might have accomplished had she become a pilot.

The Princess Lowenstein-Wertheim, a wealthy English woman married to a German prince, was an avid aviation fan, but she was content to be piloted about in whatever machine was considered the latest and best. She flew across the Channel in 1914, and in 1927, at age sixty-three, her single-engine Fokker monoplane, christened the *St. Raphael,* took off from Salisbury, in spite of her family's objections, to attempt a crossing of the Atlantic with two pilots aboard. Seated in a wicker chair in the cabin, surrounded by eight hundred gallons of gasoline, she waved gaily at takeoff. The aeroplane was sighted as it crossed Ireland and left the coast of Galway, and once more by a Dutch boat midway across the ocean, before disappearing forever.

Women like the princess and Trehawke Davies, not aviators themselves, were important for arousing interest in aviation and demonstrating its potential. Money allowed them to pursue aerial adventures in aeroplanes, marvelous toys for them, but machines that would transform modern life.

Gertrude Bacon, a member of the Aero Club at Sheppey, off the Kentish coast, and the Women's Aerial League, is mentioned among aviation enthusiasts because of her writings on aeronautics. As a young woman she made numerous balloon voyages with her father and was the first woman to make a "right away" voyage in an airship. In 1909 she arranged to have her first aeroplane flight with Roger Sommer at the first Rheims Aviation Meet, a landmark event of early aviation. The surprising lift as the ground dropped away was pure delight for Gertrude: "that glorious, gliding sense that the sea-bird has known this million years." Later, at Brooklands, she flew with Douglas Gilmour. Her journal articles and lectures gave enthusiastic support to the fledgling aviation development in England. Keenly aware that England lagged behind advances on the Continent, where Germany and France were funding aviation development, she argued that England must do the same.

Dorothy Levitt, a student of Hubert Latham, was at Châlons at the same time as Raymonde de Laroche and Marie Marvingt, but she did not win a license. Spencer Kavanagh, a balloonist and parachutist of Irish birth, took lessons first at the Blériot School, at Pau, then with Grahame-White when his school opened there. She almost certainly soloed in early 1910 to win the title: England's first woman to fly. One writer has commented that Kavanagh changed her name as often as others did their dresses.

Her real name was Edith Maud Cook, but at different times she used Elsa Spencer, Viola Fleet, Viola Spencer-Kavanagh, and Viola Spencer or Viola Kavanagh, depending on which company she was working for as an aerial performer. The two most famous firms she worked for were Spencer Bros. Ltd., and A. E. Gaudron. Her exhibition career was short-lived; she died in hospital on July 14, 1910, five days after a failed parachute leap from a balloon at Coventry, England. Spencer, who lacked the money to buy her own aeroplane, had stayed at Grahame-White's school, where she could use a machine until she felt she had mastered flying. She never earned a pilot's license in her brief career, but not because she lacked courage.

7
America Gets Wings

AVIATION TOOK OFF in America in 1910. The Wright brothers and Glenn Curtiss had company aviators who appeared at fairs and enlivened holiday celebrations around the country. Air meets were fashionable in cities wanting to prove themselves up-and-coming, and international air meets were held at Los Angeles in January, Boston in September, and Belmont Park on Long Island, New York, in October. It was a time when aeroplane enthusiasts designed and built their own machines, and two women could claim the distinction that year of "first to solo in an aeroplane."

BLANCHE SCOTT
Blanche Stuart Scott probably flew first on September 6, but without official observers at the Curtiss center at Hammondsport, New York; Bessica Raiche went up on the 26th at Mineola, Long Island, a busy aviation center with numerous official witnesses. Both ladies deserve the spotlight for their achievement, and their courage.

Blanche, known as Betty in those days, was a harum-scarum young woman, "a fresh brat" in her words, with red hair and a temperament to match. Born in Rochester, New York, on April 8, 1891, she was the only child of doting parents who soon realized they had a spirited bundle on their hands. Her father, John C. S. Scott, was a veterinarian who amassed considerable wealth with the invention of a medicine for ringworm. Her mother, Belle J. Herendeen, was a descendant of *Mayflower* ancestors whose family migrated to Rochester in the early part of the nineteenth century. Blanche inherited plenty of pioneer spunk and the energy to put it to use.

Her daredevil antics led her mother to enroll her in a series of girls' schools—Miss Nichol's School for Girls in Rochester, the Howard Seminary in West Bridgewater, Massachusetts, and Fort Edward Seminary in New York State—hoping her high spirits would be tamed. Betty matured, decided she would like to be an automobile saleswoman—she could already drive a car—and went to work for the Mitchell automobile company. With an urge to do the unusual, she approached the Willys Overland Company and suggested that she drive one of its models across the country, visiting Willys Overland dealers along the way, with a newspaperwoman as passenger to describe the trip. It would be an eye-opening first, generate publicity for the company and Betty, and was not the first nor the last of her good ideas.

The trip was a publicity success. Gertrude Phillips, the presswoman passenger, and the advertising agent for Willys Overland contacted newspapers along the way so the two women were met by state governors, representatives of the auto clubs then in existence, and the Overland distributors as the two zigzagged six thousand miles across the country. The newspaper coverage was phenomenal. Like the coverage on Cal Rodgers, the first person to fly coast to coast, arrival in a town became a three-day story: the approach the day before, the arrival, and the latest word the day after. Gertrude didn't drive, which made Blanche the important figure behind the wheel. In later years, she admitted that so much attention went to her nineteen-year-old head.

As Blanche and Gertrude approached Dayton, Ohio, on their way to an appearance at the Indianapolis auto races, they saw two aeroplanes in the air above the Wright aviation field, an exciting first for the women. The travelers joined a crowd of several thousand to watch the aerial show. At the time Blanche thought the fliers "plumb crazy." It was the first of two encounters with aviation. In California, at the end of the trip, the two women met Glenn Martin in Santa Ana. He had one arm in a cast from a crash testing his aeroplane and "looked and acted like a divinity student." He was surely daft, the women thought, and teased him mercilessly. In time, when she flew his aeroplanes, Blanche would recognize his ability as a pilot and designer.

Blanche and Gertrude were entertained in Tijuana by Governor Carranza of Sonora, who was later the president of Mexico. On their return to San Diego to pack for the trip back to New York, a reporter for the eastern newspapers called with a story idea: How about being the first woman, or one of the first, to ride in an aeroplane? Betty agreed; "I was crazy enough to do anything," she admitted.

Back across the border again on a Saturday afternoon—the story was scheduled for the Sunday-morning papers—the women discovered that the pilot had wrecked the Farman that day taking a spin. Even worse, the reporter had filed the story early because of the time difference, which left the three participants in a bind. It was too late for a denial, so Gertrude, Blanche, the reporter, and the pilot, Roehrig, were sworn to secrecy. The next day, the two travelers left for New York.

Blanche found New York City very quiet after the cross-country adventure. By chance, she met Frank Tipton, Glenn Curtiss's press agent, who was aware of the publicity generated by the cross-country drive. Would she like to learn to fly? After all, she had been up in an aeroplane near San Diego. Scott swallowed, hesitated, and finally agreed. Jerome Fanciulli, general manager for the Curtiss Exhibition Company, with booking offices in New York City, and always on the lookout for possible fliers, thought Blanche a likely candidate and sent her up to Hammondsport, aware that a woman pilot would be a good publicity gimmick.

The factory staff was less enthusiastic. Curtiss didn't think it was a good idea, but he yielded to Fanciulli's judgment. Reluctantly, Curtiss trained Blanche. After receiving a brief explanation of the machine's parts (a pusher biplane), she was set to running the machine back and forth—"grass cutting"—with a governor on the motor to keep the machine on the ground. A sudden gust of wind eddied around the surrounding hills, and Blanche found herself about ten feet in the air. From then on, she begged to have the block removed; she wanted to fly. A few days later she got her wish; she could do "hops," but she must promise not to go into the air. She hopped, gradually extending her distance, landing on the straightaway, until one day she was up unexpectedly and "circled once or twice," by her account, before landing. She had done it! Proud, scared, she claimed September 2 as the magical day, sometimes September 6.

With the years, the dates changed, but never her insistence that she was America's first woman pilot in the air. She probably was, but recognition was denied her because her solo was "accidental."

Blanche tells one anecdote from her days with Curtiss that contradicts his reputation as a serious man without humor. According to Blanche, a prominent society woman approached him one day and said she knew a lot about aviation, but she had one question: "If one has trouble up there in the air, how does one come down?" "Well, we're still in the experimental stages of aviation," Curtiss explained seriously. "Now, we've had a man up there for three days and there is some concern of his starving to death if we don't get him down."

Curtiss may not have been happy about teaching Blanche, but he recognized her ability. In October, she made her public debut at Driving Park, Fort Wayne, Indiana, as a member of the Curtiss Exhibition Team. Using a machine of Eugene Ely's, she rose twelve feet and sailed across the field. Afterward she insisted she could have "turned and circled the track, but Mr. Curtiss has absolutely forbidden me attempting the turn."

Shortly after, she married the man who had done publicity for her automobile trip and gave up flying for a while, but she couldn't stay away for long. By June 1911 she was flying with Thomas S. Baldwin at Mineola, unlearning what she had learned on a Curtiss pusher. Baldwin's machine was built for speed; his method of instruction, direct. As soon as a pupil learned the controls—the touch was more delicate than the Curtiss machine—he or she was permitted to make a straightaway, then turns. Blanche did all of these, and by August 1911 the *New York Sun* was reporting that three women fliers were in the air at Mineola: Blanche, Harriet Quimby, and Matilde Moisant. (Bessica Raiche was flying in the spring at the same time as Quimby, both women wearing trousers, which caused news comment, but there is no mention of her after that time.) The *New York Tribune* spotted the trio and hailed them as "First Americans of Their Sex to Wing the Deep Blue."

During this period, Blanche, mad about something, took off in her machine one day and ignored the rule not to leave the area of the field. She was up and free. By the time she reached Riverhead, Long Island, her temper had cooled, and she turned back toward Mineola, where she landed safely. The next day she was surprised to read that the flight was

American Blanche Stuart Scott seated at the controls of a Curtiss pusher. INTER-
NATIONAL WOMEN'S AIR & SPACE MUSEUM, INC.

hailed as a woman's cross-country distance record of sixty miles. It was
typical Blanche behavior.

Blanche flew everything, and everywhere, as "The Tomboy of the
Air," dressed in her voluminous bloomers padded with three petticoats.
She earned as much as five thousand dollars a week, out of which she
paid for maintenance and transportation of her machine, a fee to her
manager, and her mechanic. She was at the meet at Squantum Field in
1912 when Harriet Quimby was killed in a crash. Blanche was in the air
at the time of the accident and had a difficult time finding a clear space to
land; unruly crowds were everywhere, and her nerves were not steady.
With much anguish, Blanche got her machine down and, reportedly,
fainted. Exhibiting was a strenuous life, and Blanche was a daredevil stunt
flier performing ever more daring feats. She flew upside down twenty
feet off the ground, under bridges and, as a special stunt, her "Death

A typical advertisement for Blanche Stuart Scott, 1912. NATIONAL AIR AND SPACE
MUSEUM, SMITHSONIAN INSTITUTION

Dive," during which she dropped down from a great height with the throttle retarded, then pulled up one hundred feet from the ground.

In California she flew with the Great Western Aerial Circus, her reputation as a daring pilot calling for more and more dangerous stunts to live up to her billing: "A Thrill Every Second, Rain, Shine, or Cyclone"; "Watch this daring woman duplicate all the flying tricks of Paulhan"; "'The Tomboy of the Air'—The Most Famous Aviatrix in the World." Luck was often on her side. One day, in the midst of her daring dive, the carburetor flooded and the machine kept going down. Pulling the stick back quickly, the machine hit tail first. The pilot walked away, because, she believed, she was wearing a lucky red sweater. The proof was, another time, without the sweater, she landed nose down in a swamp and broke several ribs, her collarbone, and left arm. Blanche was fond of saying she had forty-one mended bones in her body, the result of numerous crack ups and two that were serious. She must have forgotten the sweater more than once.

The circus performances were more entertainment than serious aviation. During one act at the Emeryville Air Meet, a mysterious pilot, announced as Mme. Cozette de Trouse, arrived on the field in the company of Mrs. Florence Ferris, the wife of the meet's manager. Dressed in an ordinary costume, the striking blonde posed for pictures with flowers for Mrs. Ferris, then seated herself in Lincoln Beachey's aeroplane and made a quick ascent, circling the field with a few dips and curves before landing. Blanche met the mysterious aviator, then reached up and tore off a golden wig and veil to reveal Lincoln Beachey. The crowd roared and applauded the stunt. The *San Francisco Chronicle* reported that Beachey made the mistake "of trying to walk while in skirts," a certain giveaway. The act was a crowd pleaser but did little to advance aviation. Although Blanche was grounded by weather conditions one day, some thirty thousand spectators were thrilled by her performances during the eight-day meet. She showed that a woman could pilot a biplane as well as any man.

Despite her hectic career, Blanche married and divorced twice; both were nice men, and wealthy. Her explanation: "They wanted domestic wives, and I couldn't stay in a birdcage." By the end of 1916 she had given up flying, realizing that a real career in aviation wasn't possible and stunt flying had lost much of its appeal.

She sold her machine to the government when war began and turned her hand to the movie business with a studio bought for her by her second husband. This lasted a couple of years by her account; then she wrote scripts and performed in radio at station KFI, in Los Angeles, before returning to Rochester to work in radio (WVET and WARC) and at Hornell, New York (WLEA). During the 1950s she worked with the Air Force Museum at Wright-Patterson Air Force Base in Dayton, Ohio, traveling around the country boosting the museum and collecting material and memorabilia from the pioneer days of flying for the museum's collection.

Blanche continued watching and commenting on aviation developments through the years; she enjoyed membership in the Early Birds, a society of aviators who soloed before World War I, and several other aviation organizations. On September 6, 1948, she had a unique experience. Flying with Charles E. Yeager in a TF-80C, she became the first American woman to ride in a jet. Her long life was a delineation of American flying history from the first lifting off the ground by a woman pilot to women in space. She flew without earning a pilot's license; she never saw the need for one.

Blanche died at Genesee Hospital in Rochester on January 13, 1970. She loved telling people about the early years of aviation; she was never short of opinions, and her stories got better with the years. She considered herself one of the lucky ones: "Most of us got killed."

BESSICA RAICHE

Bessica Faith Raiche shared the honor, with Blanche Scott, of first American woman to solo and received a gold medal presented by Hudson Maxim from the Aeronautical Society of New York on October 13, 1910, to prove it. Maxim was the inventor of deadly explosives.

Born in Rockford, Illinois, in 1876, to James and Elizabeth Curtis Medlar and the oldest of three daughters, Bessica was an active girl with wide interests: languages, music, shooting, swimming, driving an auto, and painting—in many ways a Renaissance woman! Her father was a pioneer photographer who owned the Art Emporium Studio on West State Street, where Mrs. Medlar helped out regularly enough to learn the new art of photography and its commercial applications. The 1893

*American aviator
Bessica Raiche, a
portrait photo.*
DEAN TODD COLLEC-
TION, COURTESY OF
LYGIA IONNITIU

Rockford High School yearbook noted that Bessie, as they called her, was third vice president for her class, and a Literary Society officer. "Through nature and through art she strayed" was an appropriate comment beside her name.

Following high school, Bessica attended the Rockford Academy, a private school run by Mary L. Carpenter, for one year. About this time, her mother and father separated, as they are listed in the city directory at different addresses. Mrs. Medlar was operating her own photography business at a new address on State Street. Sometime between 1894 and 1900, Bessica studied painting in France, but, in the years 1896–97, she was listed in the city directory as assistant to Dr. C. J. Sowle, dentist. Her work with Dr. Sowle may have led her to consider a career in medicine. Certainly she learned skills that enabled her to pay her way through medical school. She and her sister Ruth both worked as clerks in 1899, according to the directory, and lived with their mother. By 1901, mother and daughters had disappeared from the directory.

Bessica entered Tufts Medical School in 1900 and was graduated in 1903. Apparently the family disapproved of her choice of profession— none of them attended her graduation—but Bessica's determination blazed a trail for women in medicine. She worked her way through school as a dental assistant and by teaching painting, with little support from her family. During this period the young dental assistant met the man she would marry, François Raiche, when he came to the office with a dental problem. It was kismet.

François C. Raiche was the son of a French immigrant who had prospered sufficiently in Portsmouth, New Hampshire, to send his son to university. The elder Raiche spoke no English when he came to America and answered every remark made to him with the word "right." Consequently, his son went through school as Frank C. Wright, although his real name was Raiche. Young Raiche was Yale Law, 1892, Phi Sigma Kappa, and crew; a practicing attorney in New York, he and his family had become proper Yankees.

Bessica's first assignment was Staten Island Children's Hospital, where she interned and served a residency, receiving specialized training in obstetrics. In 1904 she started private practice as Faith C. Medlar, M.D., first in Beachmont, then Swampscott, Massachusetts, as a general practitioner. According to Catherine Stull, the couple's daughter, Bessica and Frank married sometime between 1904 and 1907, maintained a home in Beachmont, and were actively pursuing their interest in the new heavier-than-air technology. Frank was a member of the New York Aeronautical Society, and both Raiches attended exhibitions of new flying machines and studied the latest literature about aviation.

By 1907, the couple was settled in their summer home on Long Island to be near the aviation activity at Mineola. All of the early aviation enthusiasts were there: the Wrights, Glenn Curtiss, and a throng of amateur builders with whom the Raiches fit right in. Bessica was determined to learn to fly; Frank, as his American friends called him, dreamed of building his own aeroplane. In short order, the couple did just that in the living room of their summer home. The Raiche-Crout biplane, the work of

Bessica and Frank, was the first machine to fly that was built by a member of the New York Aeronautical Society—earlier models never got off the ground. The engine was built by a Mr. Crout.

As the machine took shape, the grand piano became a carpenter's horse to support the back end. The aeroplane was a Curtiss-type pusher biplane of flimsy design: A set of wings, covered on the top with shellacked silk, had boxlike structures fore and aft, and bamboo struts held in place with wire, all of which sat on a triangular set of bicycle wheels powered by a two-cycle, forty-horsepower boat motor that turned a wooden propeller behind the pilot's seat. Like the first Wright motors, there was no throttle to control the motor's speed; it ran at full speed until the gas and ignition were cut off.

Weight was a major concern for the builders, who had the mistaken idea that the lighter the machine, the better it would fly. The builders didn't realize that the power of the motor was the key to successful flight. Bessica weighed ninety pounds, which made her an ideal candidate for pilot. Just to be sure, there was much drilling of crankshafts and other parts to reduce every possible ounce of weight. When the machine was ready, the front of the house was removed to move the aeroplane out for a trial. That was a unique learning experience; Bessica had no training other than helping to build the machine and cursory advice to pull the stick to go up, push it to come down.

The first starts were tentative, little more than grass-cutting up and down the field to get the feel of the motor. Before the aeroplane moved, the motor was started, and when it was going at full speed, the mechanics holding the wings let go and the fragile contraption moved forward, skimming the tops of the grass. The first attempt was judged a success; the machine left the ground briefly, then came down again—a bit hard, but machine and pilot were safe. It was a remarkable achievement for 1908, considering the stage of aviation, when the first test was often a disaster.

Bessica discovered that wearing a skirt was a mistake. The wind got under it, and interfered with the safe working of the controls. Thereafter, she wore riding breeches until she had leather pants, a jacket, and a helmet made. When a second aeroplane was finished, Bessica's very own, the determined flier was on board again. This one was a Curtiss-type pusher biplane with a rebuilt four-cylinder, forty-horsepower engine that could fly about thirty-five miles an hour. Ailerons for lateral balance in flight were still unknown, and because the Wrights controlled wing-warping devices, a harness worn by the pilot worked wing flaps on the upper and lower wings. If the aeroplane started to slip in flight, the pilot leaned in the opposite direction and the harness depressed one flap while raising the other to keep the machine level.

Finished on September 15, 1910, the frail machine was rolled out the next day, and Bessica settled herself in it to make the first accredited solo flight by a woman in the United States. She made several more short flights that day, but on the fifth trial, the aeroplane hit a rut in the ground at the far end of the field, and the nose jammed into the ground, smashing the front control. The aeroplane crumbled, and the pilot shot out onto the ground, followed by the seat, which hit her in the back. Dazed for a minute or two, Bessica got up, ran to the machine, whose motor was still running "at a terrific rate," and cut the ignition. As she explained later, she needed that motor for the next aeroplane.

The press followed the aviation attempts at Mineola with quizzical interest. Accidents were sure to make the news. The *New York Globe* observed on September 25 that Bessica's appearance on the field after her mishap quieted fears "that the experience might unnerve her. But it was proved this morning that she was made of different stuff." Interested spectators noted approvingly her increased skill with each flight: "The longest was about 500 yards, during which she rose from 15 to 20 feet above the ground." There were more misadventures—wind was a problem for the delicate machine—but by October 15, Bessica was flying at thirty feet and making several circles of the field, a marked advance from the straight flights, when around the country scores of amateurs "have operated aeroplanes without leaving the ground."

The Aeronautical Society of New York had recognized in 1909 that many of the aeroplanes built were ingenious but impractical. Its prize to a triplane that year was carefully worded: "winner of first prize money for design and workmanship, independent of performance." Elsewhere, amateur builders had similar results. *Flight* published a lively account of one builder in Budapest who could not contain his excitement when after repeated tries "the tail lifted from the ground"—he was still not airborne. The Raiche machines, built with little technical knowledge by enthusiastic tinkerers, were amazing for their time.

The Aeronautical Society, impressed by Bessica's achievement, held a dinner in New York on October 13 to award her with a winged gold medal encrusted with diamonds. The wording of the presentation was very specific: in official recognition of her aeroplane flight a month earlier as "the nation's first intentional solo by a woman." The society, Solomon-like, chose to recognize Raiche's intentional flight rather than Scott's accidental one.

The success of the first aeroplane led the husband-and-wife builders to construct two more, which were sold to eager buyers. Meanwhile, Bessica had designed and made patterns for the castings and supervised the building of the aeroplane that was hers. Flying this machine, Bessica continued to gain expertise. Gliding was an essential movement. She described how this was done: "In starting a glide down you shut off the motor in the air. There was no starting again. You came down, and if the glide was too steep, there was no climbing out of it."

By 1911, another bird woman had joined the crowd at Mineola— Harriet Quimby, the first woman to earn a pilot's license in the United States, followed thirteen days later by Matilde Moisant. More would follow. Bessica, like Blanche, had no interest in getting a license. She proved to her own satisfaction that she could fly and was content with that.

Bessica continued improving her flying technique in addition to helping with the Française Américaine Aeroplane Cie., a husband-and-wife venture. The company advertised to teach students to fly in two weeks for two hundred dollars, with one hundred dollars down and the balance at the end of the first week. Students learned construction along with flight lessons; the school boasted that students made circles after four days of flying. Interested persons were to give their weight; the emphasis on lightness was still uppermost in the builders' minds.

The Raiche enterprise didn't have much success; the couple's original investment was too small to attract the numbers needed. In 1911, husband and wife moved to Chicago and linked up with the Standard School of Aviation. By 1912, Bessica had organized the nation's first pilot-instruction class exclusively for women. This endeavor was short-lived; later that year the Raiches moved to Balboa Island, California, in search of a warmer climate. Bessica gave up her aviation career and returned to medicine; presumably, Frank returned to the law. Together they had enjoyed a unique experience during the infancy of aviation, which earned Bessica a place in the history books.

The Raiches' daughter, Catherine, was born in Balboa in 1914. Bessica joined the Orange County Medical Association in 1917 and was elected president in 1923. Active throughout that part of California, Dr. Raiche continued her practice in obstetrics and gynecology in Anaheim and in Santa Ana, where she was on the staff of the Orange County Hospital, concerned especially with public health problems and tuberculosis. As fearless in the practice of medicine as she was in flying, Bessica was a staunch advocate of birth control at a time when such information was illegal and was proud that she never lost a mother or a baby.

In 1925, Bessica and Frank Raiche were divorced, a pattern similar to the Medlars before them. Their daughter remembered that her father took a lot of aviation material with him to New York. Sitting in front of the fireplace "with a drawer full of papers on his lap, he'd toss papers into the fire and say, 'We don't need that anymore.'" Historians will never know what interesting material went up in smoke.

In 1931, interviewed by Gerald Bur for the *Sportsman Pilot,* Dr. Raiche admitted she still had a desire to fly, but it was on hold until her daughter finished her studies. Amused at the prospect of an instructor advising her not to be nervous at the first flight, she imagined his reaction when she would reply: "Sonny, I was flying a birdcage that you wouldn't step in when you were too young for kindergarten."

Bessica died the following year at fifty-eight when she inhaled too much chloroform to regulate pain following surgery. Her daughter recalled that Bessica had to stop her practice for about two years because of illness; she suffered from cancer. She was sorely missed in her community, where she found helping new citizens into the world as exciting as bucking the wind at Mineola.

After her death a perceptive reporter wrote, "For a woman to fly in those days was like Dr. Johnson's woman preaching: 'No one expected to see it done well, and everyone was surprised to see it done at all.'"

8
Official Bird

IN 1911, AMERICA GAINED its first licensed woman pilot, Harriet Quimby, who earned license No. 37 on August 1 by successfully completing her tests before two representatives of Aero Club of America, George F. Campbell-Wood and Baron Ladilas D'Orcy. She was an ideal choice to break the sex barrier in America: glamorous, clever, definitely a modern woman, yielding nothing to men. She was also an invented one.

Harriet, the second of two daughters, was born on May 11, 1875, in Coldwater, Michigan, to Ursula and William Quimby. Farming was not William's strong point, and the family moved to California with the hope that life would be better. Ursula, a strong woman in her own right, was determined her two daughters would have a better life than hers had been. By 1884, Harriet was attending one of the local schools in Arroyo Grande, at that time a golden land of orange groves and rolling hills south of San Louis Obispo.

In later years Ursula Quimby created a more elegant background for her pretty daughter: old New England stock who migrated west, an orange plantation in Arroyo Grande as birthplace, education by private tutors in France and America. Certainly Harriet was pretty enough and sophisticated enough to have blossomed from such a background. According to Ursula's script, Harriet's father was a member of the United States Consulate Service and the Union Club in San Francisco.

Reality was somewhat different. The early years were a hard scramble before the family moved west and tried to make a financial success of a grocery store. When it failed, they moved to Los Gatos, where their luck was no better. In 1893, William was declared an invalid and was eligible for a small pension as a Civil War veteran. Ursula became the bread-winner for the family, making herbal remedies and sewing bags for local fruit companies.

The strains of chautauqua, an education system popular in the late nineteenth century that emphasized lectures and dramatic performances in the out of doors, were still heard of in that part of California. The Methodists had built a redwood church in one of the valleys, to which important speakers and entertainers came; the Quaker medicine man set up his wagon and sold an elixir cure-all for physical problems; the Chinese workers tunneling for the Southern Pacific Railroad brought their homestyle remedies, including the golden poppy, which had replaced laudanum as an easer of worry and pain. Ursula had the materials and the know-how to make remedies (her brother in Michigan was known for his concoctions), and there was a ready market in San Francisco, the next stop for the Quimbys, where the family was listed in the 1900 census.

In the next few years, Harriet's sister, Kitty, married and disappeared from family mention; Harriet, a slender young woman in her twenties with vivacious charm, soon became known as a reporter and feature writer for the *San Francisco Call* and the *Chronicle* and, in 1902, she joined the staff of the *Dramatic Review.* At the same time, she won a place among socially prominent San Franciscans. Editors who worked with her recognized her ability—"the keenest nose for news" was one judgment. She had a talent for writing about the unusual or exotic and making readers experience it. Her success in San Francisco gave her the confidence to turn her sights east; a year later she was in New York City, determined to make a career in journalism.

New York was tougher, but rejections only stiffened her resolve. The editor of *Leslie's Illustrated Weekly* interviewed her, read some of her work, gave a tough critique, and suggested she try another line of work. Harriet admitted she had considered cooking but felt she was "a better writer than a cook," and she thought she could work well with the editor. (Her quick reply probably won her a trial.) Not long after, *Leslie's* printed her first article, "Curious Chinese Customs." There would be others. Her news sense for the unusual, or what was new, and her ability to involve the reader won her a regular position with *Leslie's* in 1904, as drama critic and editor of the women's page. She was on her way!

Harriet loved to travel—being paid to do so and write about it was heaven. In addition to traveling overseas, she explored the rich variety of neighborhoods in New York—Chinese, Italian, German, Jewish, Hungarian—capturing her impressions in print for *Leslie's* readers. Her drama columns, which appeared weekly, were informative, recommending what was good and warning about what was bad. *The Call of the Cricket* was one of the latter. "Were it not for the utter foolishness which pads out the story, the play might be more of an entertainment than it is. The plot is not a bad one for a comedy, but even the extremely young persons of this generation demand something more than milk-and-water sentiment in their love stories." Harriet was a modern woman; foolish sentimentality did not play.

There were serious articles on infant mortality—it was high in the immigrant neighborhoods; on the preservation of nature and animals—"A Woman's Moose Hunt," a story she liked because it had no killing; human interest articles such as "Hints to Stage-struck Girls"; and articles of special interest to women. She wrote about the joys of an ocean voyage—the entertainment derived from watching fellow passengers, the proper clothes to wear, the luxury of total relaxation—all of which gave working women a chance to dream. Her technique with serious articles was to introduce the subject, followed by an interview with a known authority in the field to provide pertinent comments. She avoided personal opinion as much as possible.

A 1910 editorial in *Leslie's* —"Should Women Vote?"—discussed a topic much in the news and quoted President Taft on that question. "I am not a rabid suffragist. The truth is, I am not in favor of suffrage for women until I can be convinced that all women desire it; and when they desire it I am in favor of giving it to them, and when they desire it they will get it, too." The editor agreed with Taft but reminded readers that women should be listened to—the influence of "pure womankind" would be a plus for politics. As long as the reformers didn't agitate as the English women were doing, they deserved "a fair hearing." Harriet surely concurred. Though she was not a suffragist, she was certainly a feminist. Experience had taught her that women were as capable as men, some even more so, and she had shown she could hold her own in the male world of journalism.

As her career progressed, Harriet enjoyed the comforts of success. She rented a suite at the new Victoria Hotel at Twenty-seventh Street and Broadway and brought her parents east to live with her. The Victoria was a stylish and comfortable residence for a successful journalist. She bought an automobile, a sure sign of success, and wrote several articles about women and the auto: the process of learning to drive, the excitement that came from incredible speed, and women's influence on automobile design. Driving about in her sporty yellow model, to paraphrase the words of the song, she proved everything men could do, she could do better.

In 1910, in anticipation of the coming International Air Meet at Belmont Park, *Leslie's* devoted one issue to aviation. The pictures were excellent, catching early aviators in action, the lure of sailing above the earth. Harriet attended the meet, met dashing young John Moisant, whose flying ability enchanted the crowds on the ground, and watched carefully as machines soared overhead. Flying looked so effortless; she was certain she could do it, too. John told Harriet that he had commitments during the fall, but he planned to open a flying school in the spring. He was killed in New Orleans at the end of the year, but Harriet had made up her mind.

She enrolled at the Moisant Aviation School, newly opened at Hempstead, Long Island, in April. Matilde Moisant, John's sister, was among her circle of friends. Harriet conveyed her excitement to Matilde, and in short order she, too, was taking flying lessons. Both young women took to the air despite objections from their families.

When Harriet began training, there were newspaper accounts of a heavily veiled woman, or a person, practicing flights in secret, who jumped hastily into an auto and sped away to avoid detection. Harriet knew how to get attention! The New York papers were agog, even the *Washington Post*. Who was the mystery person? Shortly, Harriet was revealed when a tire blew on takeoff, and every subsequent newspaper account of the flier's identity mentioned her unusual dress—"Woman Aviator in Trousers Flies Like Birdman." Harriet's aviation career was off with a bang. Harriet explained her reason for the disguise: If the flying lessons did not go well, she did not want the public to know; it might jeopardize her job. As for her garb, she considered the French harem skirt "clumsy and uncomfortable" for flying and had one designed especially for her: a plum-colored wool-backed satin suit, all one piece including the hood, that converted from knickerbockers tucked inside boots to a skirt by simply undoing a few buttons. It provided needed warmth without bulk and allowed her to appear feminine in an unfeminine occupation. (A costumer has noted that Quimby had several suits in purple hues but wore a practical outfit to fly the Channel.)

André Houpert, Harriet's teacher, who was taught by Blériot, had a healthy respect for the power an aviator held in his hands each time the motor started up, a sentiment he passed on to his students. Today the engine of that period resembles a ridiculous toy, but the thirty-horsepower motor with 1,250 revolutions per minute equaled the pull of thirty horses. It was not to be taken lightly, Houpert reminded his pupils.

The lessons went well and provided copy for several articles in *Leslie's*. The first, "How a Woman Learns to Fly," in two parts, described the Moisant training—a month of lessons was $750—which was similar to the cost at most other schools. André Houpert was careful and patient; Harriet had thirty-three lessons, most of them lasting only two to five minutes, over two and a half months. Explanations of the machine—its simplicity; the maneuvering needed to run it across the ground before advancing and going up; trying turns; left and right; and the ability to land the machine within a designated distance—were discussed and practiced. Always, there was the question of weather: Was the wind too strong? Was it too foggy? Would the rain stop?

The Moisant School set forth the rules and regulations for training in a pamphlet that was required reading. It set the time of instruction (5 A.M. every day except Sunday); who determined closure because of weather (the chief pilot) and the order of instruction (the business manager); how students were ranked (by proficiency); rules for maintenance of machines and lecture attendance; a full explanation of the code of the air, which determined when, how, and where to move a machine in the air; what to do in the event of an accident; and grounds for suspension (the business manager decided).

After the first week of shop instruction, Harriet discovered just climbing into the aeroplane was a challenge, its chassis and fixtures slippery with lubricating oil. The first directions from Houpert were for manipulating the switch so that the mechanic cranking the engine in front of the monoplane would avoid injury. Four mechanics held the rudder until the engine had reached the speed to move. For newcomers the sound of the uncovered motor, similar to a bolt rolling inside a metal drum, took getting used to. Once the student was familiar with the footwork for steering, the first lesson was to steer the machine in a straight line for a mile or so across the ground, an effort that seems easy but Harriet found difficult because the aeroplane "possesses the perversity common to all inanimate objects." It veered off instead of going straight. This dash across the field, if successful, might last two minutes; after another such dash, the teacher should dismiss you, wrote Harriet, "because you have had all that your nerves ought to be asked to stand." She believed that the French tradition, which kept the student's first efforts under five minutes, was the correct way to learn. Aviators who claimed they learned to fly in three days are giving the aggregate of time; lessons were seldom longer than a few minutes at a time. At the end of two weeks, Harriet had spent barely a half hour in the monoplane.

Once the straight line was mastered on and off the ground—one newspaperman referred to the hops off the ground as "kangarooing"— the student learned to manipulate the wings to preserve balance in the air. Students were warned not to elevate their wings the first time in the air, lest the machine shoot upward. The freedom, the surprise, might lead the student to hastily descend, which all too often ended in breakage and humiliation.

As the student gained experience, grass-cutting gave way to flights in the air on a different aeroplane, one with more speed and a more sensitive control. It was a happy day when the student first flew across the field and landed where a mechanic waited to turn him or her around for the return trip. Warping the wings with the wheel in front of the pilot and manipulating them to elevate or lower the machine were essential maneuvers to be done instinctively. Once these skills were mastered, the student learned to make a right turn—considered the most difficult move—and return, without landing, to where he or she started. Gradually a circuit of the field was added and the student practiced turns in either direction in preparation for the figure-eight requirement for a license.

On July 31, the *New York Evening Mail* reported that "Miss Quimby Outdoes Rival in Flying Dips." Blanche Scott had made a spectacular flight the previous day, and Harriet was not going to be outdone. Once in the air, she did a series of figure eights, then headed away for a cross-country flight to Westbury and Meadowbrook. She returned a half hour later and "made a perfect landing." Three days later the New York press reported that Quimby had won a license; she was America's first.

Harriet's tests incorporated the new regulations adopted by the Fédération Aéronautique Internationale and its American branch, Aero Club of America, in October of 1910: The pilot must be eighteen years of age; must pass two distance tests, without touching the ground, of no less than five kilometers in a close circuit, indicated by two posts five hundred meters from each other; and must make a series of uninterrupted figure eights changing direction at each post. He or she must make an altitude flight of at least fifty meters above the starting point and land the machine within 165 feet of the point, designated before the flight, with the motor turned off when the aeroplane touches the ground.

Landings were important; the Aero Club observers could require a pilot to retake the test if the landing was not exact. Samuel S. Whitt reports that Harriet was not within the designated distance on her first try and had to repeat the test the following day before winning the approval of G. F. Campbell-Wood and Baron D'Orcy. Another article written years later, in *Air Travel News,* also indicates that she missed her landing by another forty feet and had to repeat the test. Harriet's article makes no mention of this, nor of her record on the test. By her own account, she was more concerned that her oil-spattered face and clothing were "not exactly presentable."

Was it worth the effort? "Absolutely," said Harriet. The months of predawn rising, the inconvenience of weather, the expense—all were forgotten in the glow of achievement. "I didn't want to make myself conspicuous, I just wanted to be the first, that's all, and I am honestly and frankly delighted." As an afterthought, she added: "And I have written so much about other people, you can't guess how much I enjoy sitting back and reading about myself for once. I think that's excusable in me."

There was plenty to read. The newspapers were full of quotes attributed to Harriet, due to her prominence as America's first licensed female pilot. On rivalry with males: "I'm going in for everything in aviation that men have done; altitude, speed, endurance and the rest." On women's role: "She declares she has solved the problem of women's emancipation." On fear of the tests: "I wasn't a bit nervous or afraid: there is something about 'nauting' (flying) that robs you of any nervous reactions. . . . There is a certain freedom from resistance in a monoplane such as you don't get in an auto and there is exhilaration in managing anything so delicate and so responsive." On flying and health: "Flying made me healthier than I've ever been in my life. You don't know what a fine thing for the complexion a dew bath is. The atmosphere is so pure and fresh that it starts the blood circulation and will bring color to the dullest cheeks. The mist from the clouds is cleansing and grateful to a skin that has known no other than the dry earthbound air of a motor ride."

Harriet had opinions on women in aviation. Self-confidence and a cool head were essential; physical strength was not. "There is no sport that affords the same amount of excitement and enjoyment, and exacts in return so little muscular strength. . . . Flying is a fine, dignified sport for women, healthful and stimulating to the mind, and there is no reason to be afraid so long as one is careful." Despite the cost of an aeroplane— upward of five thousand dollars—she saw no reason why women should not "realize handsome incomes by carrying passengers between adjacent towns, why they cannot derive incomes from parcel delivery, from taking photographs from above, or from conducting schools for flying."

Interviewed for the New York *Evening World,* Harriet commented that neither "luck nor pluck" made a good aviator, but rather "plain common sense and reasonable care." Women were naturals for aviation because of sanity and instinct, the latter especially important because it works faster than reason. "When you think of the generations that women have relied on instinct rather than reason you will see for yourself that they have practically had their training for aviation."

In an article written for *Good Housekeeping,* Harriet had one word of warning: "Only a cautious person, man or woman, should fly. I never mount my machine until every wire and screw has been tested." She disapproved of stunts for mere entertainment; the real achievement in aviation is "to master the air as a proof of human progress." She gave credit for her success in the air where it was due: "I attribute it to the care of a good mechanic." Was flying dangerous? "Yes, so is swimming if one tries to swim through Niagara or in the ocean with its perilous undertow." It was the kind of quick response that made good newspaper copy.

In the next month, America's first licensed woman pilot made arrangements to have her success pay off. She signed contracts to fly at the Richmond County Agricultural Fair on Staten Island, the International Aviation Meet at Nassau Boulevard on Long Island—where a Moisant School promotion touted her demonstrated ability with a breakage bill for the entire course of instruction of less than five dollars—and the Inter-State Fair at Trenton, New Jersey, from late September through October. Her hope of earning enough money to retire and write seriously looked promising.

The first three days of the Richmond fair were rained out for flying, but September 2, when Quimby was to appear, was mild and clear. President Woodrow Wilson was to speak that day and, in his honor, Harriet was especially engaged by William Van Clief, head of the fair management. However, the noise of her engine being tested was not what Van Clief had in mind; Wilson was not pleased at having to speak over the motor's on-and-off roar. The moment Wilson finished, Quimby was in the air and circled the field twice over the Meadowlands and the Narrows in her machine, to approving applause from the crowd. Then from two hundred or three hundred feet, she turned down sharply, which became a trademark of her flying, and landed to more applause. Houpert, who was on hand for her performance, commented for the press: "She's the best I ever taught. I don't say this because she's a woman. Yesterday, she went up with a Gnome engine. I was sure she would break some wood. . . . They almost always do the first time. She didn't."

Harriet's second flight was scheduled for the last day of the fair, September 4, at night; it would be a spectacular first. Her party was late arriving after a mad dash and a speeding ticket for the unheard-of speed of thirty miles per hour! Some fifteen thousand people waited impatiently for the moon to rise and the start of her flight. Before takeoff, Harriet had to circle the field in her auto to warn people to clear the field for everyone's safety, then she climbed onto the monoplane with its new Gnome motor—"You feel like a monkey crawling along the chassis"—and was off. A sharp ascent brought forth gasps as the aeroplane rose to several hundred feet and headed for Midland Beach. Shortly, she turned back toward the fairgrounds and circled the track before dropping low to pass over the judges' stand. A wave of her hand brought cheers and applause from the crowd, and it was time to land. The crowd had surged onto the field again, which made landing tricky. She dropped sharply, bounced several times—once about ten feet in the air as she hit a rut—before stopping just short of the enclosure fence. The dramatic debut made headlines around the country. Her obvious satisfaction was heightened by Van Clief's appearance with a check for fifteen hundred dollars, a handsome sum for seven minutes' work. It was a grand beginning.

In the next several weeks, Harriet earned six hundred dollars at the Nassau meet, where she was the only woman to compete in the cross-country race, and a sum equal to that of the Richmond fair and the New Jersey fair. The *New Brunswick Times* hailed the pilot as "nerviest and one of the most beautiful in the world"—and with it all, "cultured," too.

Harriet joined the Moisant International Aviators, an association sponsored by the school to contract for exhibition flights. Its business agents were useful in booking appearances, leaving Harriet free to decide if she would attend or not, depending on the fee offered. The press reported that she turned down an appearance at the Chicago Air Meet because the organizers did not meet her price. A meet at Harvard-Boston failed to attract her because there were no prizes for women.

In this respect, aviation was still a man's domain; the small number of women flying meant few competitive opportunities, as Aero Club rules prohibited them from flying with men. There were high hopes for the International Aviation Meet, which ballyhooed the appearance of four women pilots in "the greatest women's contest in history," but that event never took place. Harriet flew alone in the cross-country flight when Hélène Dutrieu switched to duration; Matilde Moisant, flying alone, won the altitude prize; Blanche Scott, without a license, did not appear. The "greatest women's contest in history" fizzled. Both Quimby and Matilde Moisant left the meet, although there were still several days left.

The meet had an unexpected result: It antagonized the religious leaders on Long Island, who believed the sabbath should be observed with religious activities. Flying was not one. There was much ado about whether the meet would be held on Sunday or not. Harriet refrained from flying on Sunday because of her parents' scruples; Matilde Moisant believed it was an individual matter, and flew, if she felt like it, but not for money. The Sunday flying dispute produced an amusing cartoon in the *Morning Telegraph* entitled "The New Weight Carrying Contest," which showed a pilot at the International Aviation Meet flying perhaps fifteen feet off the ground with three men clinging to a rope tied to the machine's front wheel axle. The caption read: "The Ministers: 'Stop. Heaven belongs to us!!!'" The attempt to extend blue laws to include aviation continued to agitate the locals on Long Island, where airfield managers expected to reap a profit from Sunday exhibitions.

Early in November, Harriet sailed from New York City on the *Lampasas* with Matilde Moisant and other aviators of the Moisant International Aviators who were to fly in the inauguration festivities at Valbuena Plains near Mexico City for Francisco Madero, Mexico's president-elect. The aeroplanes, equipment, and mechanics made the long haul by train to Mexico City, the site of the celebration. On arrival at Vera Cruz the Moisant party traveled to Mexico City by train, where they were wined and dined in royal fashion. The two women appealed to Latin sensibilities: They were feminine, cultured, and knew how to please an audience. Alfred Moisant, a keen businessman, had arranged for the pilots' exhibition, reportedly for a handsome fee, and the opportunity to sell more machines to the Mexican government. The women never mentioned money in their comments to the press, then or later.

Harriet, after a rain pause, ascended on November 16 at about 5 P.M. to open the air show, but found atmospheric conditions on Valbuena Plains difficult. Mexico City's high altitude affected the engine, so she was able to get up only 250 feet, and after six minutes she landed, declaring it was "the hardest flight in terms of air conditions" that she had ever made. George Dyott, another of the Moisant group, found similar conditions and also landed after a brief flight. The show ended when an enthusiastic crowd of several hundred spectators broke through the fences with roars of *"Viva Madero!"* and *"Viva los aeroplanos!"*

On the third day, again after a rain pause, Quimby "in a bat-winged, long-tailed monoplane" won the hearts of the crowd. Flying far out over Lake Xochimilco in the late afternoon, she found her way back after more than a half-hour excursion and landed with the help of smudge fires. Another day Harriet's engine stopped in midair. Cool and unrattled in an emergency, she scanned the ground and glided down over several obstacles to a safe landing.

The exhibition ended on the 25th, with both Matilde and Harriet flying together along with Dyott, who carried a passenger. The pilots had flown almost daily, but the meet failed to attract the anticipated crowds, who complained that the promised number of fliers and aeroplanes failed to appear. Alfred Moisant had extended himself with his promises, but weather and the confused state of Mexican politics almost certainly contributed to the financial failure of the venture.

Francisco Madero was about to be inaugurated as president to serve out the term of former president Porfirio Díaz, but around the country there was increasingly fierce opposition to him. To the north, national troops fought with rebel forces, creating tension and uncertainty in the capital. In this atmosphere, people had other things on their minds than watching an aviation show.

In short order, four of Moisant's aviators quit; Quimby left, after appearing at Guadalajara and León, for New York, where she hired a new manager, A. Leo Stevens, well known as an aeronaut and an air-show organizer. Her abrupt departure avoided an unpleasant experience. Matilde, Houpert, and the mechanics were stranded for almost two weeks on a train trying to leave Mexico. Harriet missed that ordeal, although it would have made fine copy for *Leslie's.*

Harriet later wrote in *Leslie's* that she had the idea of flying across the English Channel while in Mexico but kept it secret, lest someone else would have a similar inspiration. Once back in New York, she started planning and wrote to the Blériot Company to inquire about the purchase of a new aeroplane. She knew what she wanted: a seventy-horsepower motor and a machine similar to the one she had been using in America. Armed with a letter of introduction to Louis Blériot, she sailed for London on the Hamberg-American liner *Amerika* on March 7, 1912. In the city of Big Ben, she described her project to the editor of the *London Mirror,* who, delighted with the idea, offered her "a handsome inducement" to fly as a representative of the *Mirror.* The next step was to get a monoplane.

Crossing to Paris, she met M. Blériot and placed an order with him; she also arranged for the loan of a fifty-horsepower machine like the one she used in the United States. Leaving Paris, she traveled to Harde-lot, where Blériot had a hangar and she could test the machine without attracting attention. Harriet imagined staying at a fine hotel at the seaside resort, but discovered on arrival that the resort was closed until summer. Fortunately, she found a small room simply furnished in a café and was grateful for that.

The next several days saw wind blowing at gale force, some forty miles per hour. All hope of trying the loaned aeroplane faded as the wind continued. Harriet had promised the editor of the *Mirror* to be in Dover promptly, which meant quick action. She arranged for the machine to be shipped secretly to the aerodrome on the heights at Dover and wired the editor to have photographers and reporters meet her at the Hotel Lord Warden, binding everyone to silence. From the smooth area of the heights, the Dover Castle, straight ahead on the cliff, pointed the way across the Channel. Harriet took it as a good omen.

The following day, a Sunday, was clear, bright, and promised a warm sun. Harriet's group encouraged her to seize the moment and fly—at least try the new machine—but she stuck to her no-Sunday-flights rule. Unfortunately, the next day was windy and cold, totally unfriendly flying weather. Pilot and her supporters hung around all day, getting cold and miserable, hoping for a change. It was not to be.

In the meantime, Gustav Hamel, the English aviator who had flown the Channel a few weeks earlier, had joined Harriet's group. In fact, he had tested the machine on Sunday and found it working satisfactorily. Tuesday morning, April 16, the group was on the field at 4 A.M.; there was no wind—scarcely a breath of air. Quickly, the monoplane was rolled out, Hamel took it up for a brief test, and declared it fine; then it was Harriet's turn.

Butterflies churned inside, but she appeared calm as she climbed into the machine. She had never flown a Blériot before, never used a compass before, never flown over water before. Instinct told her to get away quickly, for there were clouds and masses of fog in the distance; the wind would likely come up within the hour. Although she had layered warm clothes under her flying suit and wore a long woolen coat, a raincoat, and a sealskin stole over her shoulders, her solicitous friends handed her a hot-water bottle, which Hamel tied around her waist.

At 5:30 she was off the ground, rising in a wide turn to fifteen hundred feet from where she picked up the castle in the distance, partly shrouded in fog. She headed straight for the flagstaff, as she had promised the *Mirror* and motion-picture men she would do, and in the next instant

A confident Harriet Quimby, America's first licensed woman pilot, prepares to take off as Gustav Hamel gives a last-minute assist. INTERNATIONAL WOMEN'S AIR AND SPACE MUSEUM, INC.

she was over the cliffs headed for France. The newspaper reporters on the tug below watched as she sailed overhead and disappeared into a bank of fog; now nothing was visible, not the water, not Calais. There was moisture everywhere, so much so that Harriet pushed her blurred goggles up on her forehead to peer ahead. She knew she was flying at a mile a minute, the distance to Calais was twenty-two miles, and it was time to drop lower in hopes of spotting land.

Lowering from about two thousand feet to half that, a ray of sun struck her face; straight ahead was the sandy shore of France. Happiness struggled with uncertainty. Where was Calais? Being unfamiliar with the coastline, she decided to drop to about five hundred feet and travel along the coast to try to get her bearings. A rising wind with puffy gusts sent her inland, where she looked for a landing place, but the tilled fields neatly arranged below her discouraged her from coming down and tearing up a field. Turning back toward the coast, she decided on the beach; it was hard and empty. Jumping down from her machine in the middle of nowhere, she was soon surrounded by curious farmers and townspeople, who had heard the aeroplane overhead and came running on the double. They carried her in triumph to Hardelot, a short distance from the beach.

Newspapers the next day should have hailed her achievement. Instead, the sinking of the *Titanic* stole the headlines. Coverage on the first woman to pilot an aeroplane across the Channel was relegated to the back pages of the world's newspapers, a disappointing show after such a unique feat. On Harriet's arrival in New York City, a huge suffrage demonstration kept reporters away from their usual beat. There were none of the welcoming stories she had expected. Harriet was featured in a number of journals, including her own weekly, which published her written account of the adventure. Among her observations: The hot-water bottle that had been tied to her waist for added warmth "was cold as ice" when she landed. While Hamel's warning—that a five-mile deviation in direction could result in being lost over the North Sea—was enough to intimidate the average person, Harriet wrote: "My heart was not in my mouth. I felt impatient to realize this project on which I was determined, despite the protests of my best friends." She had supreme confidence and high expectations.

One story repeated frequently about the flight was Hamel's offer to fly the Channel for Harriet dressed in disguise. The reason given was his concern for her safety; Harriet's account in *Leslie's* is silent on this, but Elizabeth Hiatt Gregory quotes Harriet telling the story— Harriet thought it amusing—in a *Good Housekeeping* article. In *Leslie's,* she had only kind comments to make about him for his preflight assistance, but writing in *World Magazine* after her return, she expressed her disappointment that Hamel had taken Eleanor Trehawke Davies as a passenger across the Channel, thus depriving her of being "first woman to fly the Channel." In this report, Harriet had confided her plans to an unnamed English pilot, whom she "trusted very much," who, two days later, flew with a woman passenger across the Channel. Apparently, Harriet still smarted because of Hamel's betrayal.

One biographer, Henry Holden, claims that the *London Mirror* canceled its financial backing when Davies made headlines as the first woman to fly the Channel. Maybe, but the *Mirror* correspondents were on a tug off Dover tracking the flight and a second group waited at Calais for Harriet's arrival, then hurried almost thirty miles to join the landing

party on the beach with a bottle of champagne. They insisted on salut-
ing the happy pilot seated in the machine. Said Harriet: "Of course I did
so—anything to oblige these faithful recorders of the events of the day."
They not only wrote and photographed, they carried her long seal coat
across on the tug the day before, which seems unlikely if the newspaper
had withdrawn support. The coat allowed her to make the trip into Paris
looking fairly presentable, always a concern for her. Known for her dramatic style, Harriet had learned early that clothes can make the man, or
the woman.

The new Blériot machine was a delight to Harriet. She commented
to one reporter that she should name the machine *Catt* because a monoplane could be amazingly feminine when it wanted. Some considered
the new model, a two-seater, unstable because it was sensitive to shifts
in the center of gravity, but Harriet successfully carried a number of
passengers for short trips. When flying without a passenger, she kept a
heavy bag of sand in the rear seat. With its seventy-horsepower motor, it
was a speedy machine, and Harriet loved speed.

Her achievement in Europe had made an impression in America; she
enjoyed celebrity status, wrote knowingly on aviation subjects, and was
invited to a number of meets. Estimating that her training had cost
$2.50 a minute, she accepted those invitations that would help repay that
expense and the cost of the new white Blériot.

She accepted an invitation to fly at the 1912 Harvard-Boston Aviation
Meet at Squantum Airfield, which featured aviation greats: Lincoln
Beachey, Charlie Hamilton, Farnum T. Fish, Earle L. Ovington, Paul
Peck, Blanche Scott, and Harriet. As part of the meet's program, she
would fly an experimental mail delivery from Squantum Airfield to
New York City on July 7 to mark the close of the meet.

Monday, July 1, was a clear, sunny day. The crowds got their money's
worth with bomb-dropping contests, aerial gyrations, precision landing, and good, plain flying. There was talk of Harriet's competing with
Grahame-White in a speed race. She took passengers up for a brief spin
and, dressed in her distinctive plum costume, posed repeatedly for the
photographers. Shortly before 6 P.M., William A. P. Willard, manager of
the meet, climbed into the Blériot for a short flight over Dorchester Bay
to the Boston Light and back. He and his son, Harry, had flipped coins for
the ride, with the father winning. Friends waved the two off as A. Leo

Stevens, concerned about Willard's weight and the machine's sensitive balance, warned Willard to "sit tight," not to lean or move once they were airborne.

The aeroplane rose quickly to several thousand feet, continuing upward to about five thousand feet as it reached the Boston Light in the late afternoon sunlight. Circling the light, the aeroplane turned back toward the airfield, passed at full speed over the field at about three thousand feet, turned wide in a circle to lose altitude, then started the approach glide over the tidal flats at one thousand feet. Harriet habitually made a sharp downward turn to land, and, this time, when the machine turned down sharply, its white wings heading into the west, Willard fell out. The machine seemed to steady for an instant before plunging again, then Harriet's plum-colored body fell from the machine as it turned over in its downward descent before five thousand horrified spectators. Once the machine lost its weight, it righted itself and descended at a thirty-degree angle until its wheels touched the water; then the aeroplane flipped over on its back. Its damage: a few broken struts and wires.

There was no agreement on the cause of the accident or even the details of what happened. The opinions were as varied as the aviators present. Glenn Martin observed there would have been no accident if the two had worn seat belts. (The following year the loop-the-loop feat of test pilot Adolphe Pégoud would make belts essential equipment.) Earle Ovington believed a loose control wire got tangled, but the machine's flight after Harriet and Willard were thrown out seemed to negate that. Ovington believed there was a construction error—the warping lever on the machine was not the conventional Blériot cloche seen on other machines, and the control wires should have been positioned away from the warping lever, or contained some way, to prevent their becoming entangled. Paul Peck said Harriet was coming down with the power wide open, and when she threw the tail up to volplane, Willard was not expecting it and was thrown out. Since the machine came down at a perfect gliding angle, it reinforced his belief that nothing was wrong with the controls.

A. Leo Stevens, Harriet's manager, had a different opinion. He believed that Willard leaned forward, probably to congratulate Harriet on the flight, and the sudden shift in weight caused the tail, which was already higher than the nose, to flip upward, throwing Willard out of the machine as if shot out of a cannon. From his association with Harriet, Stevens believed she struggled to control the aeroplane in the instant it seemed to steady before the second downward plunge. Weight was essential for control of the Blériot, which normally flew with an elevated tail, the nose slightly down because of the forward engine weight; any change in weight distribution upset the center of balance, causing the machine to plunge. When Willard was thrown out, Stevens believed the pilot "was pitted against a circumstance over which no aviator, no human ingenuity, or knowledge, or skill or practice could have control."

Hardy, Harriet's French mechanic, insisted that the machine was in perfect order as far as the guiding apparatus was concerned. He asserted "without reserve" that the accident was due to the loss of balance in the machine; beyond that, he made no further technical comment. Privately, he may have thought the pilot needed more experience flying the sensitive machine, that her speed was too great, her abrupt descent too acute, but he kept these thoughts to himself. The death of his boss was a tragic loss. She embodied charm, competence, and tremendous confidence—too much for her own good.

Shakir S. Jerwan, a member of the first class of students and later director of the Moisant School, recalled in an article for the *Sportsman Pilot* that he rode with Harriet in her new two-seater Blériot on her second trial of the machine as "ballast" and copilot. He noticed as they flew around above Long Island that the machine had a tendency to nose over and, upon landing, he cautioned her about this. Harriet didn't take the criticism seriously, or she would never have carried a passenger on the fatal flight. Overconfidence led her to take risks, when she needed more practice on the new Blériot to learn its eccentricities.

The death of America's first licensed woman pilot, as might be expected, produced much editorial comment. Men were falling out of the skies daily, at a faster rate than women, but that was men's work. When Harriet was killed, the *New York Times* suggested that "it would be well to exclude women from a field of activity in which their presence is unnecessary from any point of view." It is debatable if women gave up thoughts of flying because of Quimby's tragic accident. Certainly, those women who were flying or training continued to do so. Like her, they found flying exciting, fulfilling, and profitable, and enjoyed pushing the barriers that kept women back.

Ironically, a few days before leaving for Boston, Harriet had dinner with a friend who advised her to quit. "I will after I make enough money to pay for my aeroplane. I feel awfully poor with the debt hanging over my head." Matilde Moisant said years later that Harriet was anxious to make money, with two elderly parents to care for. Money concerns were ingrained in her consciousness.

Even in death, the fiction surrounding her life continued. Her age was given as twenty-eight—she was really thirty-seven—she was born in California, according to her father, in the press, but her death certificate is blank. Harriet was buried first in Woodlawn Cemetery on Staten Island, then reburied in the Quimby family plot in Kensico Cemetery, Valhalla, New York, at her mother's request, where she joined her daughter on her death. William Quimby was buried in Greenville, Michigan, which he considered his hometown. The Quimby fiction ended.

In one of the ironies of fate surrounding Harriet, her article on superstition was published after her death. In it, she declared that all women pilots were superstitious and proceeded to give examples, much of it describing her own beliefs. Harriet would have us believe that all the misfortune she had experienced was the work of a small brass idol to which she attributed occult powers. "I am always knocking on wood for fear something will happen," she once wrote, behavior that is hard to reconcile with the decisive, clever woman who had forged a career in journalism and aviation.

Harriet's articles focused the public's attention on aviation and the roles women might play. She predicted that "women could and would fly passengers and freight, take aerial photographs, train students, and do everything connected with aviation." She knew they were capable—it was only a matter of time.

In 1991, the U.S. Postal Service issued a stamp honoring Harriet Quimby, pioneer pilot and trailblazer.

9

A Second Bird Takes to the Air

THIRTEEN DAYS AFTER Harriet Quimby won her license, Matilde Moisant followed her into the Aero Club of America records. Born into a close-knit French-Canadian family, Matilde (newspapers frequently used "Matilda" instead of the French "Mathilde" she was christened with) took up aviation after the death of her brother John, a charming daredevil of a flier who gave the American public something to cheer about.

Born September 13, 1878, in either Manteno, Illinois, or Earl Park, Indiana (her Aero Club of America license named Earl Park as place of birth), Matilde was the sixth child of Medore and Josephine Fortier Moisant, who came from French-speaking stock that had immigrated from Canada. Medore was industrious and made a living for his growing family by farming in the summer and working as a carpenter in the winter; in addition, he bought real estate as his earnings permitted. The 1880 Manteno census lists the family at home: Medore, forty-one; Josephine, thirty-nine; George, fourteen; John, ten; Annie, six; and Matilde, two. (When she won her pilot's license, Matilde, the spelling of her name on the license, did what was not uncommon among women fliers—she dropped several years off her true age for publicity purposes. Matilde explained several years later that she lowered her age for fear she would not be accepted as a pilot at age thirty-three.) The older boys, Alfred and Edward, were already working away from home. Louise, born on

April 18, 1883, was listed as the twelfth child, of which only seven survived beyond childhood.

By 1881 the family was living in Chicago, where Medore owned real estate and worked as a carpenter. The family spoke French at home, but the children were completely bilingual and, in future years, they added Spanish to their language skills. All had a "sound high school education"; Annie, four years older than "Tillie"—her nickname among family and friends—was the only one to attend college.

Medore died in 1887, before reaching fifty years of age, but hard work and thrift left the family comfortably provided for. Alfred—"Fred" to his siblings—took over as head of the family and in the next year moved the Moisants to California, where the Alameda city directory for 1888 listed Alfred J. as a "commission merchant." By lucky chance, the Moisants' arrival coincided with Alameda's emergence as a boom town. In short order, Alfred's ambition and business acumen were put to good use, and the Moisants were established in local society.

As opportunity arose, Alfred looked south to Central America, making his first trip to Guatemala in 1890. In the next decade the family invested in coffee and sugar plantations in El Salvador and Guatemala. The Moisants carved out an idyllic plantation—Santa Emilia—from the jungle in El Salvador; this was home to the younger Moisants for ten years. It was a time when fortunes could be made with hard work—the yearly profits from Santa Emilia averaged one hundred thousand dollars—but financial power relied on which faction was on top in the ongoing revolutions in the area. The family profited from banking positions, lost them in a government turnover, then regained them again. John, an adventurer at heart, took part in some of the fighting with the enthusiasm of a gun-slinging desperado from the West.

When aviation burst upon the scene, with its potential for gain, Alfred and John became enthusiastic supporters. Alfred moved to New York City to further commercial enterprises, with Matilde and Louise in tow, while John went to France in 1909, determined to build his own aeroplane and fly.

His initial attempt in France was a disaster, but John signed up for lessons with the Blériot School, bought a new monoplane, and passed his tests for a license, to the satisfaction of the French Aero Club. The license was transferred to the American Aero Club, which issued him license No. 13. In August 1910 he flew the Channel with Albert Fileux as passenger, an aviation first. Unconcerned by a series of breakdowns once he reached England, he was jubilant on reaching London. "We have broken a lot of wood, but we are in London," he told Fileux, in typical John fashion. His seat-of-the-pants flying style would make a name in aviation circles, while Alfred, assuming the leadership reins, would build aeroplanes and open a school to train aviators.

Alfred's vision of a thriving aviation business, building Moisant machines modeled on the Blériot and teaching would-be pilots in a planned setting of one hundred hangars, developed slowly. The grandstand with clubhouse and restaurant failed to appear; when financing and construction lagged, his big plans for family enrichment slowed. John did his part to kindle interest, making his debut at the 1910 Belmont Aviation Meet. With the cream of society present, he beat Grahame-White's time in the Statue of Liberty speed race by thirty-eight seconds (or forty-three, depending on the reporter) in a machine bought on the spot to win the applause and hearts of the American public. Months later, when the judges declared the English pilot the winner, Matilde and the family insisted it was due to "maneuvering." Actually, it was due to a technicality: Moisant began the race after the specified start time. Grahame-White won the ten thousand–dollar prize money, but John had the glory.

Following his debut, John made appearances around the South with the Moisant International Aviators. At New Orleans, he planned to try for the Michelin Cup for distance and endurance. Again, his penchant for doing the unpredictable was his undoing. On December 31, flying René Barrier's Blériot (John's machine was not in great shape), Moisant started to land with the wind at his back at a new site, when a gust upended his tail. Moisant pitched forward and out from about fifteen feet, breaking his neck. The short, daring aviator was suddenly gone, one of thirty-eight flying fatalities worldwide by the end of 1910. He died "gloriously," a "pioneer in a new pursuit," editorialized the *New York Times*, still charmed by his audacity.

Ironically, when Harriet Quimby crashed nineteen months later, the *Times* questioned the presence of women in aviation. There was little glory for her in spite of her role as the first American woman to earn a license.

Years later, Matilde enjoyed telling this story, which appeared in the *Times* shortly after John's death:

> John went to heaven, knocked on St. Peter's door, and said he would like to come in. St. Peter replied, "But you're an aviator, aren't you?" John said, "I fly, yes." St. Peter informed him, "You know, we're awfully sorry but we don't allow aviators here."
>
> "Wouldn't you let me look around? I'm kind of inquisitive, I'd like to see what it looks like up here, even if I have to go below." St. Peter agreed, and John looked around. "Isn't that Grahame-White over there, under that tree?"
>
> St. Peter looked. "Yes," he said, "why?"
>
> "Well," said John, "he's a flyer."
>
> "Oh no," said St. Peter. "He only thinks he is."

Matilde would laugh at this point, adding that Grahame-White was going to sue the *Times* because of the story.

Grief did not halt Alfred's plans. The school came into being with André Houpert as instructor and, by spring of 1911, the first class of eager students was in training, including Harriet Quimby, a friend of Matilde's, who convinced Matilde she should fly—"You have as much sense as I have," Harriet said. Matilde went to Alfred and told him she would like to fly. He regarded her seriously for a moment and asked why she wanted to fly. "Just for fun," she replied. Her brother then agreed, provided she promised not to fly commercially, a curious stipulation, but perhaps Alfred thought it reflected on the family's status. He secured rooms at the Atlantic City Hotel for the prospective flier, and Matilde started lessons on July 1, 1911.

The vagaries of weather played an unpredictable role in learning to fly. Days were spent waiting for favorable conditions, during which students learned about the machine, but this didn't require a great deal of time due to the aeroplane's simplicity. Matilde remembered she spent the first twelve days just waiting to sit in the aeroplane. On the thirteenth, Houpert called to her that the wind was four miles an hour; if she hurried she would have time "to make a run on the ground."

The old grass-cutter was called St. Genevieve, the saint who looked after aviators. It was slow, but it enabled Matilde, like Harriet before her, to learn how to manage a machine on the ground before trying the

Grasshopper for hopping off the ground for five or six feet and landing. According to Matilde: "You lost your breath, and then you got it
back again!" When the student was ready for more advanced work, a
third, slightly faster aeroplane with a thirty-five-horsepower motor,
dubbed the Goat, was used to go up, circle the field, land, then repeat
the process.

On that first day, Matilde, showing Moisant independence, ignored
Houpert's directions and drove St. Genevieve to the other end of the
field and back, using the rudder, as if in a boat, to turn around. Houpert
could hardly scold her for a good performance. Early on, Matilde, who
was a small woman, showed she had a mind of her own. She wanted
only to fly; lessons about carburetors and motors held no interest, and
she skipped them. Like her brother, she didn't think lessons were essential, if you were a natural. Of course, she was, as the official Aero Club
time records indicate. Matilde's total when she qualified for her license
was thirty-two minutes, something of a record even at that time. During
this learning period, she was in a one-seater aeroplane—alone—a fact
Matilde emphasized in later years.

Her first real flight was a thrill. The ability to control the machine
while floating through the air was magical. She felt like one of the big
buzzards she used to watch at Santa Emilia, lazily skimming over the
countryside. It was "just so wonderful." Watching her brother fly had
made her nervous, but she didn't feel that way about her own escapades
in the air. "I enjoy every minute without a thought of anything that
might happen," she said. On August 14, having progressed rapidly
through the lessons, she passed her tests before Aero Club observers
Baron Ladilas D'Orcy and William Bluet to become the second licensed
woman pilot in the United States. And, miraculously, she was ten years
younger! Her year of birth was given as 1888.

For the next two weeks, Matilde was in Chicago, a city she remembered well, strictly as an observer of the aerial antics at the Chicago Air
Meet. Traveling by train, she was interviewed by the *Findley Republican*
in Ohio about her ideas, as one of a select group, on women's dress. She
believed aviation would likely affect the style of dress; tight skirts which
prevent the female pilot from climbing into the aeroplane are out; wide
skirts that balloon in the wind are too dangerous; genuine women fliers
will wear boots and trousers, "but the fashionable devotees will probably

wear modified skirts." Helmets and the Russian double-breasted blouses are likely favorites to be copied. Matilde's new prominence made her an expert on everything feminine.

On her return to New York, plans were in the works for an international aviation meet to be held at Nassau Boulevard, which promised the appearance of four women pilots for the first time ever, the entrance of a Moisant-built Farman capable of carrying eight passengers in the passenger-carrying contests, and the presence of Louis Dubrow, automobile driver, in an aeroplane pace-making race—with a first prize of six hundred dollars and four hundred dollars for second place. There was keen interest in how well the monoplanes and biplanes would perform against each other. While the appearance of four women in the air was definitely noteworthy, the advertisements played up the presence of the "world famous aviators" Claude Grahame-White, Harry Atwood, Earle Ovington, T.O.M. Sopwith, and George Beatty—all men. Before the opening of the meet, Matilde practiced on a Moisant monoplane fitted with a fifty-horsepower Gnome engine known as the "Mile-a-Minute Machine." The engine's power enabled her to climb to a reported height of between fifteen hundred and two thousand feet on a day when no other aviators went up.

On September 23 the Nassau meet got off to a good start, featuring speed races, which were always popular with the public, Ovington's mail delivery at the Mineola post office—more than thirty pounds of letters from a height of two hundred feet—and altitude contests. Matilde appeared, dressed in a gray sweater and a leather helmet, which made her indistinguishable in the air, the reporters noted, unlike Harriet Quimby, the previous day, whose long scarf identified her as she circled the field. Stepping into her monoplane, Matilde shot upward in a cloud of smoke and soared in wide circles to a height of twelve hundred feet to win the Rodman Wanamaker Trophy, offered for "members of the fair sex." Her flight lasted thirty-one minutes. Americans were impressed by her performance, unaware that Melli Beese, in Germany, had soared more than twenty-four hundred feet that same week and chalked up an endurance record of two hours, nine minutes, in competition with men. The first American women pilots could not match this performance.

The meet was notable for the contest between the upholder of Sunday blue laws, the Episcopal Bishop Burgess of Garden City, and the promoter of the aviation meet, Timothy L. Woodruff, who considered flying a harmless entertainment. Sheriff Charles DeMott's threat to arrest anyone who flew on Sunday during the meet provoked much comment among the fliers. One flier, showing total disregard for authority, jumped into an aeroplane and took off—Matilde Moisant. Rising quickly, she flew in circles above the three deputy sheriffs' heads, waving her hand now and then at the glitter of stars on the field below.

A Keystone Cops sequence followed, with Matilde heading for the Moisant School at Mineola and the sheriff's deputies following by auto. After landing, Matilde waited in Alfred's car for the next scene. The unfortunate deputies had not reckoned with Alfred, who threatened to arrest them for trespassing, since they lacked a proper warrant for dealing with Tillie. The aviation crowd on the field muttered unfriendly comments, and in the next instant a shoving match ensued, when the deputies tried to seize Matilde. Matilde fled to another auto and left the field, followed by the deputies and Alfred in separate automobiles. It was grand comedy!

When the three deputies arrived at the home of Justice of the Peace Gittens at Hempstead to get a warrant for Miss Moisant, the justice asked: "What has she done?" "Flying on Sunday" was the answer. The justice replied that he could not see that flying was any worse than riding on the ground in an automobile and refused to issue the warrant. Matilde's adventure was cartoon material in several papers. The conflict continued to simmer locally, but the blue laws, generally, had little success preventing Sunday flying.

Early in October, Matilde shared her ideas on flying in an interview in the *New York Evening Sun*. She was never afraid when getting ready to go up or when actually flying. Matilde promised herself that the moment she had a nervous spell while flying she would give it up. "I know my limitations and I am not going to risk my life by trying to do just a little bit more than I realize I am able to do—neither to please myself or the public." She insisted that an aviator must know when not to go up as well as how to fly; the person who ignores the hoots and jeers of the crowd goading him to fly doesn't have "cold feet"; he has good sense.

As a beginner, Matilde knew she had much to learn. Fortunately, she never had a motor go dead in the air, but to be prepared she wanted Sopwith to give her a lesson on how to act "when your engine stops dead." Despite her spunkiness, Matilde had a clear head about flying, which is one reason she lived to a good age.

On November 1, Matilde sailed with the Moisant group en route to Mexico City for an aviation meet to celebrate the inauguration of President-elect Madero. Brother Alfred would arrive within a week to open the new Mexican Army Aviation School, which would be equipped with six Moisant monoplanes and two Moisant military-type biplanes, the first American-made machines in Mexico.

The newspaper *El Imparcial,* one of the sponsors of the meet, featured daily articles on the aviation activities. A smiling Matilde, seated on her machine was front-page news. A headline blared: "Aviation Field Taken by Assault, The Public Invaded the Field Hoping to See Close-up the Lady Pilots and Their Machines." The aviators had good publicity each day, but as the days went by, it was clear that the meet faced stiff competition from the horse races, the bullfight, and the overall confusion resulting from a chaotic political situation. The expected crowds were not there.

On opening day the crowd was about two thousand, probably the peak for the run of the meet. Some days the attendance was a disappointing eight or nine hundred, which added to the tribulations the fliers countered Atmospheric conditions at Valbuena were difficult, altitude affected the engines, and the fliers complained that more wind or moisture was needed to get their machines off the ground. Matilde had trouble landing on the first day and smashed part of her machine. There were long delays between flights, prompting the smallish crowd to depart early, and on a bad day the total time in the air was barely thirty minutes. As the days went on, the public's impatience and disappointment did not help the word-of-mouth publicity that usually brings crowds.

Despite these conditions, the fliers did their best to create excitement. Alberto Braniff finally got his Farman off the ground for two short flights of precisely one minute and two minutes. Matilde made several good flights, including one reportedly of more than two thousand feet, lasting twenty minutes, and concluded with a graceful, clean landing. The crowd applauded wildly as she drove past the grandstand in the *El Imparcial* automobile. When weather conditions canceled flights, unhappy spectators were given rain checks.

Rodolfo Gaona, star of the corrida, came to the field near the end of the meet, posed for pictures with George Dyott, and went up as a passenger in Dyott's Deperdussin machine to experience for himself the "majestic silence and supreme quiet of space" that the poet D'Annunzio found so moving. For aviators and spectators alike, the flight rescued some brilliance from an otherwise lackluster meet.

When the exhibition ended, there was a general feeling of relief. The exhibition group disbanded, leaving Matilde, Harriet Quimby, and André Houpert to carry on the Moisant meets arranged in other cities. The fliers with mechanics and aeroplanes traveled by train to Guadalajara and León for appearances. Aviation was too primitive to allow flights to the next destination.

Again, there was trouble with balky motors. Harriet made a respectable showing, taking off first, after much tinkering with the motor, to be followed shortly by Matilde. This time the motor stopped just after take-off and the monoplane crashed on the ground in pieces. Luckily, Matilde escaped without injury. After two days of nonflying weather, Harriet departed for New York, leaving Houpert and Matilde to carry on. Six days later the aeroplane reconstructed, Matilde braved treacherous air currents, not wanting to disappoint the waiting crowd. Houpert warned against a flight in such wind, but Matilde, asserting her own mind, went up.

Houpert was right. Maneuvering in such air currents felt "just like a little rowboat out in a heavy sea. First I'd go way up, and then I'd come way down, just as if they were pulling me down, and then letting it go," until the last push caused the propeller to hit the ground, upending the aeroplane. Matilde threw herself back in the machine, and that bit of weight threw the tail back. "That's the only thing that saved me," she confided years later. Another repair job was called for.

The exhibition in León ended, and the next stop, at Torreón, was canceled; revolutionary forces were too close for comfort. Partisan armies encircled the city as one faction battled another in the increasing political anarchy. Remembering that time, Matilde said, "We just got out. They burned the bridges after we left."

The train didn't get very far—it was sidetracked when rebel forces circled Torreón in the escalating battle in the state of Chihuahua between contending parties. For almost two weeks, the party was stranded inside their Pullman car. Thanks to Matilde's knowledge of Spanish, the group survived on food and water she brought in daily. Factional fighting was nothing new to her after her years in Central America, but the uncertainty of the situation was stressful. It brought out the best in Matilde, however. Houpert, who had watched her in numerous risky situations, credited her with bringing them safely from Mexico: "Few men could have managed our affairs as well in Mexico, and had it not been for the cool-headedness of our little woman manager, we would have gotten into serious complications at the city of Torreón."

The next several months were no less eventful. An appearance at New Orleans was scheduled for early March. Capricious weather caused a delay until March 9. Houpert and Matilde used the extra days to advertise the show and attract a crowd. Houpert flew over the city and brought traffic to a standstill, as John Moisant had done before his last flight. Opening day's high winds forced cancelation of the show for the small crowd that had braced the weather to see the fliers. Finally, on March 9, the weather cleared; a flight could be made.

A reporter for the *Times-Picayune* described the scene. Matilde walked onto the field "wearing a long grey coat, her flying cap in one hand and goggles in the other." The crowd cheered, photographers descended upon her, and the "quintessential 'girl flyer'" posed for pictures. Her qualities noted by one reporter made her irresistible to the public: "as womanly a woman as ever lived . . . attractive, beautiful, demure yet vivacious and highly entertaining." She spoke her mind, but not too aggressively, and she flew with the same nerve as her brother John.

The crowd was not disappointed. "Matilde Moisant flew her great Blériot over the same ground as her brother had. . . . Several thousand people at the city park race were thrilled by her skill and daring maneuvers." (Matilde's machine was a monoplane, but it was a Moisant model, not a Blériot.) The finale was a flying duet with Houpert that thrilled the spectators below—everyone except her sister Louise, who traveled with Matilde regularly but disapproved of her sister's flying and refused to watch her perform.

Shreveport was next on the tour arranged by Alfred, who had disapproved of Matilde's flying commercially but was not above using her to

The popular Matilde Moisant poses with one of her family's Moisant aeroplanes. Besides building planes, her family founded a flying school on Long Island and had a touring company named the Moisant International Aviators. NATIONAL AIR AND SPACE MUSEUM, SMITHSONIAN INSTITUTION promote the Moisant aeroplanes. Again, the weather was not cooperative. Heavy rain inundated the ground, leading Matilde to comment: "They call us birds but we're not ducks." She promised the press she would fly as soon as possible. Two days later the heavens cleared and Matilde gave the public quite a show.

This time a golf course became an improvised flying field. As Matilde described the scene years later, from above, the rises didn't appear threatening, but as she prepared to come down, she realized there could be a problem with the slope. "I knew I couldn't do it in front of it, but I thought I might do it over. . . . I just came like that, right in it, and it threw my machine right over, and I came right down." One wheel struck the slope, flipping the machine into the air before it landed upside down. Again, Matilde survived. She crawled out from under the machine to the cheers from the crowd, saved by the iron support for the guy wires, which kept the engine and crankshaft from crushing her. It was her second serious fall in three months, but Matilde appeared confident in public. Privately, she was having second thoughts about flying, prompted, certainly, by Louise's mounting concern.

The next scheduled appearance was at the Dallas International Aviation Meet, with Houpert, Ramón Alvarez, and Harold Kantner. Wearing a purple outfit, which delighted the photographers, she flew when the March winds permitted. While flying a brief duet with Kantner one day, she abruptly cut out over the city and realized she was not concentrating on flying; fright was beginning to take over. On the third day of the meet, high winds prevented flying. Speaking with reporters of the *Dallas Morning News,* Matilde remarked that pilot John Frisbie had been killed on a day like the present, and she was sure that the nice people of Dallas, much as they would like to see her fly, "wouldn't care to see me killed." Although she had the distinction of being the first woman to fly in Texas, a shade of caution was replacing her usual daring.

Chatting with reporters, Matilde and Houpert acknowledged the unpredictability of Texas weather. Matilde had been told that day "that the temperature once fell 60 degrees in two hours." Houpert could top that: "I once fell 100 feet in two seconds." Good trouper that she was, Matilde said she would try to break her altitude and endurance records, hoping to attract the public. Surprisingly, she declared she planned to give up contract flying "very soon," explaining that her sister refused to travel with her anymore, and "I certainly will not go alone." In the future, she would fly only for sport.

Yet on another day of the tour, she insisted she was never fearful in the air because Houpert wouldn't let her go up if the wind was too strong, or the machine was not perfectly adjusted. "He taught me all I know about flying, and I rely on his judgment." She then gave a plug for the monoplane, her contribution to the ongoing debate on machine safety: The monoplane "is safer than the biplane because there is no chance for the engine to fall on you when the machine drops. Practically all of the fatalities are the result of the engine crushing the aviator when it falls to earth." Spoken like the sister of a prominent monoplane builder.

The air meet competed not only within the weather but also with the other show in town, the Military Carnival sponsored by Battery A, First Texas Artillery. It was a weeklong run of activities—minstrel shows, the Miller Brothers Miniature Circus, a country store, the jungleland tent, which had specimens of natural history, including "two splendid specimens of Alaskan wolves" and "the longest snake in captivity"— and all clamored for public attention. It was Mexico all over again; aviators were not the only attraction in town.

Edgar L. Pike, chairman of the committee on arrangements for the meet, reminded the public that part of the proceeds from the event would be used for free band concerts in the park during the summer. "You-all come" was his plea. "The flights are as pretty as any I have ever seen, and the program is attractive." The aviators did their part to give the public their money's worth, but the Military Carnival was tough competition.

When it was over, Matilde announced she would make one last appearance, before giving up flying, at Wichita Falls, Texas, to fulfill a contract made by Alfred. With Houpert, she traveled to the Texas town accompanied by Louise, as usual. Ballyhooed in the press as her last flight, there was an expectant crowd on hand when Matilde appeared at six o'clock, after a long wait. Excited viewers pressed against the wire enclosure to get a good look as she climbed into her machine. A clean takeoff took her up swiftly, and she circled for ten minutes when the motor began to sputter, forcing her down outside the park. Minor repairs would fix it up, but Houpert warned that the wind was rising. Matilde overruled him; her last flight should be "one of my most successful ones." She would go up again.

The flight went well—she thrilled the crowd with her handling of the aeroplane as the machine sped higher and higher, until it was a mere speck. Some ten minutes later, it was time to land. Unfortunately, the excited spectators had never seen an aeroplane before and had no idea of what happened in a landing. As Matilde dropped closer to the ground, she saw people standing where the machine was headed; she would mow them down unless she did something. Nosing the aeroplane down so the tail wouldn't flip over, she let the wheels touch, then tried to bounce the machine back up, only it wouldn't go.

The *Dallas Morning News* headlined what happened next: "Woman's Monoplane Wrecked and Burned." The machine cleared the crowd before hitting propeller-first into the ground with such force that fragments sliced into the gas tank, and, instantly, the whole machine burst into flames. Fortunately, Houpert and the mechanics had realized her intention and started for the machine. Reaching the burning wreckage, they pulled Matilde out, singed and blackened from the flames, but largely unharmed. She had missed death by a hair in her monoplane. Her phenomenal luck held—it was time to quit.

Her first concern was for Louise, waiting at the hotel; send word that she was uninjured. Working her way through the crowd, Matilde admitted, "That was a close call." After five months of touring and three serious accidents, Matilde quickly reached a decision: She had flown her last flight.

Matilde, like Harriet Quimby, had a career of less than a year. Harriet's, with much promise, ended tragically, but Matilde was fortunate. She had pushed her luck far enough; she quit while she was still healthy. The years following were divided between time in California and stays in El Salvador. In time the family fortune dwindled, but Matilde and Louise enjoyed a comfortable old age with their sister Ann in La Crescenta, California.

In 1953, Matilde was named fair pilot and official hostess of the Sixth Annual Air Fair at Los Angeles International Airport. Designed to give the public a close-up view of the aviation industry, the fair also commemorated the 50th Anniversary of Powered Flight. The petite, five-foot pioneer, always interested in aviation, never flew again except as a passenger, but she enjoyed sharing experiences from her pioneer days with the public and curious reporters. Asked if she drove a car, Matilde, who had risked her life in fragile air machines, replied: "No, I don't. It's too dangerous." Sister Louise, who couldn't bear to watch her siblings fly, was always behind the wheel when the two ladies went driving.

Matilde died in 1964 at eighty-five years of age, the last of the family. She was buried, with Louise, next to the grave of brother John at the Portal of the Folded Wings in North Hollywood, a memorial to pioneer aviators.

10
Star Quality

IN THE FIVE YEARS between the first licensed woman pilot and the end of 1916, Katherine Stinson and one other American woman, Ruth Law, stand out as exceptional aviation performers. Both won their pilot's license in 1912, both established distance records for flight, both performed fearlessly in aeroplanes almost comical by today's standards. They were friendly competitors and women of great determination, and they flew an aeroplane with greater skill and intelligence than most of the men then flying. They were aerial superstars.

Katherine Stinson, the oldest of four children, all of whom were active in early aviation, was born in 1893 in Fort Payne, Alabama, to Edward and Emma Beaver Stinson. Emma was one of six children; Edward, one of nine; both came from families who had moved west from the eastern seaboard in the middle of the nineteenth century. Edward Stinson, born in Canton, Mississippi, moved around in his career; his last stopping place was the city of Aberdeen, where, as city engineer, he served with the Aberdeen Water Light and Power Company from 1906 until 1934. Emma, of an independent mind from all accounts, separated from Edward following the birth of Jack, the youngest child, in Canton, taking the four children—Katherine, Eddie, Marjorie, and Jack—with her. Apparently, the couple's parting was amicable. Marjorie once told a friend that being "smart, sensible people," her parents agreed to live separately.

Emma and her brood settled first in Jackson, Mississippi, and eventually moved to Hot Springs, Arkansas.

Emma, apparently, was a good manager and businesswoman. She started a business printing city directories while in Jackson and, when the family moved to Hot Springs, she continued this business and took in boarders to help pay family expenses. The children never seemed to want for money, the family owned an automobile in Jackson—a sure stamp of success—the two older children attended private schools at different times, and when Katherine became interested in aviation, Emma was supportive and gave her money for lessons and the purchase of an aeroplane.

Originally, "Katie," as the family called her, wanted to be a pianist. She had talent and studied for several years, including a year at a music conservatory in Indiana. At this point she had two experiences that changed her goal in life. Visiting friends in Kansas City, she made a balloon ascension with Lieutenant H. E. Honeywell of the U.S. Signal Corps. It was a pleasant experience, looking down from on high. In 1912 the idea of flying took firm shape after a flight with Jimmie Ward in Hot Springs. (In later years her sister, Marjorie, disputed the idea of some writers that Katie took up flying to pay for music lessons. Not so, said Marjorie. Mrs. Stinson gave Katie fifteen thousand dollars at different times for aviation pursuits; money was not a problem.)

Katherine, interviewed for an article in *American Magazine,* stated that her mother "never warned me not to do this or that for fear of being hurt. She never reproved my sister and me for playing with boys. I suppose she thought it would do our little bodies just as much good to be exercised and trained out of doors." Katherine's luxurious curls and soft southern voice belied a steely resolve.

She had little trouble convincing her mother to let her go to Kinlock Field at St. Louis early in 1912, where she had a flight with Tony Jannus in a Benoist biplane. She loved it and begged for instruction, but Jannus's boss, Tom Benoist, felt females were unsuited for flying—if she didn't crash, she would surely catch pneumonia. Lessons were few and far between; there was scant encouragement from the young men hanging around the field. By May, Katherine had had enough and went to Chicago determined to enroll in Max Lillie's flying school at Cicero Field.

Maximilian T. Liljestrand, a Swede, was an enthusiastic aviation promoter. He had opened a flying school at Cicero Field near Chicago, where he earned a reputation as a careful, sane flier—"not at all showy," Katherine recalled—using a revamped Wright aeroplane. When Katherine first approached him, he refused her because he couldn't visualize a woman in a flying machine except as a passenger. He was not an easy sell, but Katherine could be very persuasive, and she didn't take no for an answer. In desperation she plunked down her last $250 in front of Lillie, saying she wanted to learn to fly. That decided him—$250 would get her 250 minutes; they were off. Very quickly he realized she had a talent for handling the levers on the dual-control machine.

During her training period, her first flight alone was a memorable near disaster, as she recalled it years later. She had barely gotten up when the motor stopped. She remembered thinking: "Here is Mr. Lillie down below, and he has the $250 and I have the plane in the air and not knowing how to get it down." Lillie shouted for her to "come down, come down!"—beckoning to her, talking her down by conversation. Showing unusual deftness, she landed just inside the circle on the field, for a precise landing, a neat performance for a beginner and, more important, both pilot and machine were uninjured. Remembering the incident, Katherine felt she couldn't fail, because people were very helpful; they were "all boosting for you."

After three weeks of instruction, Katherine applied to take the test for FAI (Fédération Aéronautique Internationale) certification. She passed her tests on July 19, 1912, earning license No. 148, issued on July 24 by the Aero Club of America—the American representative of FAI—to become the fourth U.S. woman pilot. The cover of *Aero and Hydro* featured her as "the only feminine Wright pilot in the world." For the next two months she remained at Cicero Field, making practice flights whenever possible, then moved with the Lillie School to Kinlock Field in the fall, before returning to the family home in Hot Springs for the winter.

The following spring, Katherine and Emma formed a corporation to pursue aviation development. Katherine was president; Abner Cook, vice president; Emma, secretary-treasurer. The capital investment (less than ten thousand dollars, according to one source, although ten thousand was the figure given repeatedly by sister Marjorie) was enough to pay for an aeroplane and start the oldest Stinson child on an aviation career.

The Aero and Hydro *cover showing Alabama-born Katherine Stinson on her Wright Model-B biplane.* LIBRARY OF CONGRESS

The aeroplane, a modified Wright B, was covered with layers of dirt and oil. Katherine took the machine apart and cleaned it up, examining every part. She noted that there were a lot of crossed wires that were beginning to rub, "so first thing you know, you'd have a little cut, a wire just worn out." She removed all the old wires and put in new ones, and "cleaned the whole thing up." The men on the field ribbed her for her careful scrubbing—"You'll be washing it with a toothbrush"—but when she had finished, the machine looked like new, and it was airworthy. All of her flying career, Katie insisted on a well-kept aeroplane. If something went wrong with an automobile, you could stop and tinker with it; in an aeroplane there was no place but down if something went wrong. She had no good-luck rings or pins, no reliance on anything but a well-maintained machine. Confident of that, she was ready to begin her flying career.

And what a career it would be! Beginning in Cheyenne, Wyoming, America's newest aviatrix would thrill and amaze the public, her appearance a sure drawing card. The first thing her agent did was drop three years from her age and bill her as "The Flying Schoolgirl." Her demure

manner and long brown curls added to that impression. For two week-
ends in July 1913, she performed with A. C. Beech, a new Wright flier, at
Cincinnati's Coney Island Park, where the president of the Queen City
Aero Club presented her with a box of chocolates and Beech with a box
of cigars as tokens of their honorary membership in the Aero Club.

The weather was not ideal for flying, but Katie amazed the immense
crowds with her long flight along the river and her low dive, fighting
strong winds, to greet the *Island Queen* coming up the river. The anxious
crew on the ground wished her down, but she was enjoying herself. The
press reported she did aerial stunts, then glided down to "a very pretty
landing."

Actually, in 1913 Katherine did no sensational stunts—she knew the
slow Wright machine wasn't built for that—and she was a careful flier.
Curious spectators at county fairs were allowed to sit in the aeroplane,
and she answered endless questions about it. Then two or three times a
day she would make flights and land on a specific mark after a long glide,
always a crowd pleaser. An unsophisticated public viewed aviators as
people with otherworldly qualities; just to see Miss Stinson or stand close
to her was a thrill. The stunts came later.

J. C. "Bud" Mars, the well-known Curtiss aviator, called flying in this
period "a trick." "The crowd came out to see a stunt and they never could
realize what a genuine stunt they were witnessing if the ships flew at all.
In the air, the pilot was constantly busy keeping his ship on an even keel.
Those crates lacked the inherent stability possessed by modern planes, and
responded unpleasantly to every little gust of wind. . . . Flying, in those
days, required the ability of a balancing genius, the agility of an acrobat,
and the brain of a lightning calculator." When the press described fliers
as "dare-devil" and "death-defying," the writers "came nearer the truth
than they suspected," said Mars. Lincoln Beachey and Eugene Ely, who
gave meaning to the press's adjectives, were taught by Mars. Both died
early.

In France, as Katie was beginning her exhibition career, Adolphe
Pégoud, a test pilot for the Blériot company, amazed the aviation world
by performing a corkscrew twist and a looping loop upside down while
testing a new machine. Secured with a seat belt, he dove steeply about
three hundred meters and was carried upward in a circle of about one
hundred meters by the impetus, until he was in normal flying position

again. *Flight* hailed the accomplishment: This feat shows "the aeroplane is a safe, dependable machine in the hands of an experienced flyer."

In America, Pégoud's achievement was hailed as the elixir to cure the doldrums in fairs around the country. Scientific men declared his flight a trick, an impossible feat, but fair managers offered large sums to the plucky Frenchman to loop in America. Pégoud declined. However, Lincoln Beachey, seeing the financial possibilities, ordered a new aeroplane sturdy enough to loop from the Curtiss works in Hammondsport. In the following year he earned an impressive eighty-four thousand dollars from exhibitions at fairs. William Pickens, the aviation agent and manager who handled Katherine, used an apt oil-well term to describe the Frenchman's effect on exhibitions: "Pégoud's feat sprung a 'gusher.'" In time, Katie would take to looping, not to be outdone by a man.

In the meantime, she hit the exhibition circuit at full speed after her success in Cincinnati. She appeared in Pine Bluff, Arkansas, and Helena, Montana, in August and September. During October and November she performed in El Paso, Texas; Helena, Arkanas; Phoenix, Arizona; Beaumont, Texas; and New Orleans, before going to San Antonio, where the family was now settled for the winter. Helena, Montana, was memorable: Katie became the first aviatrix to fly U.S. mail. With approval from Washington, a post office was installed at the state fairgrounds, and Katherine made daily flights during the week of the fair from the temporary substation to the Federal Building in downtown Helena. The altitude in Helena was a new experience for Katie. Ever cautious, she would not carry any passengers, because she was concerned about her motor's ability in the rarer air.

The young aviatrix quickly discovered that exhibition life was anything but relaxed. Each time she moved to another town, the aeroplane had to be cut down into three sections, wrapped in tissue paper, and put into three big crates. On reaching her destination, the crates were unpacked, the parts were assembled and checked to be sure all the bolts were in, then the machine was tested to see if it worked. It became routine—tedious but necessary. The thousand-dollar fee Katherine commanded for an appearance was not all profit. Part of that sum paid her mechanic's salary, maintenance, fuel, and living expenses in a series of hotels, yet over the years she earned a substantial amount.

The year 1914 proved even busier for the "schoolgirl" pilot, who emphasized her girlish appearance with simple clothes and long brown

curls tied with a ribbon. The Corn Show at Dallas featured her for fourteen days, she had two engagements in eastern Texas before returning to
San Antonio for the Fiesta Week in May, then it was up north to Hal-
letsville, Kentucky, and Cicero, Illinois. She flew for the Federation of
Women's Clubs at Grant Park, Chicago, and exhibited her machine at the
Coliseum. If she had a few days off, she carried passengers at Cicero for
twenty-five dollars a flight. In July she flew at Alexandria, Minnesota,
followed by an appearance at Valley City, North Dakota. Kansas City
followed (her sister, Marjorie, who was just licensed, joined her there),
then Lamar, Colorado. From August to October she had engagements
in Chicago, three towns in Michigan, and Fresno, California. In November she appeared with Marjorie at a suffragette fund-raiser in Nashville,
where the Nashville Equal Suffrage League was meeting. Undoubtedly,
Katherine supported the suffragette movement—she was her mother's
daughter, with a mind of her own. She used an aeroplane to prove women
equal with men.

A reporter gave his impressions of a flight with Katherine at Over
land Park, Kansas City. He could hardly believe his eyes; the famous

Katherine Stinson gassing up her Curtiss at Tanforan, California. SAN DIEGO
AEROSPACE MUSEUM

aviatrix was a "girl who looked like a sophomore in high school . . . someone who might be wondering whether she might have to take Caesar again in the fall." After introductions, he noticed "a peculiar and interesting cloud formation just above." He kept his thoughts to himself. The pilot went up alone first to test the machine and an air pocket over the valley, leaving the uncertain reporter below. On landing, a strut was broken by one of the mechanics who caught the plane, and it was sundown before the strut was replaced. The reporter had plenty of time to imagine "more accidents than could happen this century" while he cooled his heels.

Finally, all was ready; he was strapped in and warned, "Don't touch the controls or that wire beside you." The precaution was useless, for he wouldn't touch his ear "if all the chiggers in Swope Park had been encamped thereon." The motor was cranked, they shot ahead for a hundred feet, and the ground dropped away as people, animals, buildings shrank to diminutive size. The feeling of security was amazing: "Even when we hit the air pocket, it didn't matter. . . . We talked in a sort of futuristic language that included only nouns and sounded like a whisper beside the noise of the motor. . . . Of course we laughed and hollered in unison, 'This is the life.' I know I wasn't scared because I meant every word of it. It was glorious."

Coming down provided the only real thrill in the air, when the machine dropped several hundred feet at a time, a bit like a roller-coaster. The lights on the field beamed up toward the aeroplane, and soon "the field itself was sliding under our wheels. The earth seemed indeed a mundane thing and life upon it prosaic and commonplace. I'd have gone up for the rest of the evening if the gasoline had held out." Katherine had made another convert.

That winter she was in San Antonio, where her family was living. Sister Marjorie, just eighteen, had won her license at the Wright School in Dayton in August; the sisters housed their aeroplanes at Fort Sam Houston in a hangar leased from the U.S. Army, with the understanding they would vacate if the space was needed. The sisters continued practice flights, often carrying passengers for a fee, while their brother, Eddie, acted as mechanic and Jack was an occasional helper. About this time, Marjorie began to give Eddie flying lessons.

San Antonio was familiar territory; Katherine had made a night flight there the previous winter, when she was still gaining experience as a pilot. She had fastened two auto headlights on her biplane, then had four friends park their cars at four corners and shine their lights on a middle spot, which she aimed for when landing. That flight caused quite a stir. Newspapers were flooded with calls about "strange lights in the sky and a buzzing sound"; some people, shaken by the strange occurrence, were certain "Judgment Day was here."

With the new year, the exhibition season was shaping up to be a particularly busy one. *The Billboard,* the publication that featured news in the entertainment world, printed the list of upcoming fairs for 1915. One page, which listed only states through Indiana, had thirty-five checkmarks indicating possible appearances by either Katherine or Marjorie. It would be a big year for Katherine, who had decided that if Beachey could loop, so could she.

She would need a proper machine; the slow, fragile Wright wouldn't do. To that end, she began to draw sketches of the kind of aeroplane she wanted, one that would be sturdy enough to withstand strain from speed and air pressure. It would be enclosed—no more sitting exposed on the bottom wing. She went to the Partridge-Keller Aeroplane Company in Chicago, which built an enclosed, single-seat tractor biplane with an eighty-horsepower Gnome motor salvaged from Beachey's machine after his fatal crash in March. (Katie had bought the damaged monoplane from Beachey's estate, but when it was repaired, she decided it wasn't right for her—too fast. She then went to Partridge-Keller to have a new machine built around the motor.) Walter Brock supervised the construction, incorporating some of Katie's ideas. It was hoped the more powerful Gnome motor would correct the danger of stalling at the high point of the loop ascent.

While Katherine waited for her new machine, she worked with youngsters in Texas, forming model-aeroplane clubs to encourage an interest in aviation. In July she was ready to test the new machine and coaxed Art Mix, Beachey's former mechanic, to join her on exhibitions, to care for the motor. (Katherine used several mechanics at different times: her brother Eddie; O. H. "Bud" Snyder, who served the Stinson family machines at Ashburn, near Chicago; Frank Champion, who accompanied her to the Orient; and Rudolph "Shorty" Schroeder, also at Ashburn.)

She practiced daily at Cicero, trying different acrobatic stunts as she became familiar with the aeroplane. She looped the loop there for the first time, perfecting and fine-tuning, until she felt confident to perform publicly. The unexpected provided an extra thrill for several thousand spectators, attending a Sunday program at Cicero.

The *Chicago Tribune* described the three loops the aviatrix performed before the motor suddenly quit on the fourth attempt, the valve snapped, and the purr of the engine stopped. Many people turned away to avoid the inevitable tragedy as the machine fell downward, three thousand feet. At the last moment, Katherine was able to bring the machine upright for a safe landing. The ground crew rushed to assist her and, weak from fright, she was helped to the shed. Interviewed later, she was still shaken. "The horror of the silence after that motor stopped will stay with me all my life. I didn't know what to do for just a moment. Then I began to fall. I knew it would be fatal if the machine ever lost its balance. So I just turned its nose straight down and asked God to help me." When she felt the wheels touch the ground, she lay back in her seat, too weak to move. "I would have fallen if I had attempted to stand. I would have cried if I had opened my mouth." As frightening as that experience was, it did not shake her resolve. "I'm going to loop the loop again, and then I am going to execute the 'death drop.' And this time I am going to do it on purpose."

From then on, the name "Katherine Stinson" on a program was sure to draw a crowd. A Pickens advertisement in *The Billboard* combined straightforward and upside-down wording to illustrate "little Katie Stinson's" acrobatic ability. In spite of the publicity generated by her daring feats, she was known in the flying community, especially among the mechanics, as a safe and sane flier who was meticulous about maintenance. Unfortunately, the same could not be said about her teacher, Max Lillie. The year after he had instructed his famous female student, he was killed in a crash, due to the negligent state of his machine. The Wright Company went out of its way to disassociate itself from his machine—it wasn't really a Wright biplane, Lillie had made too many adjustments on it, and it was in dreadful condition. Lillie's death underscored Katie's concern for maintenance.

Appearances throughout the fall won Katherine a national following. She once told an interviewer that she found the usual flights monotonous, that she started doing acrobatics because they were more challenging. They also attracted bigger crowds. By the time she finished her appearances during Market Week, August 2–7, at Grant Park, Chicago, newspapers around the country were hailing her achievement—looping. On Labor Day she looped at Caro, Michigan, and later at the Michigan State Fair at Detroit, working her way by stages through the Midwest to Arizona and California. She was warmly received in Tucson, where she carried mail again, met with youth groups and aviation enthusiasts, and was filmed in flight by the Cuauhtemoc Film Company of Tucson, before leaving for California. In San Francisco she was hailed as "the first pilot to fly at night." Although not actually true, the claim was good advertising. The preparations in the Bay City pleased her: "There was a beautiful lawn, illuminated by hundreds of lights for starting and landing." Newspaper accounts of her flights were glowing. Traveling south to Los Angeles, she decided to try skywriting using magnesium flares that released a stream of light and smoke at the touch of a button. Before a large crowd of newspapermen gathered outside of Los Angeles (the city authorities did not want her flying over inhabited areas), she traced the abbreviation for California—"Cal"—in the darkened sky, pictures of which were flashed to newspapers nationwide. Landing was tricky. Katherine complained later that the field was lit by only a few pine knots, unlike the conditions in San Francisco; even more disconcerting, her motor stopped just as she was coming down to land. Although the flight made history, she could see the need for improvement, particularly to prevent the flares' smoke from blinding her. *Aerial Age Weekly* reported the event and observed that she had done it "to eclipse the feats of her male competitors."

Katherine was not shy about voicing her intention in a Los Angeles interview: "When I looped in Chicago last July, it was a bitter pill for the male loopers to swallow, but I accomplished all their stunts and in my case went them one better." (She added a snap roll on top of a loop.) When she heard that Art Smith was skywriting at night with flares attached to his plane, she decided she would do it, too. Both the press and Katherine played up her competition with the men; it made good copy. A Los Angeles reporter watching her night flight wrote that she used her aeroplane "like a great invisible pen, writing in molten fire on the curtain of the night." Reporters were impressed by her "perfect control": The graceful handling of the aeroplane; the rapid, confident ascents and soft landings; and her soft, southern accent charmed them.

The Los Angeles success was soon routine. Katie lit up the Chicago night sky with a drawn-out "S" over Grant Park to celebrate the New Year, before returning to San Antonio for the winter. The family was busy at the end of 1915 with plans for an aviation school, with Marjorie and Eddie as teachers. Katherine was an interested observer but took no part in teaching or managing the school. Some of her earnings may have financed the school; family records are not clear on that point.

The past year had been successful for Katie; the Partridge-Keller machine was marvelous for stunt flying. In 1916 the Stinson name played coast to coast. In May, at Sheepshead Bay in Brooklyn, the "most daring woman aviator in the world" raced Dario Resta, a renowned auto driver, around the speedway and crossed the finish line seventy-five feet ahead of him. Spectators watched with disbelief as Stinson dropped to within six feet of the track, flying sixty miles an hour, to cross the finish line ahead of her competitor, an act that was popular from coast to coast. The meet, a benefit for the National Aeroplane Fund of the Aero Club of America, was an eye-opener for easterners, who watched enthralled as the young pilot dropped bombs and looped over the field.

She played a repeat performance at the Sheepshead Speedway during the Military Naval and Aviation Tournament, held soon after. She arrived at the speedway at night after a flight from Brighton Beach—the first indication of her approach was the buzzing of a distant motor. The grandstand crowds searched the sky as the sound grew louder; next, they saw the magnesium flares light up as the aeroplane flew over the west end of Coney Island. There was a roar of approval as the lights traced somersaults in the sky before burning out. Within minutes, the machine drew closer and another tube of light appeared, tracing twists and a final loop at a thousand feet over the field.

There was more. At nine hundred feet, Katherine turned off the motor, dropped vertically to one hundred feet, and volplaned the remaining distance, to land. Applause and honking horns filled the night air, as the delighted pilot climbed out of her seat. She knew she had scored a hit. Recounting the trip for the press, she said, "After I left Coney Island I didn't know just where I was, for my fireworks had blinded me, and I was afraid I wouldn't be able to find a good place to land." She knew the speedway was large enough, but "wasn't sure just where it was."

The applause was tonic; she would go up again. The mechanics were hustled to get more flares, they checked the machine, and at 10:30 the tireless pilot was up again, turning two more flip-flops "while the planes streamed white flares." The New York press wrote glowingly about her performance before fifty thousand, her youth, and her brown curls. They liked her ingenuous manner: "Looping the loop is the easiest thing in the world. Except that you get lost sometimes, and have to hunt around to get your bearings again."

Katherine could be as busy as she wanted at this stage of her career. She was probably the best-known woman flier in America, but she was not the only one. Blanche Stuart Scott was still flying, although she would soon retire, and Ruth Law was making headlines for her daring flying. Ruth would become Katherine's closest competitor—they were friendly rivals. Katherine's long-distance flights were instigated by Ruth's record flight in November 1916. Katherine couldn't let anyone, male or female, get ahead of her.

Back in Chicago, Katie had "Shorty" Schroeder spend two weeks doing a major overhaul of the Partridge-Keller machine. In a test hop, she reported the motor was running much better, its performance improved. She would be ready for the next tour.

Meanwhile, her reputation had crossed borders. In late June, Katherine began a tour of western Canada, with a four-day appearance in Calgary, Alberta. There had been little aviation in the prairie provinces, so news of her appearance created much excitement. She performed her usual repertoire: bomb throwing, acrobatic tricks, and night flights. She filled dates at Edmonton, Brandon, Regina, and Winnipeg, attracting large crowds and acclaim. At Camp Hughes, near Brandon, the aviatrix was threatened with arrest when she landed unannounced. Explaining that she had come to entertain, she was told "Carry on!" and sixty thousand troops turned out to see her.

The tour was not without incidents. Returning to Brandon, where she had been made a princess of the Sioux by Chief Waukessa (reportedly, the Stinsons were one quarter Cherokee), the Gnome broke a piston, and an emergency landing in a wheat field left the looper on its nose. A farmer came along, studied the machine, and asked: "Is that one of them newfangled threshin' machines?" Katie had to laugh in spite of the fix she was in. Together they got the tail down, and the farmer guarded the aeroplane while she went for help. At Regina her last flight was memorable for the locals. When the aeroplane headed vertically down from a great height, people watching at a distance were convinced the pilot had crashed. The municipal switchboard "buzzed with eye-witness reports from all over town."

Back in the United States, the fall fair season started up; Katherine was sought after in many places, among them Massachusetts, Tennessee, Virginia, and Iowa. *The Billboard* for October 14, 1916, commented that the contract at Richmond was for "the largest amount paid any aviator for a fair engagement this season." In November the Pickens office announced that Miss Stinson would make a six-month Orient tour, starting in December.

There was much to be done to get ready. She would need two aeroplanes; the second was insurance in case of an accident. She arranged with Emil Matty Laird to borrow his small machine, with a sixty-horsepower Anzani motor—its size would prove useful in small areas. She had to pack clothes that would be warm, not showy. It was announced that mechanic Frank Champion would care for the machines, and Katherine's mother, Emma would accompany her. William Pickens made all arrangements for the tour. On November 25 the party sailed from San Francisco.

Her debut in Japan was arranged when Katie received a cable on board ship from a Japanese woman who wanted the women of her country to see a woman do an extraordinary feat never done before in Japan. The feminist supporter offered twenty-five hundred dollars; Katherine accepted. It would be a night flight with lights—the works. Accordingly, she made her first flight in Japan on the night of December 15 on Aoyama Parade Grounds outside of Tokyo. Huge bonfires lit the field, and hundreds of police were present for crowd control. The awaited performance lasted fifteen minutes: loops, twists, and tracing the letter "S" in the night sky, for a delirious crowd that threatened to mob her on landing. Flowers were everywhere—wreaths, horseshoes, bouquets. Katherine remarked years later in an interview: "I didn't know whether I was expected to get killed, when I saw these arrangements, all those flowers." Her appearance excited the country; she was hailed as "Air Queen."

After the Tokyo flights, Yokohama, Nagasaki, Osaka, and Nagoya were next on the tour. Everywhere there was great enthusiasm—government officials and the public alike were caught up in an outpouring of feeling. There were few hitches during Katherine's flights, a rarity considering the winter weather and the crowded topography, but while she was flying at Nagoya on January 15, the Anzani motor suddenly stopped. Intense vibration, a trait of the Anzani, had caused a crack in the crankcase. A newsman on the scene wrote that the machine plunged "like a falling arrow until the rudder re-commenced to operate" at little more than one hundred feet above the ground. The Laird machine was damaged slightly on landing. The motor was sent to a local foundry to be rebuilt, while a spare fifty-horsepower Gnome was fitted into the Laird. When she was not flying, Katherine visited local model-aeroplane clubs and fan clubs that sprang up overnight; she was frequently photographed in a kimono—it was comfortable, and beautiful. She watched a performance of a Japanese play in which the characters were dressed like aviators, but she didn't have a clue about the plot. Everywhere she went, women greeted her as an emancipator for demonstrating women's potential; wearing a kimono made Japanese women feel she was one of them. She was showered with gifts and money, and collected "a bag full of medals." For her part, the aviatrix found the Japanese very accommodating, quick at sizing up a situation, and with a "no problem" attitude, which endeared them to her.

China was a different matter. The crowds were large, extremely curious about the aeroplane, and uncontrolled. Whoever made arrangements for the flights lacked any idea of what was involved. More than once, Katie found it impossible to take off because the crowds surged around the aeroplane on all sides. The first time this happened, she realized the webbing intended to keep people at a safe distance was useless. She asked the consul, who spoke little Chinese, to explain to the local dignitary that the rolled-up webbing should be held by people along the path of the aeroplane to improvise a barrier. The looper had no brakes, which meant that people had to keep clear of the takeoff area, some fifty yards at least, or the machine couldn't go up.

It was a fiasco! In desperation, Katie got out of the machine, took the hand of a Chinese man on one side, and the hand of another man on the other side, trying to form a ring to move people back. The consul knew what she was trying to do but couldn't explain it in Chinese. The crowd was vastly amused and kept asking in Chinese, "Why don't you fly?" They thought the aeroplane went straight up. The consul insisted she *must* fly; people had been waiting all day. There was an ominous tone to his command.

Slowly, as Katie formed a line on each side, pushing people back, she was able to inch the aeroplane forward, making a big noise with the gas to scatter those close up, until people finally understood what she was trying to do. When enough room for a quick ascent was cleared, she took off quickly. She was up, but landing soon became a problem. Below her, an uncontrolled mob drifted about the field. Instead of looping and dropping from on high, Katie contented herself with flying in circles while she tried to figure out a landing site.

Spotting a big yard ahead enclosed by a fence, she could see people in uniform walking about. She had no idea what it was, but she knew the growing crowds outside made landing dangerous. She landed quickly near the fence and motioned to the men to help roll the machine inside the enclosure; that done, they began to climb all over the aeroplane, examining everything. Eventually she positioned it to keep it from harm. Years later this experience, one of thirty-two flights made in China, was the only one of her flights Katherine mentioned in an interview. It made a lasting impression.

Her flight in Peking, a private premiere for the president, who presented her with three thousand dollars, was followed by appearances in Canton, Hong Kong, Tientsin, Nanking, and Shanghai—to thrilled multitudes, who watched her aerial stunts with awe. It was a great relief, however, to return to Japan in April 1917, where she was received royally and with greater public decorum. There, events in Europe and America's entrance into the war caught up with her. The tour was shortened, and Katie sailed home on April 27, 1917, arriving in San Francisco three weeks later.

On her return, *The Billboard,* in a long article, mentioned some of the adventurous pilot's impressions from her trip: The two cultures intrigued her; each had something to offer the rest of the world. Chinese writers had "mastered the art of delivering sterling thoughts in sugar-coated fairy tales"; the Japanese were "the most polite people I ever met." Her feminism rebelled at the idea of walking ten paces behind a man, as Chinese wives had to do; no American woman would do that! She was glad to be home, glad she was an American.

The coming of war changed aviation in America. Aeroplanes, recognized as an important weapon in Europe, already three years into the war, became the focus for an industrial revolution in America. The old, leisurely, one-model-at-a-time production was finished. Manufacturers geared up to meet the challenge, among them Glenn Curtiss, who was producing the new government JN-4. At the same time, civilian aviation activity ceased and schools around the country were taken over by the military or closed.

Against this background, Katherine planned a distance flight to break Ruth Law's record of the previous year, but to do this, she would need a different aeroplane. She had contacted Curtiss before she left for the Orient about the kind of machine she would need, and gradually the "Junkshop Hybrid," the nickname the mechanics had given it, was assembled from parts belonging to other experimental models. To continue flying during wartime restrictions, she volunteered to assist the Red Cross in its fund drive by flying from Buffalo to Washington with stops at New York City and Philadelphia. It was a chance to help the war effort and further the distance-flight goal. When the United States had declared war, Katherine offered her services to the military, but she received a polite turndown. No women need apply.

Katherine was not nonplussed. She found ways to keep busy with recruitment promotions, Red Cross drives, and appearances at a few fairs. In the late fall the Curtiss JN, a hybrid with clipped JN-4 wings and an S-3 triplane fuselage, was ready. First tests by company engineer Roland Rohlf showed it was nose-heavy; a nearly fatal crash sent it back to the shop for balancing and repairs. There were more adjustments before Katherine began practice flights to get acquainted with the ninety-horsepower OX-2 motor. In the late fall, pilot and machine were ready; a small mirror positioned in the cockpit allowed her to present a clean face before climbing down, on landing.

On December 5, 1917, twenty thousand soldiers at Camp Kearny, near San Diego, scanned the sky in anticipation. Shortly before noon, Katherine's special aeroplane, *Speed Scout,* was spotted in the distance. Flying in low, it looped once over the parade grounds and landed. Standing on the reviewing platform, she announced she would make a nonstop flight to San Francisco. The applause and cheers were thunderous from the assembled troops, who were treated to a special afternoon performance of aerial stunts.

Six days later the determined aviatrix rose before dawn and took the trolley to the North Island ferry landing. She had a quick breakfast while waiting and forgot to pay, in her haste to get on the ferry. At 7:31, the heavily fueled Curtiss took off from North Island and headed north. Sticking to the coast for the first lap, then over Los Angeles, the pilot plotted a northern course over a piece of Mojave Desert toward the eight-thousand-foot-high Tehachapi Mountains and the pass.

By noon, Katie was having hunger pains; breakfast was hours ago. She admitted years later that she was sorely tempted to land and get something to eat, but she gritted her teeth and the OX-2 engine continued its steady beat. The hours ticked by as the Curtiss passed over the California landscape: Bakersfield shortly after noon; Madera at two o'clock; Mission San Jose at four; and in forty minutes, the historic city on the bay. Making a wide turn over the San Francisco harbor, the Curtiss landed on the Presidio parade grounds, neatly swept in anticipation of its arrival. A tremendous din from the waterfront—horns, sirens, whistles—greeted the aeroplane as it touched down. An Aero Club observer clocked the time: 4:41 P.M. The record distance was 610 miles in nine hours, ten minutes, a national record for distance and duration; the Curtiss had used all but two gallons of its seventy-six-gallon tank. Katherine was fond of saying she was "the first person to travel from San Diego to San Francisco between meals." It had been a grueling experience; in the future, food would go with her. One advantage of such a flight was the opportunity to meet famous people who were equally impressed with her. In Los Angeles, she met and was photographed with America's heartthrob, Douglas Fairbanks Sr.

During her winter rest in San Antonio, Katie planned her next flight. If she wanted to fly, she had to find some kind of official support. Reports from Europe indicated that aerial mail delivery was proving rapid and efficient. In the United States, war regulations dictated military aviators should carry the mail on military aeroplanes, but there was no organized system. That would come later when the Postal Department assumed responsibility.

Katherine applied to the War and Postal departments and, because of her sensational California flight, received permission to fly from Chicago to New York City in her Curtiss. Supplied with a ration of malted-milk tablets and swathed in woolens and leather, she took off unannounced at 7:37 A.M. on May 12 from Grant Park. A new 24-cent stamp, featuring a blue aeroplane on a red border, was issued for air-mail use on the sixty-one letters she carried. The flight ended abruptly when the engine threw a valve, and, coming down on a farm, the aeroplane ran into a tree. The structural parts were quickly repaired, not so the engine.

On May 23, having been sworn in by the postmaster at Chicago, with her machine in good running condition, she started again for New York. It was tough going; strong winds fought her all the way and, after ten hours, she ran out of fuel at Binghamton, 150 miles short of her goal. Coming down on a muddy hillside didn't help. The machine nosed over; a new propeller was needed before the flight could resume. Mechanics worked all night to ready the Curtiss. On takeoff, the hillside location proved unsuitable. The machine flipped over on its nose again; mud had worked into the engine. More repairs were needed. Six days later, on takeoff the machine turned turtle again for the third time within a week. Katie, strapped into her seat, hung upside down a few inches from the ground. Finally, a third try was successful, and sixty-one letters were delivered on June 2, when the Curtiss landed at Mineola, Long Island. The distance recognized by the Aero Club for the Chicago-Binghamton flight was 601.763 miles, bettering Ruth Law's record of the previous year; newspapers headlined the railroad mileage: 783 miles. Newspaper accounts credited her with distance and endurance records (ten hours, ten minutes), even "first to fly the mail" (not correct—others flew with official recognition before Katherine), and played up the success of a nineteen-year-old "slip of a girl." Despite the poor landing at Binghamton and the subsequent takeoff failures, her flight demonstrated the aeroplane's potential for mail service. Today, stamps from that flight are highly valued collectors' items.

Katherine's next venture was a flight for the Red Cross. At 11:50 A.M. on June 24, Katie took off from Buffalo, flying a new military-type, two-seater Curtiss JN, with wings forty-five feet in length—loaned especially for the flight. The second seat was convenient for carrying her luggage and Red Cross literature. She had exactly fifteen minutes of instruction from Curtiss's head instructor on the new machine before winging her way south, with stops at Rochester and Syracuse, arriving at Albany at 6:45 that evening. The next morning, her flight was delayed until ten o'clock to ensure a noon flight over New York City. Guided by railroad maps, Katie had bombarded towns along the route with cards urging folks "down there on earth" to do their bit for the Red Cross one-hundred-million fund.

At 12:15 she landed at Governor's Island in New York Harbor for a welcome by Aero Club and Red Cross officials, and lunch. Her next stop was Philadelphia, with another large welcoming party of Red Cross officials and newspaper reporters; then, finally, she arrived in Washington, where a large white canvas cross marked her landing spot on the polo grounds near the Washington Monument. The field was packed with automobiles and people who had waited hours to greet the young aviatrix at the end of her 670-mile flight. The last 373 miles from Albany made another distance-record flight for an aviator flying to Washington. Before landing, the pilot gave the waiting crowds a fifteen-minute acrobatic performance, ending with an eighteen-hundred-foot nosedive and glide to the ground.

Red Cross officials greeted her and presented her with a check for fifty thousand dollars, as the first donation from the Washington area. This, together with more contributions than expected from Buffalo, was presented to Secretary William McAdoo at the Treasury Department shortly after eight o'clock that evening. The flight, the longest Katherine had flown, had given the new giant machine a fine christening. Reporters on the scene all commented on the pilot's youthful appearance; her age, given variously as nineteen or twenty-one, remained a public mystery.

From Washington, Katherine took a train to Chicago, where she packed up her Curtiss machine and traveled to Canada for appearances. In late June she flew into western Canada, visiting the ranching communities. On July 9, as the Calgary Exhibition was in full swing, she took off at 6 P.M. from the gopher-hole-pocked field north of town to begin a flight to Edmonton, an outpost of civilization at that time, carrying a mail pouch with 259 letters. She had been granted a special dispensation by the postmaster general at Ottawa to make the mail flight. Two hours and five minutes later, she landed at Edmonton, where an enthusiastic crowd greeted her. Elsewhere, this would have been a night flight, but, as reported in *The Curtiss Flyleaf,* in Western Canada, in the summer, it is possible "to read a newspaper in the open as late as 10:30 at night." Expectations ran high, following her flight, that western Canada would see increased aerial-mail development—the potential was there, with good topography and climate, according to Canadian commentators.

Back across the border again, Katherine applied to the U.S. Aerial Mail Service to become a member. Captain Benjamin Lipsner was dumbfounded. He listened, then declared that some time in the future her application might be considered. He didn't know Katherine. She went to Postmaster General Albert S. Burleson and, in short order, the air-mail service was told to add her name to the list of pilots, all men. When she asked that Wright controls be put on the Curtiss aeroplane, Lipsner demurred, pleading cost, and was overruled by Burleson.

On September 26, Katherine made her first flight as an employee, flying the Washington–to–New York route via Philadelphia, the only air-mail route at that time. Her escort was Maurice Newton, who led the way with Katie flying close behind, each carrying 150 pounds of mail. Three hours later the two aeroplanes landed at Belmont Park, at Elmont, Long Island, which had been donated by August Belmont for the government's use, with Newton touching down first. On the return flight the following morning, Katie took off first, Newton second. Some newspapers, treating the flight as a race, hailed Katie as the winner when she landed first in Washington. Newton was furious, as were the other male pilots, and because of this misunderstanding, and the ill feeling it generated, Katherine left the service without fanfare. In December, Lipsner, increasingly unhappy about Postal Department interference with his prerogatives, resigned in protest.

Still anxious to do something useful during the war period, Katherine joined an ambulance service organized under Red Cross auspices and went overseas shortly before the end of the war. There are claims that she flew around London before shipping to France, but this is highly unlikely. Her stint in France as an ambulance driver was brief, thanks to the armistice. The *New York Times* reported on her return, March 20, 1919, that she had been delegated to fly mail between Paris and Koblenz, the command center for American forces in Germany, but she was "forced to give up aviation because of a heavy cold contracted while driving an ambulance." The "heavy cold" was then diagnosed as tuberculosis.

Katherine was never robust—"fragile" and "frail" were frequent descriptions in the press—and her exhausted body had little strength left to fight the disease. Six long years would pass, the first two spent confined to total bed rest, before she won the battle. By that time, flying was no longer possible. She moved to Santa Fe, New Mexico, for its healthy climate and became interested in architecture, especially the Pueblo Indian and Spanish Colonial styles. She won a prize in 1927 for plans for a house costing less than six thousand dollars, and built and restored several structures in Santa Fe, "using remarkable sensitivity in building," according to the *Santa Fean Magazine*. In 1928 she married Miguel A. Otero Jr., a former aviator and the son of a former territorial governor, and settled down to life as a housewife.

In 1953, Katherine and Marjorie appeared together at the National Aeronautic Association dinner commemorating the fiftieth anniversary of the Wright brothers' flight at Kitty Hawk. Also present was President Dwight D. Eisenhower, who spotted Katherine among the guests and went over to shake hands. "I remember you down on the border in 1916, when you were flying there," said the president. "I was a second lieutenant and I saw you fly at Fort Sam Houston. Gosh, how I marveled at the new-fangled planes and your ability to handle them." (Eisenhower, who had a private pilot's license, flew a Stinson Reliant in the Philippines in the late 1930s for interisland transportation.)

In 1962, Katherine suffered a stroke and became a semi-invalid for the last fifteen years of her life, a sad ending to a brilliant career in the air. She died on July 10, 1977, at age eighty-four.

Of the many women who flew in the years before 1916, Katherine Stinson was one of the very few who could have picked up after the war where she left off, if her health had permitted. She had the ability, the intelligence, the spirit. As she had learned years before: "If you are going to let other people decide what you are able to do, I don't think you will ever do much of anything." She knew that flying was not a matter of gender. "There is nothing about flying that makes it unsuited to a woman. It doesn't demand size or strength." And she loved showing the world what a woman could do.

11
Superstar II

RUTH LAW, A NEW Englander with just a hint of reserve, obtained her pilot's license, No. 188, four months after Katherine Stinson, to become the sixth American woman pilot. (Bernetta Adams Miller was the fifth.) Like Stinson, whom she resembled in nerve and daring, she was instantly taken with flying, pursued it confidently, and made a good living during a long career. Of the many recognized women in early aviation, Ruth Law was the only one who had a successful career after World War I.

In August 1912 the *Boston Herald* described her as a "slip of a girl who likes to fly 75 mph at Saugus racetrack . . . a slim young woman who has yellow hair, blue eyes and a low voice. She looks like some high school girl whose principle business might be wrestling with Ovid's translations." In short order, the girlish appearance would give way to competency. She checked the machine before each flight—being a mechanic is part of an aviator's responsibility, or should be: "When your engine suddenly stops when you're 2,000 feet in the air, it's some comfort to know that if anything can be done, you can do it," Ruth said. Not yet a licensed pilot, Ruth practiced her trade through the summer of 1912, totally absorbed in the enjoyment that came from flying. It was what led men and women to take up wings, not fame, not money. Ruth commented succinctly: "There's too little money for the risk."

Born into a proper Daughters of the American Revolution family in Lynn, Massachusetts, in 1887, Ruth Bancroft Law and her brother, Rodman, were the adventuresome children of staid parents. Ruth's mother once remarked that she felt like a hen who had hatched two ducks. Both children had a daredevil streak that all the education and refinement in the world could not dislodge. Rodman, who was a year and a half older than Ruth ("We were almost like twins," she said), led his sister in a parade of games and outdoor sports that made a tomboy of her. Rodman, known as "the human fly" for his feats scaling buildings, performed leaps from high points with a parachute (he made the first public parachute jump from an aeroplane and leaped from the hand of the Statue of Liberty); he was one of the original stuntmen in the movies, with Pathé, before he pursued experiments with rockets and plans to cross the Atlantic. His interest in the aeroplane as a vehicle led Ruth to follow suit; she was a keen observer when the Burgess Aviation School opened at Marblehead. The years at Miss Livermore's School in New Haven, Connecticut, had not subdued her.

Tired of watching the activity on the field, she begged one of the boys to take her up in his machine. From that moment, she was determined to enter the school but met a wall of refusal. Finally, she convinced Phil Page to take her on; July 1, 1912, was scheduled for her first lesson. Waiting on the field, she watched Harriet Quimby and her passenger fall to their deaths at Squantum during the Harvard–Boston meet. Amid the mass hysterics, her practical mind looked for a reason for the crash, and she decided, to her own satisfaction, that the Blériot monoplane was to blame, not the pilot. Convinced that the Wright biplane was a safer machine, she sent her husband to Dayton.

Charles Oliver was an understanding husband. Also a native of Lynn, he had married Ruth in 1910 and realized soon after that domesticity was not Ruth's main interest. He encouraged her interest in aviation, and became her manager and chief supporter when she began her professional career.

Oliver tried to enroll Ruth in the Wright School, but without success. Orville Wright refused "absolutely" to teach her, convinced that women were "entirely unfitted for the nervous strain and that women ... have no mechanical ability"—he would not be responsible. However, Orville willingly sold her an aeroplane for seventy-five hundred dollars—twenty-five hundred dollars down, the balance in installments. Oliver made all the arrangements, and the machine, a Wright Model B, was shipped to Marblehead, where Ruth continued lessons with Page on the old Saugus racetrack. In later years she said she also exchanged the use of her machine for lessons with another young flier at the field.

As important as the air lessons were shop lessons with an elderly German mechanic at the school, who taught Ruth to grind valves, take a motor apart, and put it together again. As a result, Ruth firmly believed that aviators, in a pinch, must be mechanics. With experience, she could "anticipate what would happen to the motor by the sound of it, and be able to get down." Of course, as she was quick to acknowledge, "there was a lot of luck entered into it, too."

Early on the morning of August 1, Ruth soloed; impatient with waiting, she took the aeroplane up without her instructor's knowledge. Getting off the ground was easy, but it was "quite another matter to stay right side up after you get off." At five hundred feet, she realized she didn't know how to get down. Wobbling around in the air, she pulled herself together, aware that "until I had confidence I could not make a landing." The Wright aeroplane did not fail her; it was "very simple to learn to fly, because it was a natural flier." After fifteen minutes spent calming her fears—anxious friends waited below, knowing she had no business in the air alone—she felt fairly composed and "more by good luck than ability made a very fair landing. After I landed, I thought I was quite some aviator." But good sense prevailed; she continued to practice daily, weather permitting. Reportedly, on one practice flight with Arch Freeman, her teacher, she climbed to seventy-eight hundred feet.

On Labor Day, Ruth made her first exhibition appearance, flying at Narragansett Park in Providence with Lincoln Beachey. Before a crowd of ten thousand, she showed aerial mastery, doing figure eights and banking well on the turns. She had accepted the date because she felt the need to earn some money. Flying made money disappear at a fast rate—the cost of oil, gasoline, and rental of a hangar were constant—and there was five thousand dollars owed to the Wright Company. She received five hundred dollars for her first exhibition flight, mainly in one-dollar bills. "It looked like a fortune when I threw it on my bed in the hotel. It was the first money I had ever earned in my life." As a beginner, she was paid half of what Beachey received, but that didn't bother her a bit. As her reputation grew, she was very well paid, because there were so few women doing exhibition flying.

Appearing on a program with Beachey ensured being seen by a good-size crowd. The weather was not ideal—a drizzling rain lasted throughout the afternoon—but the two aviators and Samuel A. Libby, a parachute artist, were not deterred. Beachey performed a series of spirals, dives with his hands outstretched, and the glide for which he was famous. From a height of several thousand feet, he made a vertical dive with the motor cut off, and landed on the racetrack in front of the grandstand—an area of about seventy-five feet in width with a straight-away of possibly five hundred feet. The crowd, seemingly oblivious of the weather, was on its feet throughout much of Beachey's performance.

Ruth went up without incident and was warmly received by the crowd, who admired her graceful maneuvers. Her landing gave the crowd a thrill, as she descended rapidly near the first quarter post on the mile track, with so much speed that her machine bounced over the gully outside the track. One strut snapped, but machine and pilot were uninjured. Replacing the strut was minor; Ruth had learned to whittle as well as take a magneto apart. Yet she still had a lot to learn. Exhibition flying demanded good judgment in sizing up locations, in adapting the machine to new dimensions. At the end of her flight, the crowd surged onto the field, despite warnings from the police, to inspect the young woman pilot—dressed in black satin bloomers, a red sweater, a black head covering, boots, and goggles—and her machine. It took the sound of Beachey's motor starting up to make the excited fans give way for another flight.

Beachey, at that time America's most famous aviator, was friendly and helpful to the novice pilot, offering advice on clearing the trees near the field. "Now, Ruth, you see those trees at the end of the racetrack? You only have to just miss 'em by a little. Don't try to go up too high, you might stall and fall." With all his success, Ruth found Beachey a modest person, contrary to the opinion others had of him. After his exhibition, nobody could find him. According to Ruth, he left the area quickly, and "when the newspapermen wanted him for an interview or pictures, he was gone."

As the only woman flying in the East, Ruth was a prime subject for newspaper articles whenever she appeared. Following her debut at Narragansett Park, she spoke up frequently for women in aviation. Ingrained in her personality from years of copying her brother's actions was the knowledge that anything he could do, she could do, too. In the press she expressed herself this way: "I believe a woman can do anything a man can do and do it just as well, with the exception of anything which requires great strength." Aviation, generally, did not require that kind of strength. She believed, however, that men were more apt to be successful at flying than women, because "it's an adventurous business and most women prefer other things than adventure." She herself, a tomboy, loved adventure. She touted flying as a "fine and dignified sport for women, healthful and stimulating to the mind." She might have added that nothing could compare with flying for sheer, "dizzying" fun. When she became a regular on the exhibition circuit, receiving fifteen hundred dollars for an appearance, she marveled that she was paid so well for "just having a good time."

Along with the fun, there were moments of anxiety. Flying at the same Providence fairgrounds, Ruth narrowly missed serious injury. The weather was miserable; high winds spelled trouble for a fragile aeroplane. Before a large crowd, Ruth agreed to go up simply out of ignorance. Later, she knew better. About two hundred feet in the air, a gust of wind caught the machine and pitched it around like a feather, threatening to turn her upside down. The machine dropped rapidly downward, blown by gusts of wind, hit an automobile that had taken refuge near a shed, sheared off the top of the auto (there were seven people inside), and demolished one wing, then spun around and crumpled the other against the shed. Miraculously, none of the five children and two adults in the auto were injured, nor was Ruth.

In November, she attended a Staten Island meet where she was billed as trying for an altitude record. On the appointed day, she reached fifty-five-hundred feet according to her barograph, a record for American women, but the Aeronautical Society of New York did not announce the record until it had studied the instrument. The *Staten Islander* advertised "Free Aeroplane Ride with Miss Ruth Law" to the man or woman presenting the most coupons from the newspaper at the paper's office "before six o'clock on Thursday, November 14, 1912." The free ride would take place at the Oakwood Aerorace on Sunday, November 17. The aviatrix was flying every day and taking up passengers for a fee; each received a certificate indicating the holder "has had an aerial experience." The accumulation of hours in the air grew, and on November 18, having performed the required tests at Oakwood, Ruth Law received her license from the Aero Club of America. She was a bona-fide aviation pilot, entitled to enter any meet sanctioned by the club.

That winter, Ruth and her husband went to Sea Breeze, near Daytona Beach, Florida, where, in agreement with the Clarendon Hotel, starting on January 1, 1913, the newly licensed pilot took hotel guests and other interested people for aeroplane rides. It was a perfect arrangement: The hotel could boast an unusual attraction, Ruth earned money during the slow aviation season, and the couple enjoyed the balmy southern weather. The Olivers kept this arrangement for three years.

On one occasion a young man came running to the hangar around closing time, asking to be taken up—he was leaving the next day. Ruth agreed and the two took off. As she recalled years later, it was late afternoon, absolutely calm, no wind. She went up the beach, "the usual flight," then back again, toward the hangar, and prepared for landing. Suddenly, at about three hundred feet, the machine started down without any motion of the elevators on her part. Immediately, she knew something was wrong and turned off the motor. She eased the aeroplane down and, because there was no wind, made a perfectly good landing. The young man hopped out, paid his fee, and left. Ruth went to the back of the machine, her original Wright, for a look. Said Ruth, "We used to joke about them [the early Wrights] being put together with stove bolts—well, it was no joke, they were put together with stove bolts. And the bolt that held the elevator arrangement on the end of the tail of the plane had broken loose and was swinging free. . . . I had no elevator or directional guidance for the plane." Fortunately, the perfect calm and the ability of the Wright biplane to float down like a bird had saved pilot and passenger.

The Florida season had its comic moments. One year the Brooklyn Dodgers, in Florida for spring training, wanted something unusual for their opening game. Ruth was hired to throw the first ball from her aeroplane. Wilbert Robinson, the Dodgers's manager and known for catching high pop flies, would be the catcher. Just before takeoff, she realized she had no baseball to throw. "Here," said her mechanic, "you can use this. It's about the size of a baseball," and he handed her a grapefruit. It looked about right, and Ruth thought nothing more about it. Up in the air, ready for the throw, she zeroed in on Robinson, let the grapefruit fly, and hit Robinson on the chest, knocking him flat on his back.

Ruth was horrified, but the Dodger fans roared at another example of Dodger daffiness. Robinson flattened by a grapefruit was as funny as three of his runners occupying third base at the same time—which happened on occasion.

Ruth met a variety of people, generally wealthy enough to winter in Florida. Not all were ready to accept the new vehicle of travel. John D. Rockefeller declined an invitation, saying, "I'll wait until my wings grow." Surprisingly, men were less eager to go up than women, who apparently enjoyed a change from the sameness of resort life. *Aero and Hydro* reported in March that the "capable Wright pilot" made a long flight with Dr. H. F. Bigger of twenty-one miles in twenty-seven minutes, flying at eighteen hundred feet. If true, that was good flying for the time.

One hotel guest who insisted on going up begged to be taken down when scarcely ten feet off the ground, then wanted Ruth to put on the certificate that they had flown at a thousand feet. She refused, but he bragged to one and all that he had been up a thousand feet, which was all that interested him. As the Florida season ended, America's newest pilot was reported to have fifty thousand dollars' worth of contracts for the coming season.

That news may have been for advertising purposes, but the schedule of appearances for 1913 was impressive: the Easton Home Week Celebration in Allentown, Pennsylvania; Newport, Rhode Island, for the midsummer season; Hempstead, Long Island, carrying passengers and making a record flight at Garden City; the Mount Holly Fair Grounds in New Jersey; the Fall Meet at Oakwood Heights, Staten Island, where a flight lasted twenty minutes in bright moonlight; and in December, flights at Hackensack, New Jersey. Then it was time to head south for the winter season. Ruth's aerial jaunts with passengers from the Clarendon gradually lengthened, but the news that Pégoud had looped in France had yet to influence her.

On May 30, 1914, Ruth began a week's engagement at Oakwood Heights, Staten Island, and later in June she was flying again at Newport, thrilling the resort guests with a moonlight fight. In August she teamed with Rodman for a brother-sister act in Salem, New Hampshire. She piloted, and Rodman made a parachute jump. Appearances in the Midwest followed, until it was time to return to Florida. Exhibition flying had taken on a different look; spectators, no longer content with graceful turns and up-and-down maneuvers, expected thrills for their entrance fee. Ruth continued to carry passengers at exhibitions and to try for altitude records, but her flying was less exciting than that of some of the men. Of course, she was still flying the Wright biplane, which was unsuited for acrobatic feats. The Wright Company disapproved of stunting and did not build that kind of machine.

In April 1915, Ruth appeared at Louisville, Kentucky; in June she flew for the local Auto Club in Cincinnati and was featured on the cover of *The Billboard*. In July she substituted for Katherine Stinson at the Letter Carriers' Convention in Dayton. The site of this performance was a small racetrack, its infield full of trees, smack in the center of the city, with buildings and high wires to complicate flying. Ruth thought it "probably the worst field that I have ever attempted to fly from." Apparently Orville Wright had doubts about it, too. No one had ever tried to fly from that field.

Ruth took the aeroplane up, performed, and landed safely. After her flight, she chatted with Orville, who congratulated her on the flight, on being able to do it there. He wasn't much for publicity, Ruth thought, but he was curious to see whether the flight could be done or not from that site.

Next, she flew for a week at the Kentucky State Fair with George Mayland, a parachute jumper. Ruth flew the aeroplane, and Mayland jumped out; the point was to land him in front of the racetrack grandstand, which took considerable practice. Always, there was the wind to consider—its strength, its direction. Usually parachute jumpers landed miles away. Here, the pilot guaranteed to land the jumper in center field, "right where people could see it." The act was a big hit and started Ruth thinking of bigger thrills. The sameness of performance was beginning to pall. She completed her contract in Shreveport, Louisiana, in October, and decided it was time for a change.

She sold her faithful biplane, bought a Curtiss pusher with a one hundred–horsepower motor that could do loops, and had it outfitted with the Wright levers she was partial to. As she had done before, she spent time in the shop learning the intricacies of the new machine, taking the motor apart and reassembling it to her satisfaction. When she felt acquainted with it, the Curtiss was crated and shipped to Florida, where the wide beach provided a great practice site.

For ten days or more, she tried all kinds of rolls and vertical dives but no loops until her husband admonished, "You don't really have to do this. You don't have to try to loop, if you don't want to." That did it. On the next ascent, at a height of about fifteen hundred feet, she dipped the aeroplane back and pulled back the elevator. The machine went straight up, "and the plane went over like a bird." It was easy! She did another loop to be sure she could and landed, to great excitement, on the beach. Charles said, "You didn't have to do it the second time!" but Ruth felt otherwise. At that time, fliers didn't know if a particular machine would go over or not—"everything was new, everything was trial and error then," she recounted years later. She was a stickler for finding out a machine's capability.

On January 17, 1916, she gave a public exhibition of looping and acrobatic flying at Daytona Beach, which was a sensation. The new aviation season was about to begin, and Ruth's new acrobatic routine would be a sure crowd pleaser. At Hammondsport, New York, she showed her stuff in an exhibition that kept all eyes on her. In May, at the Military and Naval Tournament at Sheepshead Bay, she won second place in the altitude competition with a height of 11,200 feet, a new women's record recognized by the Aero Club of America. Competing against male aviators, Ruth placed second in bomb dropping and third in the speed race.

Ruth decided to try for the altitude record because she wanted to do something somebody else hadn't done. The sun was shining when she took off late in the afternoon, and it continued to shine the higher she went. With an eye on the registering barometer, she tried to coax the aeroplane higher—she could still see sunlight. To her amazement, it was dark when she returned to the field, where her anxious husband waited. The record was fine, but he lectured her for staying up so long.

The summer season brought appearances in Chicago, for the Conference of Associated Advertising Clubs, and elsewhere in the Midwest—Downs, Kansas; Fargo, North Dakota; and fairs in Mason City and Des Moines, Iowa, and Rochester, Minnesota. Mason City provided one of those incidents that aviators prefer not to have: Leveling off at fifteen hundred feet before starting a loop in a night flight, Ruth's aeroplane suddenly dropped from fifteen hundred feet to five hundred before stopping. Ruth landed immediately to investigate. The aeroplane was fine—all parts worked—but the nervous manager wouldn't let her go up again to loop. The next morning, pilot and crew met to consider what had happened. Ruth realized after looking around the area that she had flown over the top of a blast furnace shooting hot air skyward. In the dark she couldn't see it, and she had not had time to check the area carefully on arrival in town. Apparently when she passed through a blast of hot air, there was no resistance, and the machine fell. Fortunately, it stopped at five hundred feet.

Flying at the Iowa State Fair, the prize of the summer season, she had another near disaster. Her contract called for performing directly in front of the grandstand for day and evening stints. Before beginning her appearance, Ruth had fixed a tiny gasoline cup to the bottom of the carburetor; for the few seconds needed to loop, the motor would run upside down and gas would be fed by gravity. But the motor sputtered and refused to work properly while Ruth warmed up the machine for the first exhibition. Someone had been working on the special carburetor, and it needed the services of a factory expert to restore it. Ruth attached a stock carburetor to the motor and made a hurried takeoff before the waiting crowd.

Once in the air, everything worked well until she started the third loop. Upside down, over the small center field of the fairgrounds track, the motor quit. She was about five hundred feet in the air with little choice—somehow she had to land in the center field, where poles and other equipment were in place for the evening fireworks. She calmed her panic, searched the ground, and saw a narrow pathway that just might do. Leveling off, she brought the aeroplane down and, as the wheels touched the earth, the heavy claw brake on the rear of the undercarriage dug into the ground. Another brake on the front wheel dug in, and the machine came to a stop, right side up, at the fence separating the field and the racetrack. On the track, a twenty-five-mile automobile race was in progress when Ruth made her emergency landing. The spectators held their breath, waiting to see if the machine would crash through the fence into the racers. Once again, luck was on her side.

From then on, Ruth had a carburetor made that could not be tampered with, and decided "never to fly an airplane unless the pilot's seat was out in front and the landing gear equipped with three wheels that would prevent a nose-dive or ground loop, no matter how rough the landing field might happen to be." Tractor machines were already in use, but Ruth stuck with her pusher, convinced that it had many advantages over other small aeroplanes.

She was maturing as a flier. In an article for the *Brooklyn Eagle,* Ruth wrote: "The more I fly, the more careful I become. I know I took many chances when I first began driving my plane. . . . It takes time to teach you the full dangers you run. . . . It takes a skillful flyer to avoid risks."

In October, Ruth appeared at the International Wheat Show at Wichita, Kansas, then stopped to consider her next move. She wrote years later that she had been flying for the amusement of other people and had become a bit fed up with it. She would make one flight for her own pleasure—if possible, a nonstop flight from Chicago to New York City. Victor Carlstrom, a pilot for the Curtiss group, had attempted a similar flight on November 2. At Erie, Pennsylvania, a distance of 432 miles, a leak in the gasoline pipe brought him down, but it was a distance record for the United States.

Ruth asked Glenn Curtiss for the loan of a fast aeroplane with a two-hundred-horsepower motor, like Carlstrom's, to try to break the nonstop flight record, but was turned down. "Mr. Curtiss was afraid that I would break my neck instead." Her own looping model, with a few changes, would have to do. Auxiliary gas tanks were added to boost the fuel load to fifty-three gallons, rubber hose was used for gas lines, every connection was wrapped with bicycle tape, and an aluminum shield attached in front of her feet gave some protection from the cold. Every nonessential piece, including lights, was removed to make the load lighter. With these changes, Ruth hoped "the collapsible plane would not shake apart on the longest flight it had ever attempted."

Ruth had gone into training for the trip, sleeping in a tent on the roof of Chicago's Morrison Hotel to get used to the cold and taking a rigorous course of exercise. Satisfied that machine and pilot were in good shape, takeoff was scheduled for early Sunday, November 19. Arriving at Grant Park at 6 A.M., precious time was lost because the engine wouldn't start due to the cold temperature—the air and gas wouldn't mix together in the carburetor. Finally, at 7:25, central time, with James S. Stephens, an Aero Club representative observing, she rose into the air.

Sitting exposed in front of the wings, she was thankful for the layers of silk, chamois, and wool under her leather jacket, her wool and leather face mask, and helmet and goggles. The rolled map in the case strapped to her

Ruth Law, the "Queen of the Air," carrying her map box and gear for her long-distance flight from Chicago to New York in 1916. During this flight, she set a new American record for the farthest nonstop flight (590 miles from Chicago to Hornell, New York). LIBRARY OF CONGRESS leg allowed her to check the route plotted with Lieutenant J. A. McAlser, of the Hydrographic Survey Office; the cuff of her glove carried compass notations for the cities and towns along the route as she flew steadily east, ticking off the landmarks below, with an eye on the compass. The brisk fifty-six-mile-an-hour wind promised her in Chicago died out; there was no push from behind. Flying between three thousand and five thousand feet, she followed the compass directions sewed to her glove. Over Cleveland, it was snowing and bitterly cold; as she passed Erie, she was confident of making a new record. The question was, How much farther could she go?

Ten miles west of Hornell, New York, the motor began to sputter, a sign that the gas supply was going; two miles from the town, the tanks empty, she turned the motor off and glided down onto the racetrack outside of Hornell, where it seemed the whole town was waiting to welcome her. Hornell was a planned stop for refueling the machine; it was also a timely stop for its hungry pilot. The official landing time was 2:10, eastern time, just five hours, forty-five minutes after takeoff. She had flown an incredible 590 miles, a new American record for men and women.

Hot coffee and scrambled eggs restored the pilot, who had to be helped, numb from the cold, to a waiting automobile for the short ride into town. An hour and fourteen minutes later, with a full gas tank, she was off for the next stop, Binghamton. Ruth hoped to push on from there, but as daylight faded, unable to read her instruments in the dark, she decided to stop at Binghamton for the night. Spotting a racetrack, she landed just as Samuel Davis of the Glad-Hand Committee drove by. Davis, totally thrilled to meet the aviator, gave her a ride into town once the Curtiss was tied to a tree for the night with a police officer to guard it. It had been a good day of flying in spite of the morning delay. The distance covered nonstop was an American record, and she had broken the world's record for continuous flight by a woman. Only one person in the world had flown farther: Sub-Lieutenant A. Marchal, who flew from Nancy, France, to Chelm, Poland, a distance of 812.5 miles. If only the engine had started earlier, but Ruth gave up thoughts of what might have been and concentrated on dinner and a good night's sleep.

The following day, sensational headlines hailed Ruth's triumph. Two points, in particular, were stressed: the age of the aeroplane (an old model

New Englander Ruth Law seated on a Curtiss, the model used for her long-distance flight. INTERNATIONAL WOMEN'S AIR AND SPACE MUSEUM

Curtiss and small at that), and Ruth had paid all expenses. In her comments to the press, Ruth was confident the flight from Chicago to New York could be made nonstop. She would try again as soon as she could get a bigger machine. Obviously happy she had done so well, better than the man, she hastened to say the fact that she was a woman didn't make any difference. "I suppose I ought to say that I am in favor of woman suffrage—but what has that got to do with it?" If she was hoping the headlines would play down "the little girl" aspect, she was wrong. Her youth and sex were emphasized.

An editorial in the *New York Times* backed up Ruth's view. "Aviatrice" or "aviatrix" were good words for Miss Law, but since she had showed all the qualities—"courage, endurance, skill, sense of direction and position"—required for navigation of the air, "there is no necessity, and hardly an excuse, for giving her a name that emphasizes the fact, professionally irrelevant, of sex." Unquestionably, she belongs "in the rank of the great aviators."

The editor had one criticism: "It was, however, a serious oversight for her not to take along something to eat on the way. Food, judiciously selected, would have made her task far less exhausting, and helped her to endure the cold of the upper airs." All true, but space on the Curtiss was limited, any food would probably have frozen, and Ruth was so bundled that just working the levers was difficult. Eating would have been impossible.

The next morning at 7:23, Ruth was off on the last lap of her flight, landing at 9:37:35, the official time according to Aero Club records, at Governor's Island. The flight from Chicago totaled eight hours, fifty-five minutes, and thirty-five seconds, faster than any other form of transportation could accomplish. Numb from the cold, she remained still for several moments after her aeroplane stopped; then Aero Club officials undid her seat belt and helped her down. Slowly removing gloves, helmet and mask, she gave a big smile, despite stiff lips and a face blue with cold. Walking briskly for several paces until the circulation in her feet quickened, she collected her skirt and climbed into the automobile waiting to carry her to the quarters of Major and Mrs. Carl F. Hartmann, where she washed and powdered her face, and had breakfast.

During breakfast, the "Queen of the Air" described what was almost a near miss. Starting from Binghamton, she neglected to refill the gas tanks in her haste to depart. Flying low through morning fog, she had difficulty finding her landmarks, relying first on the Susquehanna River, then, to the east, the Delaware, and finally the Hudson. As she reached Manhattan, the machine started to cough. Remembering that one tank was placed too low to feed any more gas once it got down to two or three inches in the tank, she dipped down to coax gas into the carburetor, then leveled until the next dip to keep the motor working. Using almost the last gas, she rose higher to have room to glide down with the wind and land on the island. "One hundred and twenty-five pounds of nerve and pluck" was Aero Club president Alan R. Hawley's description of Ruth. He had it right.

Meeting with reporters after breakfast, she was asked, "You have made the longest flight a woman ever made, haven't you?" Her reply was pointed: "I have made the longest flight an American ever made." For her it was a warm-up for another try to fly Chicago to New York in one day, or even a transcontinental flight. Aero Club was offering a prize of twenty thousand dollars for such a flight. Ruth thought it was doable in three or four days, a definite improvement over Cal Rodgers's forty-nine-day trip in 1911.

There were accolades and honors galore. Aero Club held a reception on the afternoon of November 23; on December 2, Ruth was guest of honor at a dinner at the Waldorf-Astoria, attended by President and Mrs. Woodrow Wilson, celebrating the lighting of Miss Liberty; on December 18, another dinner in her honor, luminous with dignitaries—including the discoverers of the North and South poles—was given by the New York Civic Forum and the Aero Club of America at the Hotel Astor with Rear Admiral Robert E. Peary as toastmaster. "America's premier aviator"—the title bestowed by *Scientific American*—was presented with a check for twenty-five hundred dollars by Aero Club in appreciation of her achievement and its furthering of aviation. Victor Carlstrom, who could not be present, was presented with a gold watch.

More than one dinner speaker pointed to the flight's beneficial effects: American machines and motors were shown to be capable (even ordinary ones)—no special equipment was needed for success; distance flights were not a circus stunt but a serious extension of aviation; and the popular mind was encouraged to consider a career in aviation. Of all the speakers, perhaps Eleanor Gates, an ardent feminist, caught the spirit of the evening best in her comments as reported in *Flying.* "It is easy to get a dinner if you are a man. You get one if you are a such-and-such degree Mason, or a naughty Elk, or just because it's time to have another dinner. But for a woman to sit in glory at the Hotel Astor she must do something superhuman."

By now, Ruth's flying ability was legend. Only weeks before, on the evening of December 2, memorable for the lighting of the Statue of Liberty, she had looped over Miss Liberty as the floodlights came on for the first time ever. It was a glorious celebration with President Wilson, Mayor John P. Mitchel, French Ambassador Jules Jusserand, and the Atlantic Fleet present, plus the countless thousands who watched from every vantage point. Thanks to Henry Doherty and George Williams of Cities Service, an electric utility company, with an assist from Ralph Pulitzer, publisher of the *World,* New York threw a grand party for the statue, now transformed from "night shrouded bulk" into a "Glorious Goddess," permanently ablaze with freedom's message.

Ruth's part entailed carrying a heavy load of electric lights under the wings to spell out "liberty" and magnesium flares on the wing tips, all of which would light up on cue when the floodlights came on. Getting up was a concern, but the Curtiss made it, flying in "a bright rain of fire" that thrilled the cheering thousands on ships and shore. The cheering continued up the length of Manhattan as the president and dignitaries made their way to the Waldorf-Astoria. At the dinner that followed, Ruth was on the dais with the honored guests.

Among those seated with Ruth that night was Ralph Pulitzer. It was a fortuitous meeting. On January 12, 1917, Pulitzer and Ruth initialed an agreement that provided financial assistance from the *World* if Ruth succeeded in purchasing a European aeroplane superior in speed and carrying capacity than existing American types. The newspaper would pay for the expense of the European trip, the cost of the machine, and expenses incurred in a proposed transcontinental flight from the Pacific Coast to New York before July 1, for a sum not to exceed ten thousand dollars. All information and interviews resulting from such a flight would belong exclusively to the *World*. The aeroplane would remain the property of the newspaper until the completion of the flight, whereupon title would pass to Ruth as compensation for her services. If permission could be obtained, Ruth would make a flight between London and Paris under the auspices of the *World* before returning from Europe.

Ruth and her husband left for Europe on January 14, where the reality of war soon ended any hopes of acquiring an aeroplane. At Liverpool her baggage was checked carefully when she said she was in the flying business. A scrapbook with clippings about night flights and dropping bombs aroused more suspicion—she might be a spy—and her party was held incommunicado at Liverpool until a cable to New York established it was safe to allow her on English soil. Leaving her luggage in London, she went on to Paris, where it was immediately obvious that French aeroplanes were not being sold for export.

A visit to Le Bourget, described in the *World,* left Ruth impressed with the advances in French aviation. It was a city of hangars, each capable of housing scores of machines, where every type of flying craft used at the front was seen. The newest and smallest machine, resembling a hummingbird, was flown for her benefit. Instead of a long bill, it had a machine gun that fired through the propeller. She did succeed in flying over Paris in a Morane-Saulnier monoplane, which she would have bought if this had been possible. It was light, sleek, with a motor superior to any in America, capable of making a fast, steep climb. Flying at several thousand feet, Ruth leaned over the side to look down and discovered the speed of the aeroplane. She lost her breath for an instant, felt as if her head would come off, and discovered later the powder on her nose was gone, yet sitting behind the windscreen was comfortable; speed and wind pressure were not noticeable. Before returning to the ground, Ruth had the aeroplane stand on one wing, dive, and spiral to show its stuff, an exhibition that left her an ardent admirer of French aviation.

Returning on April 4, by way of Spain to avoid possible submarine attack, Ruth sang the praises of French aviation. French aeroplanes were lighter, easier to handle, and capable of greater speed. "Just think of those Morane machines getting up 6,000 feet in seven minutes. . . . Many of them could climb almost 1,000 feet a minute—and it took me an hour and a half to get up to 12,000 in my little old biplane, when I made the altitude record. Our materials and bodies should be refined and lightened." She couldn't buy an aeroplane, but she had seen the tremendous effort put forth by the English and French to defeat the enemy, met the boys of the Lafayette Escadrille, and chatted with Lieutenant Georges Guynemer, an ace with more than thirty aeroplanes to his credit and gave Ruth a ring fashioned from the button of a German airman's coat. She also brought back with her a French trench dog, named Poilu, who was photographed with Ruth in all the newspapers.

Two days later the United States declared war on Germany. Like Katherine Stinson, Ruth was eager to serve in any way possible, preferably flying overseas. That was not to be. Instead, she flew to promote recruitment, the Liberty Loan Drive, and the Red Cross Ambulance Service. She bombed Midwest cities and Army camps, dropping leaflets and paper bombs urging people to subscribe to the Liberty Loan by buying bonds. Flying over cities in Ohio and landing at rallies in city parks prompted an outpouring of giving; the Ohio National Guardsmen gave a whopping $1,421,500, an average of $59.18 a head. From Ohio, she went to Nebraska, Kansas, and Missouri, touching down in Oklahoma, before swinging back to St. Louis and the cities of Illinois en route to Chicago, on a strenuous ten-day tour. The paper bombs she dropped bore a message on each side: "A Liberty Bond in your home or a German bomb on your home! Which is *your* choice? Mine was a bond. Buy yours today. Ruth Law." On the reverse was: "If you can't fight, your money can buy a Liberty Bond to keep off German bombs. Buy your bond today. Ruth Law." Everywhere, people responded to this novel appeal from the sky.

In July, Ruth persuaded Major Franklin Henney, the army's chief recruiting officer in Chicago, that flying exhibitions might stimulate recruiting. Wearing an army uniform by special permission, she made night flights as part of a special one-week drive by British and American forces to sign up young men for the service. Fastened to the lower part of her machine was a sign twenty-eight feet by four feet with brilliant electric letters spelling out "Enlist." That plus the showering of magnesium flares from the tips of the wings was an eye-catching display for the crowds in Grant Park. Wherever she flew that year, the "Enlist" message drew crowds of people eagerly scrambling for the white cards dropped from the sky. Millions of people got the message; Ruth had the satisfaction of encouraging thousands to join the army, many of them trying for the Aviation Service. By early 1918 the Aviation Service had more volunteers than it could handle with its limited amount of equipment.

In December, Murray Hulbert, a Democratic congressman from New York, introduced a bill in Congress to let women serve in the military. While he wasn't urging women to join up, he felt that some "intrepid, persistent spirits, like Miss Law" would be of greater value to the government using their flying skills in some capacity. Ruth, for her part, lobbied members of Congress, wearing her modified uniform, with little success. She flew over the White House upside down and landed on Pennsylvania Avenue (she had walked its length the day before, looking for hazards), hoping to change the male world's thinking, but without success. She had set two altitude records for women, 11,200 feet (1916) and 14,700 feet (1917); she could loop, dive, and spiral with the best of them. The army missed a good pilot.

The previous summer she had written a provocative piece for the *Chicago Herald*—"Go Get the Kaiser"—telling what she would do if she had a chance to bomb the kaiser, and how she would do it. Her visit to France provided her with solid information on conditions at the front and, as an experienced acrobatic flier, she had the know-how to fly combat missions. Ruth used the article to argue that women could play a vital aviation role by ferrying supplies and men behind the lines and delivering messages, if not actually assigned to the front, releasing men for frontline duty. She admitted that most women were not prepared for the "intense nervous strain of flying and fighting," but were perfectly capable of "plain, unspectacular flying." In her enthusiasm, Ruth sounded as bellicose as any man; she itched to serve in a meaningful way. Fast-forwarding to World War II, the military finally saw the light; women learned to fly and performed the kind of service Ruth had envisioned.

On June 8, 1918, an article in the *New York Times* highlighted a public-relations problem Ruth was having: She was accused of being a German spy. Apparently the accusation originated in Birmingham, Alabama, shortly after she appeared there the previous October. Sources claimed that Ruth was arrested in Atlanta as a spy (she had never been in Atlanta), and from there the accusation followed her around the country wherever she appeared. A schoolteacher in Indiana reported she was a German spy and really a man disguised as a woman. Finally, Ruth addressed the rumors in Washington, where she was arranging for a license to make further flights for the Red Cross. It is hard to believe that people gave serious credence to such a bizarre tale, but during wartime people frequently become phobic. Possibly her experience in England prompted the rumors and, as happens in the childhood game of telephone, distortions grow by leaps and bounds. In Washington, officials ignored the rumors. Her patriotism was unquestionable, and she was issued licenses to make flights for various causes and to lecture by no less an entity than the War Department.

In 1919, after the war ended, Ruth traveled to Japan, China, and the Philippine Islands, giving exhibitions in Japan and the Philippines. In Japan, she was enthusiastically greeted by massive crowds. In an interview years later, Ruth said that interest in aviation was great—"literally millions of people" attended. She had never seen such crowds in her life. Like Katherine Stinson, she found women were particularly keen; she was invited to address a women's club there.

In China, unsettled conditions did not encourage Ruth to fly. She and her group of five, which included her husband, visited Gunn Tom, who had learned to fly in America as Tom Gunn, before returning to China.

Traveling by riverboat to Canton, the party became aware of armed guards near them as they sat on the deck after dinner. Tom explained that guards were customary to keep pirates from boarding as third-class passengers and, when the boat crossed a certain point, coming on deck at the same time a boat from the shore came alongside to kidnap the passengers.

Hardly more reassuring was an invitation from a provincial governor, who offered payment in gold for an exhibition in his hometown and assured Ruth it would be perfectly safe—he would send a group of soldiers to protect her and the aeroplane. Ruth decided it "wasn't a very good place to give an exhibition, if one had to be protected by soldiers."

The Filipinos, by contrast, were friendly and enthusiastic about aviation. Ruth performed the same stunts and flights as in America. During one exhibition, on April 4, she was asked to carry mail by José Topacio, director of the Bureau of Posts, who organized booths to sell postcards, printed by the Aero Club with a two-centavo stamp, for Ruth to carry. The cards were canceled with a special mark: "Aerial Mail Service Bureau of Posts, Philippine Islands. Miss Ruth Law." With more than a thousand cards gathered in a bag, Ruth took off and, flying over the Manila Hotel, dropped the bag on the roof twenty feet below, where the cards were then distributed through regular channels. This performance was such a success, it was repeated the following day with cards for sale at several places around Manila.

Home again, the expected interest in aviation with the end of the war did not appear. Ruth flew in Canada on a short tour notable for racing Gaston Chevrolet, a famous automobile racer, and signed up with stunt pilot Al Wilson to fly for the season. By 1921 she had her own flying circus, complete with three aeroplanes and two male pilots. The constant demand was for new and more daring feats; Ruth and her troop tried to oblige. Stunting on a rope ladder, hanging from an aeroplane, then dropping into a racing auto was one; wing walking was another. The two male pilots' specialty was having a man step from the wing of one machine to the other without a ladder. The two aeroplanes flew close enough together to allow the walker to stand on the top wing of one, grab the lower wing of the other, and climb in.

Ruth's specialty was climbing out of the Curtiss Jenny cockpit, up over the front and the motor, onto the top wing, where she stood up while the pilot looped the loop three times. Verne Treat, an ex–army pilot from San Francisco, piloted the aeroplane. Ruth had complete confidence in him—"he could handle any situation." Several times, centrifugal force flattened Ruth against the wing, until she and Treat came up with a solution, a small harness over her shoulders. Four very thin woven-steel wires, attached to the wing, had hooks on the end of each to fasten to the harness. Ruth performed this chore while sitting on the edge of the wing at fifteen hundred feet. Standing up, she was held upright while the pilot looped. Three loops were fine, but when she tried a fourth, there was too much pressure on her knees—she went flat.

Another time, performing with a fireworks display, the promoter of the show, concerned about rain, fired the works off early just as Ruth flew by. In a curtain of rockets, bursting bombs, and Roman candles, the startled pilot did her three loops as advertised. She remarked afterward, she felt like "a participant in the last days of Pompeii." Of all the stunts,

Ruth Law racing Gaston Chevrolet, the famous automobile racer, in Montreal, *1919.* NATIONAL AIR AND SPACE MUSEUM, SMITHSONIAN INSTITUTION

car racing was her favorite. She liked the challenge of flying as low as possible to the auto on the ground. She confided, "I could always beat the autos on a half-mile track, but on a mile track they often won."

In October 1921, a tragic accident, resulting in the death of Madeline Davis, a stunt performer, hastened the end of Ruth's circus days, and her flying career. Davis had hoped to join the Law circus and promote a career in the movies. Her death was the final straw for Charles Oliver, who had watched a career of unnerving performances. The *New York Times,* commenting on the tragedy, editorialized that the accident caused indignation as well as horror, justifying the demands around the country for regulation to prevent "any repetition of accidents like this one." One could see that the days of flying circuses were numbered.

Ruth finished an exhibition in Trenton, New Jersey, in 1922, where, one morning, she picked up the newspaper and read that she was retiring from flying. Charles Oliver, devoted husband, backer, manager, and staunch supporter, had given the announcement to the press without consulting his wife. Reportedly, he explained to Ruth, "I can't stand the strain of seeing you in danger. You've tempted luck long enough. To please me, give it up!" She did, on the spot. His loyalty and hard work over the last ten years had helped build a successful career. Ruth knew she owed him something and gave up flying.

In an interview in 1936, she admitted she would have liked to try for the $150,000 prize offered before World War I by Lord Northcliffe, the British aviation enthusiast, for a flight from Newfoundland to Ireland. Ruth's brother, Rodman, was working on plans for this when the outbreak of war in 1914 made such a flight impossible. Ruth regretted that she did not try after the war. "I could have been the first to do it." But when Charles Lindbergh succeeded, she cheered.

The sudden end of a life of suspense and constant motion was too abrupt. After ten years of living on excitement, Ruth struggled to keep her nerves under control and had a nervous breakdown. In one of many interviews years later, she confessed, "The nervous strain of exhibition flying in those days was intense." To combat it, she did fancy needlework, keeping hoops, scissors, and floss in her machine to make eyelets while waiting on the ground. "It was very soothing." It was an unusual admission from a woman who had said that a real aviator lacked nerves: "What is called bravery is simply lack of nerves."

The Olivers settled in California, first in Beverly Hills, then San Francisco. Ruth kept one memento from her flying days, the walnut propeller from the Curtiss that made the distance record. She remained interested in aviation and attended various functions to talk about the old days, but kept her promise to stay out of aeroplanes as long as Charles was alive.

One day in 1947, after Charles had died, she accepted a ride in a new private plane with a friend. Flying at one thousand feet over the California landscape, the pilot suggested she might like to handle the controls. Ruth's first reaction was to refuse, but she didn't want him to think she was afraid, "so I took the controls and flew that airplane." A rush of memories came back as she handled the stick. For a time, she thought of buying a machine and flying again, but she resisted the temptation. Her days were filled with club activities and bridge. Flying had been too long ago.

Ruth Law Oliver died on December 2, 1970, at age eighty-three. She is buried in Lynn, Massachusetts. Her obituary in the *Lynn Item,* December 5, 1970, closed with these fitting lines:

> *Come take a trip in my airship*
> *And you can flirt with the sun and the stars.*

12
Little Sister

MARJORIE CLARE STINSON did not take easily to the role of little sister. The third of the four Stinson children, she had an independent mind, a common trait in that family, that caused rumpled feathers on occasion. She held strong convictions that all the honeyed, southern tones in the world could not hide.

Born in Fort Payne, Alabama, on July 5, 1896, she moved with the family to Canton, Mississippi, where life was pleasant, if uneventful. Once her mother, Emma Stinson, separated from her father, Edward, and moved the family to Hot Springs, Arkansas, the tempo of life picked up. The comfort of life in a town filled with relatives disappeared (Marjorie's first-grade teacher was an aunt), but as Marjorie stated more than once, "We children never lacked for anything" in the world outside the cocoon.

Marjorie saw her first aeroplane in 1912, a Curtiss biplane piloted by Jimmie Ward, "right there in Hot Springs." She was in high school—to go to the racetrack for the exhibition was out of the question—but an understanding teacher allowed her to stand at the window, where she saw the aeroplane fly, not very high or far, but it did fly. It was on this occasion that sister Katie was allowed to go see the aeroplane and make arrangements for a ride. Dressed in a hurriedly sewn white serge suit,

Katherine made her first passenger flight with Ward, and the rest is history.

Marjorie was still a schoolgirl, busy with Shakespeare and the social antics of high school, but once Katherine went off to learn to fly, Marjorie's interest in things aerial perked up. Her brother Eddie was eager to fly almost from birth. One day, left to their own devices as youngsters, she and Eddie cut up sheets, attached them to pieces of wood, and rigged up a flying machine on a wagon, which they planned to race down a steep hill the next day. Fortunately, the weather saved them from disaster. A storm that night reduced the aeroplane to a mass of tattered cloth. After high school, Marjorie spent a year at Millsap College in Mississippi before deciding what she wanted to do.

With Katherine's example before her, she persuaded her father to let her take up flying at the Wright School. Traveling to Dayton, Ohio, in mid-June 1914, she had time to plan her approach: She would introduce herself, offer the check for tuition, and ask to be accepted in the school, explaining that she had flown six times with Katherine and was used to the air. To her dismay, she was told she needed parental permission because of her age—she was not yet 18. While she waited for a telegram from her mother, Marjorie met Orville Wright, who took her out to the flying field and showed her the original hangar, the old launching device used before wheels were added to aeroplanes, the school machine, and introduced her to the man who would be her teacher, Howard Rinehart. Since 1910, Orville had changed his mind about women flying. The Wright School had graduated its first woman pilot, Mrs. Richberg Hornsby, a few weeks before Marjorie appeared.

June 26, 1914, duly enrolled as a student, Marjorie went up as passenger with Rinehart in a Wright Model B and had a five-minute introduction to the two levers that operated it. The left stick worked the elevator; the right lever warped the wings to raise or lower a wing or to bank the aeroplane on a turn. The left lever had an additional lever hinged on top that turned left or right and controlled the rudder. The two sticks moved only forward and back. In addition, a white twine string tied on the skids brace in front indicated if the machine was flying straight: Straight back, all was fine; to the left or right at an angle, the machine was skidding or sideslipping; to correct this position, the pilot had to fly in the direction

Marjorie Stinson (left) and her older sister, Katherine, seated on a Wright biplane. SAN DIEGO AEROSPACE MUSEUM

the string pointed to. Marjorie quickly discovered it wasn't as simple as it sounded.

In the factory, a balancing machine, rigged up on a wooden horse with a motor, provided the same practice as flying. The motor, when started, unbalanced the machine; the student had to work the sticks to balance it again. Working on this machine was a daily routine until the student's reactions became second nature. On days when the weather was bad, students spent extra time on the machine.

Marjorie's class consisted of four men—one a gentleman from Japan— and herself. When Lieutenant Kenneth Whiting from the navy was added the next day, she began to worry that the six-week deadline she had set for obtaining a license might be too short; the more students, the less flight time on the school aeroplane. Another dread was the chewing out Rinehart did after a poor flying effort, always within earshot of the others. She found this more "humiliating than being a minor."

The first Sunday of the course there was no flying. Marjorie noted in her diary: "They don't fly here on Sunday so it seems a very long day."

Marjorie Stinson preparing to train on a Wright biplane at the Wright School in Dayton, Ohio. INTERNATIONAL WOMEN'S AIR AND SPACE MUSEUM

On poor-weather days (no flying in the rain or high wind), there was nothing to do except work on the balance machine. When the motor went bad, time was lost waiting for a new one. In the meantime, Marjorie moved to the DeLong's celery farm across the railroad tracks and the road bordering the Wright field, saving a commute from the city. Celery grew luxuriously in the level field, and the DeLong's cultivator (really a lawn mower made by DeLong) kept the weeds down, and "the place looked good." Her classmates occasionally came to dinner at the farm, where the talk was all about aviation.

Oscar Brindley, one of the Wright aviators, arrived at the field with a new machine called the Tin Cow. He had so much help from the interested students that everybody forgot to put water in the radiator; once in the air the cow came back "gently to pasture" in a hurry. The days passed quickly, too quickly for Marjorie, who continued to worry she would not qualify within the six-week time limit that she had bet a reporter of the *San Antonio Light* was a sure thing.

The second Sunday, a grand day for flying, Marjorie rode a couple of the ponies at the field. They were hard to catch. Then on July 6, she had three short flights in the morning, for 15 minutes of flying (the air was puffy), and two more flights in the afternoon, for ten minutes. Orville Wright came out and made some practice flights, the students watching every move. The week went rapidly. Marjorie made six flights one day, giving her such confidence that she felt she was ready to make a landing by herself. Four days later she was eager to get Rinehart out of the aeroplane and fly it herself. She thought she might try telling him "that a lady likes to see him walking about the field"—he had an admirer among the ladies working at the field—but she felt too junior to speak up. Gradually Marjorie's flights lengthened—one was seven minutes. Then a storm came through, and flying stopped.

There were diversions sometimes: a circus, the Hofbraü (Marjorie didn't like beer), fishing, and kite flying. Shortly before she soloed, she went to Sunday school. If it looked as if she had suddenly taken to religion, "not so," said Marjorie in her diary. The following day, the school routine continued—one of the students smashed up while flying with Rinehart, but by afternoon the machine was repaired and Rinehart tried it alone.

On July 22, Marjorie wrote in her diary: "Rinehart doesn't say much to me. I do believe I am doing all the flying myself, but could only be sure if he stayed on the ground. He just sits in the plane with hands folded." Actually, Rinehart warned her that day he would test her soon by cutting the motor. Without looking at him, she was to land quickly when the motor quit. Two days later, while flying over a cornfield (Marjorie had a weakness for stands of tall corn), the motor suddenly stopped. She noted in her diary, "With the grace of what little altitude I had and his presence (if not his help) I got back in the field without any breakage."

The weeks rolled by. Sunday school again on July 26, pony rides in the afternoon on the field. On July 25, Rinehart was married, a surprise to his students—no flights that day. Motor trouble slowed the number of lessons; a spark plug was lost in flight. Marjorie figured that the speed of the school machine was about forty miles an hour, maximum and minimum, which meant "you can't be perfectly dumb and fly this plane too. The reason is that you are given barely what is necessary and no more, there is no reserve, and therefore there is no allowance for errors."

The weather was either rambunctious (no flying) or puffy wind, when flights were challenging because of the dipping motion as the wind blew, then slacked. The English student, Mr. Brewer, used the morning newspaper as a windbreaker inside his coat. Marjorie succeeded in making several flights of four and six minutes, with Rinehart glued to the machine. "I don't need him at all, but it isn't flying etiquette to tell him so," she complained.

On the 31st, sister Katie came to town. Marjorie had hoped to finish training before her sister found out, but here she was, "running into Dayton between her flying engagements." Marjorie felt that Katie lacked confidence in her little sister's ability; she herself was very confident. The last thing she wanted was to worry Katie. Apparently she felt some unease, however; years later Marjorie wrote that she needed more practice landing as the tests approached, but her paid hours of instruction had ended and her money was used up, too. She wired her father, who sent her thirty dollars for an additional thirty minutes of practice time.

On August 1, Lincoln Beachey was exhibiting nearby. The Wright group was in attendance. Beachey raced around the field and did his death-defying drop for the entranced spectators below. Marjorie thought she was pretty good until she saw him. Now she was discouraged. The Curtiss biplane with a Gnome ninety-horsepower air-cooled engine performed the most graceful figures she "ever hoped to see." On Sunday, Katie left. Marjorie's license tests were scheduled for the next day.

Unfortunately, a broken propeller shaft and wind in the afternoon canceled the tests. Marjorie noted in her diary, "A little war has started up in Europe." The following day, August 4, "something broken" precluded flying. Finally, in the afternoon, she did one flight with Rinehart, then a two-minute flight alone and a set of figure eights alone. It was great without Rinehart—"I knew exactly who was flying then, and I could almost hear the other students' sigh of relief when I stepped out of the plane leaving it all in one piece, that they might later fly in it." Eureka! She had done it. If only she could go faster than forty miles per hour.

The next day was almost anticlimactic. She made another set of eights, did the altitude flight, and again walked away from the plane, leaving it intact for the remaining students. It was six weeks to the day; she earned her pilot's license after four and a half hours of instruction. Many fliers learned in a shorter period—Matilde Moisant for one—but perhaps four and a half hours was a better time investment. Marjorie's career lasted longer than Matilde's.

Very quickly, Marjorie settled into her flying career. The first order of business was finding a machine. New ones were costly; a used one adjusted to personal taste was preferable and cheaper. Marjorie found a Wright B, formerly flown by Roy Waite for exhibitions, that needed considerable repair after a crash. The price of her machine was less than the five thousand dollars or more for a new model from the Wright factory. With the help of mechanic Daniel Kiser, the machine was painstakingly put together at Cicero, near Chicago. When ready, she flew more practice hours in the air and carried paying passengers. In the middle of August she joined Katie at Overland Park in Kansas City, Missouri, for her public debut. The flying sisters were a drawing card.

Marjorie followed her debut with an appearance at the Brownwood, Texas, Fall Fair on October 7, 8, and 9 before crowds who cheered her maneuvers and lined up to shake hands with the "plucky little aviator." Her Wright B was damaged in shipping, requiring Eddie and Marjorie to work on it through the night and day to ready it for flying. On the last day of the fair, the new pilot almost had a serious accident, when treacherous winds tossed the machine about, pushing down on one wing and up on the other. The day was unusually hot—"and the pilot was unusually inexperienced," commented Marjorie later—which perhaps explained the situation. She admitted afterward that she was frightened, but "practiced muscles and steady nerves" rescued her from danger. Realizing the wind at the east end of the field was troublesome, she performed the rest of her flights to the west. Brownwood sits in a valley sheltered by hills. A slight breeze in the city could be a stiff wind higher up, as Marjorie had discovered, but she went up again, so as not to disappoint the thousands of farmers and visitors gathered from the towns around. The consensus in the local newspaper: She was one fine aviator. An important element in the success of her flights was the Boy Scout troops present on the field who kept the area clear of people. Their help was invaluable, and Marjorie published her thanks in the newspaper. When the fair ended, the Stinson party—Marjorie, Eddie, and Emma, who worried her daughter was too young to be traveling alone—left for San Antonio.

Before settling in for the winter, Katherine and Marjorie made an appearance together in Nashville under the auspices of the Nashville Equal Suffrage League, which hoped to raise consciousness for women's suffrage. The *Nashville Banner* ran an advertisement with banner headlines on November 17 for the "Most Sensational, Thrilling, Death-Defying Event Ever Shown in Your City!" scheduled for 3 P.M. the next day. Katherine would race her machine against the latest Overland auto driven by Marjorie. It was unusual, perhaps, but hardly death defying. Still, the event seemed to please the Nashville citizens and visitors who filled the State Fair grandstand or stood in the chilly air on the hillside across from the grandstand to watch. A local railroad crew backed up their cars on the track near the racecourse and waited patiently for the chance to see an aeroplane in the air. When it was over, the event was judged "interesting," particularly for showing the ability of the aeroplane to make sharp turns, whereas the auto could not cut corners on the track. At the end of the flight, the aviator flew over the grandstand and released a shower of Kewpie dolls attached to small parachutes with the suffragette colors. Unfortunately, the wind carried them out of reach of the grandstand, onto the field. Kewpie dolls, the creation of Rose O'Neill Wilson, were a staple at carnivals and fairs in 1914. Real dolls—there were many imitators—are identified by their red heart and the O'Neill label on the base. They are collector's items today.

On their return to San Antonio, the sisters leased the army hangar on the field at Fort Sam Houston, for their aeroplanes, with the understanding that if the hangar was needed, they would vacate. During the winter, Marjorie carried passengers and continued practice flights, which helped create public interest in aviation. Both women visited schools to organize and speak to model-aeroplane clubs. Before the school year ended, a meet was held in May, featuring many different designs in the air. The prize for the best model was an aeroplane ride with one of the Stinsons.

Seguin, Texas, home of the Seguin Fire Department's annual May celebration, signed up Marjorie to appear, in addition to promised entertainment for all ages—races for cash prizes, a baseball game, dinner, and not one but two grand firemen's balls. Miss Marjorie Stinson would "illustrate peace and wartime uses" of the aeroplane. The war in Europe had stimulated interest in the use of aeroplanes for attack purposes, and bomb demonstrations were popular. A temporary fort built on the Bauer Park field at Seguin was the target for attack with flour bombs. Real explosives were costly and dangerous. The celebration, advertised in German to attract the surrounding German communities, promised "*Moderne Luftkriegs Methoden by Fräulein Stinson.*"

To show the peacetime potential of aeroplanes, Marjorie was sworn in as an aerial-mail pilot, to deliver mail from the Bauer Park flying field to the post office in Seguin for disposal, using a special cancelation stamp reading "Aero Post Seguin, Texas, May 19th" to mark the first aerial-mail flight in Texas. On the first flight, messages from the mayor of Seguin to the mayor of San Antonio were carried in a pouch on the seat next to Marjorie. Looking very young in her white tunic and pants, Marjorie was photographed on May 24 being sworn in by Postmaster George D. Armistead at San Antonio. Interested spectators included Emma Stinson; Katherine Childs, a child movie star; and her mother, Mrs. Childs. (Marjorie was also flying in a movie being made by Excel Motion Picture Company.) After one flight between Seguin and San Antonio, made with considerable press, the project ended without explanation. One drawback to flying the thirty-mile trip on a regular schedule was the unreliability of aeroplane motors. Also, air-mail service was still in the planning stage nationally.

The movie enterprise paid fairly well and provided lots of laughs. Marjorie's part in the rather loose plot called for her to make off with the child star because of a divorce dispute. With Baby Katherine belted in the seat beside her, Marjorie took off, circled once, and, following instructions, headed toward the camera for a close-up shot. The first time she was afraid to get too close; the second time, as she headed straight for the camera, an unexpected puff of wind sailed the aeroplane straight into the cameraman, knocking him and his machine to the ground. Fortunately, no one was injured. Since the camera was operating until the moment it was hit, *A Romance of Earth and Sky* had an exciting, real-life sequence.

Like her sister, Katherine, Marjorie flew on the exhibition trail with appearances at Menomonie, Wisconsin, and Bogalusa and New Orleans, Louisiana, where a bonanza rained from the sky. In agreement with local merchants, she flew over downtown New Orleans and dropped the *Daily States* noon edition from the sky, which offered coupons for free merchandise in the local stores. Some of the choice items included a quart of ice cream; a half-pound box of chocolates; one free piano roll; one bottle of Swat, the great mosquito lotion; and a twenty-five-dollar credit on a piano or a player piano. New Orleans dwellers were urged to be in the commercial district between 12:30 and 2 P.M. "The youngest woman in the world to pilot an aeroplane" would also make exhibition flights at the Fair Grounds, showing the use of aeroplanes in war and, weather permitting, take up passengers one at a time during her two-day appearance.

That spring, Marjorie was appointed a lieutenant in the United States Aviation Reserve Corps, an organization formed by Albert Lambert of St. Louis, the pharmaceutical magnate, to develop a roster of trained pilots who would be available, in case of war, for national aviation service. Marjorie, the youngest member and the only female, received a gold insignia pin of the corps, one of her proudest possessions in old age. The group was more for show than performance, but it anticipated the need for trained fliers.

In early fall, Marjorie was at Fort Sam Houston again. Covering a large spread of Texas ground, the fort was ideal for flying. Eddie, who had gone to Dayton to learn to fly, returned to San Antonio to train with Marjorie because of crowded conditions at the Wright School, bringing four interested Canadians with him. With the arrival of the First Aero Squadron from Fort Sill, Oklahoma, commanded by Captain Benjamin Foulois, as well as a growing number of other students, Marjorie and Eddie decided they needed their own space independent of army approval. "Being chivalrous," Marjorie wrote years later, "they [the Army Squadron] let me keep the wooden hangar, and they used tents," which worked temporarily. Needless to say, the army fliers were amazed to find a woman teaching men to fly on a Wright B aeroplane.

The Wright had undergone some changes. The wings, instead of warping by the pilot's maneuvering a small lever on the top of the right-hand stick, were now rigidly braced, and a small section, removed from the outer trailing edge of all four wings, was hinged to the wing, to form flaps, or ailerons. This change reduced pilot fatigue. When more Canadian students arrived, they informed Marjorie the Canadian Aviation officials wanted them to learn another method of control, the three-in-one, with all movement centered in a steering wheel that rocked back and forth for the elevator and turned for the ailerons. The mechanics went to work to find parts: An auto lost a steering wheel, a separate hand grip mounted on the wheel shaft worked the rudder, the elevator controls were connected, "and we had a plane with two distinct and complete ways to fly it," Marjorie recalled. She stuck with her Wright system; the Canadians used the wheel method. As with the aileron change, she took the machine up to see if there was any interference in the air between the two controls. There was none. She was ready to teach.

Toward the end of December, after scouting the countryside, Marjorie and Eddie found a parcel of land on the South Loop that would be an ideal flying field—it was flat and free of obstructions. Brother and sister clambered over the site, anxiously looking for rattlesnakes but, to their relief, found none. Meeting with the town fathers in January, Marjorie presented a petition to lease the five hundred acres of city land they had chosen for the Stinson School of Flying. Fifty acres were reserved by the U.S. government for an experimental farm, and a small parcel was used as a cemetery; otherwise, there were no claims on the land. Marjorie voiced one objection: The sight of graves being dug would not be encouraging to amateur students in the air, nor make for good flying.

However, on the plus side was the field's location along a road much traveled by tourists—the rich and leisured class, who regarded flying as a sport and would furnish students to the school. For good measure, Marjorie told the commissioners that Houston and other cities were eager to obtain the school, but the school would remain in San Antonio "if a suitable tract of land could be obtained at a reasonable rental." The *San Antonio Express* predicted the lease would be drawn up shortly, providing for a nominal rental and annual renewal. Marjorie's pitch was effective—its practicality appealed to the city fathers—and the growing prominence of the Stinson name in aviation had a certain leverage.

Even before the move to the new field, the school had graduated the first four students, who came with Eddie, and started training six more, who arrived within weeks. Joseph Gorman, the first Canadian graduate, won his license on December 4, 1915, after two weeks of training on Marjorie's "flapper" Wright. The observers for Aero Club were Lieutenants Ira A. Rader and Thomas S. Bowen of the army squad. There were three machines in use, reworked Wrights built from parts bought by Emma at a government sale. Marjorie kept the Wright system, the Canadian students used the three-in-one wheel, and Eddie installed dual wheels on all the aeroplanes like those on the French Deperdussin to conform with aeroplanes in use overseas. Students usually flew both systems.

Gorman had written to the Naval Department in Ottawa, Canada, in November to explain his move to San Antonio from Dayton. He liked the Stinson School for several reasons: There were enough machines and instructors to avoid long delays, the Wright control was used throughout (the wheel was not installed yet), and the flying field was the same as used by the army squadron. A bonus for Gorman was the presence of thousands of troops, which, in addition to the regular course, provided training in scouting work and observing troops on the terrain below.

Gorman's test flights were admirably performed and loudly cheered by the group on the ground. Marjorie had given him a last bit of advice: "Don't forget, Mr. Gorman, start your glide at once if the engine stops." It didn't, and the young Canadian went through his figure eights in consecutive flights, landing within ten feet of the designated marker on the second. Then, before the weather changed, the machine was gassed and oiled, and he took off for the altitude flight. Climbing in wide circles, the barograph strapped on the seat beside him, he continued upward until he more than surpassed the required height, before cutting the motor and gliding down to a gentle landing. (He could land anywhere he chose on this test.) Lieutenants Rader and Bowen signed the proper forms for Aero Club of America certification, and Canada had another volunteer for the Royal Flying Corps. Herbert MacKenzie, the second Canadian graduate, finished his tests on December 5 and left that night with Gorman for Canada. Both men were in England in the new year, training with the Royal Navy.

At Christmastime, Marjorie made a special flight for the children of St. Joseph's Orphanage and the Protestant Orphans' Home. She decided it would be a nice gesture to shower gifts from the sky for the children, many of whom were regular visitors to the field and had caught Marjorie's eye. The *San Antonio Express* explained her reasons: "If you could only see the utter amazement clothing their countenances when someone is in the air—why, you'd appreciate what I'm getting at." The flight wasn't charity; it was a thank-you for the lift she got from their smiling faces. There was a bit of feminine attitude, too. "Men Santas have had the stage long enough," said Marjorie; she would show what a modern Santa could do, minus the reindeer. On December 30, gifts and candies rained down from the sky (Emma was cautioned to select only toys that would survive the drop safely), and when the flight ended, the pilot joined the children to hand out presents to those who failed to get something from the "shower." Souvenir cards were also dropped, undoubtedly designed by Emma.

On January 19, 1916, the school moved to its new location, which is still known as Stinson Field, though greatly reduced in size. The field was ideal. Marjorie never tired of praising it; the ground was level, with no hills for miles to cause adverse currents, air holes or bumps, or sudden wind puffs that veer over hilltops. The main part of the field was rolled; it was as hard and smooth as a floor. Otherwise, the far reaches of the field were a tumble of mesquite and sagebrush. In addition, the genial winter climate (the first students lived in unheated tents without suffering, according to a newspaper account) allowed for aerial activity through much of the winter season. A hangar and a machine shop for the care of aeroplanes were under construction, with quarters for the men next on the list. Tuition was $250 for four hours of training, Marjorie's records note, but there is confusion on that score. A copy of a Stinson contract indicated four hundred dollars as the tuition fee, cash in advance, with the number of hours blank. Another time, Marjorie said the fee was four hundred dollars for four hundred minutes. She was consistent, however, on two other points: There was no deposit for breakage, and the use of the school machine for license tests was free. Students paid the Aero Club five dollars for the license, which came in a blue leather cover.

Running the field was a family affair: Emma was business manager and raised chickens and sheep on the side; Marjorie and Eddie were instructors; Katherine made occasional appearances but never taught, even though her name appeared on the stationery designed by Emma. By April, news of the Stinson School was spreading. *Aerial Age Weekly,* under the headline "Youngest Flyer in America a San Antonio Girl," described the personnel, the school equipment, and the students already successfully graduated. It was excellent publicity.

Writing in 1929 for *Liberty* magazine, Marjorie explained her method of teaching. In case there were doubts about her ability among the young men, she made several short flights to show she could fly safely and the aeroplane was in good order. A lecture followed (as a woman, she felt she had a right to talk a bit) to explain there were only three things to consider in flying: the direction (left or right), the banking (using rudder and ailerons), and the ascent or descent, with examples to clarify each point. Remembering her own training, she promised that each student would have as much control of the machine as possible, but in an emergency she must have control; she would ground anyone who did not relinquish all control at a given signal. "The air is no place to settle a difference of opinion about how to fly." Pointing to a fire extinguisher within reach on the aeroplane, she assured the young men that, if pressed, she would use it, since she couldn't possibly win a physical argument with a heavier student.

That settled, the men drew lots to see who would take the first joy hop. To fill the bill, Marjorie would be flying continually, but since it was for a good cause, she was willing. The first flights lasted about ten minutes, enough to get the embryo pilots used to being in the air and to give them a chance to look around, followed by short flights, which introduced the rudder control to them. The trademark white string was tied on the skid brace in front for directional control. Overcontrol or undercontrol of the rudder made the string fly back at an angle; the error was corrected by flying in the direction in which the string pointed. The string also served as a stall indicator, but Marjorie didn't tell her students about that or how to correct it, because if they stalled, as the string registered, it was too late.

After twenty minutes' practice on the rudder (a lesson usually was four to five minutes), the student was given both the rudder and ailerons to handle, and flying became a little more intricate. When the student was sufficiently advanced, he was given full control, with the addition of the elevator. At this stage, Marjorie said, "I merely sat in the plane and folded my hands," but on many occasions she unfolded them quickly to "get the plane out of a tight place." The students learned to make turns, alternating left and right, wide and easy at first, then gradually tilting the aeroplane and tightening the turns until they could make a sixty-degree bank with confidence. That is when they began to develop flying instinct. Unlike most other training schools, at the Stinson School students flew alone for the first time when they took their tests, which lasted about an hour. That was the Wright method of training.

As important as air time were the discussions following a lesson. Everyone critiqued the performance; each student told what discovery he had made, what error, and how to correct it. Marjorie felt these sessions were very helpful to the students. When they were able to correct an error while flying, she added another skill—landing without power. It was required for the license test but, more important, said Marjorie, "Spot landings without power were an every-flight occurrence." Once a student worked the controls instinctively, Marjorie could then teach him to actually fly in six days.

A stream of students followed in short order after the original four were licensed. Marjorie realized later that she was flying continuously

Marjorie Stinson (right) congratulating her pupil, Marcel Dubuc, on finishing his flying course in record time. LIBRARY OF CONGRESS

for six hours a day. On one particularly cold day, oblivious of the weather, she sat on a lower wing of an aeroplane, concentrating on a succession of students' performances, until one student called a halt. Blue from the cold, her teeth chattering, Marjorie was taken to the nearest household, where she warmed herself near the oven and "drank all the coffee that had been prepared for the family breakfast." When she had thawed out, she walked back to the field and resumed flying. Thereafter, she admitted, she had a teacher's pet; she did her best to get that young man licensed as quickly as possible—in three hours and forty-five minutes. He was not the fastest; Marcel Dubuc from Montreal passed his test after three hours and forty minutes.

Occasionally the school heard from former students overseas. Their letters were full of shoptalk about aeroplanes and how they performed. Gorman was flying a bigger machine with "lots of horsepower." English fliers, he wrote, "used the rudder a great deal and never land unless we are dead into the wind"—this where sea winds "often rise to 50 miles/ hour." Another former student wrote that the government plane was so stable "you can let go controls and she flies herself beautifully, climbing slightly." Its drawback: "no great speed and can't climb fast." The "flying schoolmarm" was proud of her graduates.

Of her many students, eighty-three by one statistic, John Frost, vice president of the Frost National Bank of San Antonio, was unique. He soloed in four hours and passed his tests in May 1916, winning license No. 498, which was usually the last Marjorie saw of her students, but on the following morning, Frost was back again in his Pierce-Arrow roadster. Marjorie landed to see what was wrong—she had been chasing coyotes around the field—and was stunned when Frost said he wanted to take some advanced flying lessons. That sounded interesting, and she agreed. Frost took twelve hours of training; bought a Curtiss JN, "the latest and raciest plane to be had in those days"; laid out a field on his estate; and built a hangar. When the United States entered the war, he was ready and served overseas, winning a Distinguished Service Cross.

During the years the school was operating, one student had his money returned to him with the explanation he would never learn to fly. He habitually froze in the air, holding the controls in a rigid grip that endangered himself and his instructor. Marjorie and Eddie tried talk sessions on the ground, but he froze the next time up. On the day his money was returned, the student inveigled John Frost into taking him up. Too late, Marjorie ran out to stop the flight. Shortly after takeoff, the aeroplane crashed into the mesquite. The student died on the way to the hospital; Frost was in shock but recovered quickly.

The school was running at full speed from daybreak often until night, when bonfires marked the landing place. Sixty-seven lessons were given in one day, a school record that saw Eddie in the air most of the day, with Marjorie doing her share. Canadians were still the greatest number, together with a few National Guard men and civilians. Flying schools around the country were enjoying similar popularity. The cost of lessons was usually a dollar a minute, but a deposit for breakage could raise the price, and some schools charged for the use of a school machine to take license tests.

The continued fighting in Mexico between contending factions brought the local National Guard to Fort Sam Houston before it moved to the border. Marjorie flew for the troops to show what an aeroplane could do and carried cameramen up to photograph the sight of hundreds of tents on the field. She demonstrated bombing techniques, using a floral bouquet instead of the usual flour bombs. Whoever caught the bouquet won a ride with her. Sergeant E. W. Edwards, the largest man in camp, well over six feet, outreached his competitors to win. The losers groused the machine would never get off the ground with his 240 pounds. But it did.

Marjorie, in a letter to her brother Jack years later, recalled another student, named Arbuckle from Oklahoma (nicknamed "Snake"), who was very anxious to learn and couldn't wait to take his tests. When he was ready to go up alone, the weather seemed fine, and Arbuckle took off and began his first set of eights. As he lined up to begin his first turn around the pylon—the Wright was not a speedy machine—the sky darkened rapidly, and a norther (a high, rough wind) blew in. The gang on the ground got the white sheet used to signal a flier down and began to wave it frantically in the center of the field. Arbuckle flew on, oblivious of everything except trying to keep the machine steady and together as he made his turns. When he finished, the norther had subsided a little, and he landed all right, considering the gusty wind. The gang rushed out to meet him, and all he said was, "I had no idea it would be so much bouncier without the instructor aboard. I didn't think the lack of weight would be so noticeable." Marjorie told Jack, "He learned to really fly in the norther." She had a warm spot for him.

One of her most interesting students was Francisco Montes de Orca, from Mexico. He spoke no English; Marjorie spoke no Spanish. All instructions about flying were relayed to Orca through his interpreter, making the learning experience a little awkward in the beginning. Fortunately, he was an excellent student. "Had he not been an exceptionally apt pupil in the air," Marjorie recalled, "the lessons might have proved to be hazardous for us both."

Not all her students were so bright. One young man always flew with the wing low. He seemed sensible on the ground and "on an even keel," but he never flew level. During one of his many sideslips in the air, Marjorie turned to see "whatever in the world he could be thinking about." It turned out he wasn't thinking—he was just gazing at the day moon and chewing gum. On the next flight up, the gum was stuck under the wing, and "the plane flew level for his first time."

During the early months of 1916, Walter Brock, a well-known English builder and pilot, was working at the Stinson School, building new machines for Katherine, Eddie, and Marjorie. On rainy days Marjorie worked with Brock during construction of the aeroplanes, drawing diagrams and copying detailed drawings, experience that taught her a great deal about design and helped her find a job with the government during the war. Two of the aeroplanes, when finished, were flown by Marjorie and Eddie during the summer at Ashburn, the new Aero Club field near Chicago; there, they continued to teach a few Canadian students. Eddie used his Brock regularly; Marjorie probably crashed hers in Ohio. Katherine never flew hers; it sat in a hangar at the school until Emil Laird took it up one day in early 1917 and crashed. Laird built and flew aeroplanes in the early aviation days. Marjorie didn't think much of his flying ability.

Brock called Eddie's machine the Caudron, the French design it resembled. It had a new wing curve, a square elevator, and was stronger to carry a sixty-horsepower Curtiss engine. Marjorie's model, like all the Brocks, was a speedy tractor, a one-seater, strictly for exhibition. Earlier, her favorite machine had been a pusher with a new wing curve, a more streamlined edge than the standard blunt Wright lead edge, covered with doped aeroplane linen. The September 18, 1916, *Aerial Age Weekly* reported that Marjorie flew "the tractor," with its fifty-horsepower engine, "perfectly" the first time at Ashburn, that she was making daily practice flights "preparatory to the exhibition season." A new machine took time to get used to; Marjorie was a careful flier.

She flew at Chicago Heights on the Fourth of July and was listed as a guest with Katherine at the Aviation Day Banquet given by the Chicago Advertising Association. Shortly after, Marjorie was scheduled to appear at Napoleon, Ohio, then Cleveland, where the Industry Exposition Fair was to take place on Labor Day weekend.

For the first time, Marjorie's luck in the air failed her. She crashed her machine at Napoleon and had to borrow an aeroplane for her appearance at Cleveland. Described as "a model used in the United States Army, so constructed that the driver cannot see directly in front of him," the machine was probably a Curtiss tractor or possibly Eddie's Caudron. Certainly Marjorie knew both models, but their different control systems, together with her lack of practice on the tractor, made flying a very different experience.

Takeoff was smooth, according to the *Cleveland Plain Dealer*, but no sooner was the machine barely ten feet off the ground than the young pilot stopped smiling and was seen pulling anxiously at a lever that apparently refused to work. Pointing the aeroplane toward the lake, she turned back abruptly as the machine shot upward. In the next instant, the machine seemed to stop, and a cry went up, softly at first, then shrill: "It's coming down—she's falling!"

The thousands watching below in horror were galvanized into action. Ignoring the police, they raced the ten blocks to where shattered wood and twisted steel marked the machine's fall. A streak of blood colored the length of the machine's floor, the wheels were pushed up through the floor, and the body of the machine was twisted completely around. The injured pilot was taken to German Hospital—miraculously, still alive.

Interviewed the next day, Marjorie admitted to being cut up and sore, but "accidents are bound to happen and until one gets my neck I guess I'm in the business." Marjorie was a trouper. She had a telegram sent to her mother to keep her from worrying. Commenting on the accident in her first and only explanation, she wrote that she had realized the machine wasn't at the height it should have been and a series of scary prospects flashed through her mind: The machine might turn upside down (she wasn't strapped in); it might land on top of her. Unable to stop the engine, the aeroplane "hit the ground head-on going at 50 miles an hour." Except for this brief explanation, Marjorie never mentioned the accident again, so we don't know what really went wrong. Like most fliers, she shut it out of her thoughts; there were more important things to occupy her mind, such as students and machines.

Over a year's time, the constant use of school machines took its toll. Magnetos needed reworking weekly, if not daily. Captain Townsend Dodd of the Army Squadron became a regular at the school, working on magnetos. Grover Loening, an early builder, worked on the collection of parts bought by Emma in 1916 for $350 and fashioned a modified Burgess H aeroplane, used for advanced training. A biplane with a tractor engine, it was designed so that the pilot and wheel control were set back from the engine and propeller. It was very different from the open-front Wright, with pilot and student seated on the lower wing, looking like "so much laundry hung out to dry"—according to Marjorie's description.

When the Aero Club of America had called attention during the summer of 1916 to the need to train men to make "America first in the air," Marjorie responded. James S. Stephens, vice president of the Illinois Aero

Club, speaking in Chicago, deplored the lamentable condition of American aviation in the military action in Mexico. Aeroplanes had demonstrated their usefulness in eliminating the element of surprise and were needed to save American lives, but as John T. McCutcheon of the *Tribune* wrote: "Uncle Sam, inventor of the aeroplane, has only one in service at the front."

In early 1917, to correct that situation, Marjorie organized the Texas Escadrille, patterned after the famous Lafayette Escadrille. Its purpose: to train primarily Texas civilians to serve in the American flying corps. Robert Shank, a Stinson graduate, shared teaching duties with Marjorie, Eddie having left for the Curtiss School in Newport News, Virginia, to join up. A majority of the group of nineteen were from San Antonio, a few from other Texas cities, and four were from out of state. All were eager to win their license and serve in the Aviation Service.

The men became familiar with the Wright pusher and the more up-to-date Burgess and Brock models, which stood on the field. To introduce the controls, Marjorie used a toy model, dipping it first to the left while a student indicated the proper lever on the big machine, then to another position while the student again indicated the right lever. After this session, students were taken up one by one for their taste of aerial flight. Another time, the students were lined up and told to push against the bottom wing of a tractor machine to experience the power of the machine as the propeller and engine worked at different speeds. When the engine speed reached its fastest point, the aeroplane began to move in spite of the best efforts of the men to hold it. In the process, they learned that the engine and wings could withstand much more force and power than appeared at first glance. Daily, Marjorie took the men through the steps that would ready them for their tests.

The declaration of war on April 6, 1917, changed flying in America for good. The military took over aviation activity; civilian flying ceased except for public-service appearances. Schools like the Stinson School were soon closed, their male personnel absorbed by the military. When the war ended, the free-spirited adventure that early flying had been became regulated, organized, and bureaucratic.

Marjorie knew from her sister's experience that there was no place for a woman in wartime aviation. She ended her flying career as it had begun—flying at a fall fair in Texas, this time in Tyler. According to the contract signed by William Pickens and the East Texas Fair of Tyler, Texas, Marjorie would be paid $1,250 each day, "in equal installments," for two flights a day during the five days of the October fair. It was a fitting end.

The Stinson School closed in late 1917. It never made money. As Marjorie observed in later years, "small schools did not charge enough instruction tuition to survive on that alone, even with no salary to the instructors." The costs of good maintenance, fuel, parts, mechanics' salaries, grounds, and buildings were constant. Marjorie put all the money she earned in appearances back into the school, but it always operated close to the edge, with one overriding compensation: knowing that the school performed a badly needed service when few good schools existed. Writing about it in later years, she observed, "Stinson School started on that basis; it didn't just happen. And I would do the same thing again, under like circumstances."

Marjorie had only two women take flying lessons. Though neither of them soloed, Marjorie was confident that both could have safely flown alone had they chosen to. Marjorie had no doubts about the ability of women to fly aeroplanes; their record was there for all to see. In interviews and articles she voiced her opposition to separate flight records for men and women. Women had proved they could compete with men and, certainly, physical strength was not a requirement. But the cost of training was a deterrent. The military services had trained men in great numbers during World War I, creating a sizable reserve air corps; many of these pilots went into civilian flying. Women lacked that opportunity, and the cost of lessons (anywhere from five hundred dollars to twenty-five hundred dollars) was a further hindrance. She was fond of pointing out, however, that once women learned, "they stayed taught."

In 1929 she wrote to the National Aeronautic Association to argue against a suggestion by Amelia Earhart and others that one or several events at the upcoming national air races at Cleveland be exclusively for women. Marjorie was having none of it. The suggestion was an affront to Raymonde de Laroche and the pioneer women who knew nothing of male superiority in flying competitions; women such as Hélène Dutrieu, Ruth Law, and Katherine Stinson had provided excellent examples for men and aided their success. To create separate contests for women would instill in public opinion the idea that women are not as reliable or skillful as men in piloting, which would prevent women from obtaining pilot's positions and create inferiority feelings. As an old flier, she knew there was "no place in aeronautics for an inferiority complex—among women or men."

Marjorie concluded the idea was "mediocre, mid-Victorian and un-American in 1929." Her ire at full boil, she wrote that she would much rather be an "also flyer" in all competitions than a winner in an amateur competition, such as Miss Earhart's plan proposed. It was a tenet of faith: Women were not amateurs!

In 1918 Marjorie moved to Washington, D.C., with money borrowed from a friend. There, she worked first with the army, then as an aeronautical draftsman with the Navy Bureau of Aeronautics. A letter of introduction to Admiral Gregory from W. T. Pratt summed up Marjorie in a nutshell: "She is not a fluffy ruffles sort of person, more intent on meeting some young man in the corridor, but strictly on the job, always tending to her own business. I think you will like her."

Marjorie stayed with the government until her retirement. She kept her interest in aviation alive in a variety of ways: She received a license to fly civilian aircraft in 1919; in April 1919 she flew from Bolling Field to the Polo Field near the White House to aid a Liberty Bond drive; she was issued a Department of Commerce pilot's license, No. P 1600, in 1928 that was valid for four years; in 1927 she helped organize the Early Bird Society, an organization for aviators who had soloed before December 17, 1916, and attended the first meeting in Chicago in 1928. (When an application for membership arrived with references to "he," she crossed out each one and wrote in "she.") She visited Panama in 1928 and flew the length of the Panama Canal in an army plane. She would have preferred piloting herself, but army regulations prevented that. Visiting at the same time were Charles Lindbergh and Lieutenant James Doolittle, in an assembly of famous fliers.

Marjorie enjoyed writing and contributed a number of articles on aviation subjects to various publications, reporting on new developments, the Cleveland Air Races, flying in the early days, women in aviation, and the new air service between Washington, D.C., and New York City. (Passengers had earphones to hear their favorite radio programs!) In 1941 she presented a script on flying to the War Department that was broadcast on more than five hundred radio stations.

She had an idea for an article comparing carrying passengers in 1914–18 with the modern jet service of 1958, for which she wanted to use some of the lyrics from "Come, Josephine, in My Flying Machine." She wrote to Shapiro, Bernstein & Co. Inc. for permission and was turned down. She wrote again pointing out how she planned to use the lyrics— "We loved flying so much we burst into song about it"—and received permission. Marjorie commented she guessed that the "examiner for the publisher would have been far too young to have understood the connection between the title 'Come, Josephine' and the subject matter, anyway."

Writing—letters, articles, complaints—was much a part of the older Marjorie. Her Christmas card for 1953 showed a picture of Marjorie in a Wright Model B just after qualifying for her license, with the caption "Celebrating 50 Years of Powered Flight, 1903–1953." Inside was this verse:

> *Greetings and Wishes for*
> *Worlds of Good Cheer*
> *Flying to You Swiftly*
> *This Yuletime of Year.*

She got a kick out of writing verses to share with friends.

As the years passed, she became a zealous defender of Katherine's and Eddie's aviation reputations, taking up the pen when she thought writers denigrated them. Orville Wright was another cause; she chastised members of the Early Birds who criticized him. A stickler for accuracy, she frequently took writers to task for passing off misinformation in the name of aviation history. Marjorie had the facts, sources, dates, or a photograph to prove her point. She maintained a wide correspondence with early fliers and willingly shared information, pictures, and negatives with interested persons. She amassed a large collection of clippings and articles on the Stinsons and other aviation topics, a marvelous treasure of material, which she gave to the Library of Congress.

Family relations were not cordial in later years. Marjorie visited Katherine only once and saw Jack, her younger brother, infrequently and not always happily. Marjorie had a poor opinion of Katherine's husband,

Miguel Otero and, being Marjorie, she didn't hesitate to express it; the closeness the sisters had shared as youngsters evaporated. She missed Eddie especially. He had been killed in a crash in 1932.

Marjorie never married. She wrote once to a friend that if Katherine, being cute and smart, couldn't do any better than she had done, she (Marjorie) didn't "have a Chinaman's chance." Another time, when asked how she managed to stay single, knowing so many nice aviators, her reply was, "They haven't all proposed."

Less comfortable with the show-business aspect of early aviation than Katherine, Marjorie lacked the kind of personality that thrived on exposure. In later years she preferred to place Katherine and Eddie in the spotlight. Her writing showed wit and common sense—the latter, perhaps, was the real reason she remained single. She liked both her parents and figured that if they hadn't been happy married, perhaps it wasn't such a great idea.

Nostalgia for the early days of flying was strong, despite her interest in the advances in aerial technology. A poem found in her collection probably best expresses her sentiments on the changes in aviation.

> *"The Move Forward"*
> *Once a flight was alright*
> *If you landed upright,*
> *No laws, big skies,*
> *free ai-ah.*
> *Now it's rulings on this*
> *regulations for that*
> *Fair well faithful Wright*
> *rocking chai-ah.*

Upon her death in 1975, her ashes were strewn over Stinson Field in San Antonio from a Curtiss 1931 pusher by arrangement with George Long, a member of the Daedalians, a national fraternity of military aviators. Marjorie had come home.

13
More Rare Birds

OTHER WOMEN HAD taken to the sky in the years before the end of 1916. Although less well known than the Stinsons and Ruth Law, they are visible evidence that women were fascinated by the aeroplane and were eager to try it, provided their family and financial situation allowed. For a few women, aviation was a lifelong pursuit; once experienced, its pull was irresistible. Flying offered excitement, freedom, and an exhilarating feeling of being above the mundane world on the ground.

JULIA CLARK
Julia Clark (sometimes spelled Clarke), the third woman to obtain a pilot's license in America (No. 133), is something of a mystery. Often listed as English and the daughter of a minister, she was born in Bangor, Michigan, December 21, 1880, according to her license certificate. (At the time of her death, *Flight* confused her with Lily Irvine, who was English, reporting that Julia Clark was the name "adopted by Mrs. James V. Martin," and apparently writers continued the error.) She was born Julia Charles to Mrs. Etta Charles. The father's name was not given. Julia was thirty-one years of age when she won her license at the Curtiss School on North Island, San Diego. Within a month, thanks to William Pickens's publicity efforts, she had lost three to eight years of age, to make her more appealing to the public.

According to Julia's own account, she was once a stenographer for "one of the big Aero Clubs of the country," which gave her an opportunity to observe the sport and talk with many of the men fliers. The upshot was predictable: She would learn to fly. Julia had married J. N. Clark, who was reported to be in Ironton, Iowa, at the time of her death. The Clarks were not living together when Julia took up flying. Her mother, when interviewed after Julia's death, said that watching Louis Paulhan at the 1910 Los Angeles meet had triggered Julia's interest in flying. The Charles family and Julia had lived in California for about three years prior to 1912.

When Julia determined to learn to fly, she went first to the Wrights for lessons and, when they refused, she sought out Glenn Curtiss, who also turned her down. Rejection only made her more determined. She bought an aeroplane, a Curtiss biplane; hired a teacher, Lansing Callan; and proceeded to practice on the same field as the Curtiss School. When she had learned to fly a little, Curtiss came to her and said that if she had made up her mind "to get smashed" and nothing could change her plans, he would teach her the rest of "the art of cloud exploring."

Within a month Julia was flying as well as any of the men, and she soloed on May 19, 1912. She sensed that "the men do not fancy my flying" because "they hate to admit or have it proven that a woman can do anything a man can." She was outspoken about her ambition: to make fifty thousand dollars in two years of flying. It was a lot of money, but Julia reasoned she was "playing an unusual role." She had a keen sense of the show-business aspect of flying and hoped to enrich herself from it. Apparently, she was the main support of her mother and two half sisters who had moved to Denver after three years in California.

As soon as Julia passed her tests, she signed to appear on June 21 and 22 in Springfield, Illinois, in an air meet billed as a "Three Ring Aerial Circus." Appearing with the boy aviator—Farnum T. Fish, age sixteen—Julia, "the Winged Suffragette," would fly in the race of nations. Aerial baseball, altitude trials, and mail-carrying flights each day would give the crowd "a run for its money." The publicity churned out by Pickens touted Julia as English, which may have started the mistake in her nationality.

Julia arrived in Springfield about a week before the meet. She had done little practicing since her tests in May. Once her machine was uncrated and assembled, she took it up late in the afternoon of the 17th to practice new tricks for the coming meet, which advertised her as the "first woman to fly in the middle west." According to the *Rocky Mountain News,* she may have had a premonition of disaster. Using a machine rejected by another aviator, which she had tagged No. 13, she left a note asking that she be cremated if she were killed.

The Curtiss machine went up easily, circled the fairgrounds, then, as it prepared to land, the tip of a wing struck the limb of a tree in the center of the racetrack enclosure. The machine fell to the ground, turning turtle, pinning the pilot underneath. Her skull was crushed, there were several serious breaks, and Julia died a few minutes after reaching the hospital, never regaining consciousness.

Marjorie Stinson, who researched the question of Julia's nationality, wrote of the crash: "Her plane was gathered up and shipped to the factory, but Mrs. Clark's remains did not fair so well. She was abandoned at the morgue, with a broken skull, shoulder and thigh, dead, unclaimed." When word arrived from her mother, the body was taken to the Metcalf undertaking establishment and prepared for shipment. On the evening of June 19 her body was shipped to Denver on orders from H. C. Ulen, whose company had employed Julia in earlier years in Chicago. Ulen paid the expenses Julia had incurred in Springfield and accompanied the body to Kansas City, where another Ulen employee took over for the journey to Denver. Julia's husband remained in Ironton. According to the *State Register,* H. C. Ulen spoke very highly of the deceased, who "had been deserted by her friends in the aviation world."

Julia's career ended before she debuted. Her proficiency as a flier is questionable—we cannot really judge. There is much we don't know about her life, but one distinction is hers, a dubious one: She was the first woman pilot in America killed in an aeroplane crash. Poor Julia! Two weeks later, Harriet Quimby became the second woman pilot to die in a crash.

BERNETTA MILLER

Bernetta Adams Miller followed Katherine Stinson to become the fifth American woman to win a pilot's license. Born in Canton, Ohio, on January 11, 1886, Bernetta was graduated from Genesee (New York) Normal School. She tried to establish a career in business but gave it up for flying.

Bernetta A. Miller learned to fly at the Moisant Aviation School on Long Island. Here she is standing in front of a Moisant monoplane. CRADLE OF AVIATION MUSEUM, GARDEN CITY, NEW YORK

In the summer of 1912 she enrolled at the Moisant School in Mineola, on Long Island, New York, where Shakir S. Jerwan was the instructor. For the next two months and three days, she followed the same course of instruction under Jerwan's tutelage as Quimby and Moisant had before her: first, grass-cutting in the single-seater machine with only verbal comments, gradually progressing to short straightaway hops. Bernetta wrote years later that she came closer to death in the grass-cutting stage than when flying thousands of feet in the air or in landing.

Apparently, the chief construction mechanic had been working on the machine and had whittled away part of the block that kept the machine from taking to the air. Suddenly a surprised Bernetta was in the air, before hitting the ground. It could have been serious, but she was only shaken up. When she had mastered control sufficiently, she advanced to a fifty-horsepower Gnome engine Moisant monoplane, on which she practiced for a month for her pilot's tests.

By early September she was ready, but the weather was uncooperative. Finally, on September 16 she completed her tests in a manner that was pure Bernetta, before Aero Club observers club secretary Delano and

Lieutenant Gustave Salinas of the Mexican Army. It was a night flight. The *Sun* described her flight as something out of the ordinary: "Moon Blinks to See Girl Win Air License." Her competency was apparent in the confident way she took off—holding steady in choppy air—and headed skyward fifteen hundred feet, as required before turning downward to perform ten figure eights around flags held by observers. Writing later about her test, Bernetta said the darkening sky and evening mist made distinguishing the markers difficult. When it was time to land, she flew over the landing area several times, unable to see the marker. Fortunately, the observers on the ground realized her predicament and raised a white sheet so she could land "in proper order." The *Sun* congratulated her on landing but twenty feet from the designated spot.

Following measurements of the landing, the sealed barograph was taken for examination and ten days later "the little leather booklet" reached her, the official proof that she was the 173rd to receive the Fédération Aéronautique Internationale aviator's license. Bernetta always counted herself the third woman in America to win it, unaware of Julia Clark and Katherine Stinson, who preceded her.

Learning to fly an aeroplane proved easier for Bernetta than finding the right costume for flying. The shops offered nothing, she told journalist Elizabeth Hiatt Gregory years later, that would individualize a person. Consequently, she dreamed up her own costume: a hunting suit, which included boots, of course, with a hat especially designed to stay on the head. The costume seemed all right then, but "now it is a scream."

As a member of a very select group of women, Bernetta dreamed of a career in aviation and was disappointed when it failed to develop. She was not interested in exhibition flying, being much too rational to indulge in the acrobatic activities that were part of flying at that time. She signed on as a Moisant flier and flew regularly to gain experience, but she eschewed the carnival aspect of exhibitions.

In October, Bernetta was chosen to demonstrate the Moisant monoplane to the government in College Park, Maryland, where the Army Signal Corps had a training school. She had no illusions about her choice. Many people considered the monoplane to be particularly dangerous and difficult to fly because of the prominent success of the Wright and Curtiss biplane models. Bernetta knew the Moisant Company hoped she could overcome some of the fears by showing "if a mere woman could learn to fly one, so surely could a man."

Recalling her experience, Bernetta wrote that her arrival at College Park came at a bad time. A fatal crash the day before, its cause unknown, made the army pilots, Henry "Hap" Arnold among them, greet her with tolerant skepticism and no real enthusiasm. Their feeling was: "It was bad enough to shovel up a man; they did not welcome the idea of having to shovel up a woman."

Harold Kantner, another Moisant pilot, was also at College Park with Bernetta. A careful pilot, not given to stunting, he was killed later in an aeroplane accident. Kantner had made it clear to Bernetta that he did not approve of women's flying, which did not contribute to the venture of demonstrating the monoplane. Bernetta readily admitted that Kantner was a better aviator than she—he was a year ahead of her—and, more important, he was an excellent mechanic.

During the week at College Park, Bernetta seemed to get all the publicity, which didn't help relations with Kantner, although he made a memorable flight from the airfield to Washington, D.C., and returned. She remembered being questioned endlessly by reporters at the Willard Hotel: "Why do you want to fly?" Another reporter studied her at a distance for hours, behavior that translated to Bernetta as "how queer journalists thought aviators were."

Orville Wright had come to College Park to investigate the Wright aeroplane crash. A date was arranged to introduce Bernetta to him. On that day one of the pilots had taken up one of the rebuilt Wright biplanes and was stunting with it, instead of giving it a shakedown flight, when Wright appeared on the scene. Bernetta recalled, "A madder man I had never seen as he made a rush from the field. It was not time for introductions." She made a number of flights during the week but kept no log. While none of the flights was far or outstanding, "at least there were no accidents." Unlike aeroplanes the army pilots flew, the Moisant monoplane landed with full power, because there was no way to regulate it. Wing loadings were probably never more than three or four pounds to the square foot, and the pilots knew nothing of aerodynamics.

Bernetta was told to try landing with what is known today as a "dead stick." A briefing might have helped first. The sensation of gliding through the air without power was eerie; the wind whistling through the wire, uncanny, For a pilot who had never made a bad landing, this time it was bumpy—fortunately, on bicycle tires.

Adding to Bernetta's discomfort, the field at College Park was not a suitable flying field. The takeoff and landing area had woods on one side of the uneven field, while train tracks, telegraph poles, and wires bordered the other. There were no nearby emergency landing spots, other than swampy earth with stumps of trees still standing, which were not always visible from the air. The field was a far cry from the Mineola site on Long Island.

The Moisant demonstration failed to change the government's opinion on aeroplanes. Biplanes remained the choice for the infant flying service. However, Bernetta enjoyed her visit, found Washington people friendly, and regretted later that she had not agreed to fly over Washington during a suffrage parade. Uncertain of her bearings in a strange landscape—"geography has such a way of changing when one is in the air"—and realizing she was inexperienced, really a fledgling flier, she declined the offer to be the first woman to fly over Washington. "Sensible" was the word for Bernetta.

Returning to Long Island, she continued to practice, hoping to extend the women's altitude record. On January 20, just ahead of a fierce winter storm rolling in from the west, she reached eighteen hundred feet, the cold so intense that she had just decided to come down when the dome of the oil register on her machine cracked with a sharp bang. At once, oil spattered her face, almost blinding her. Acting quickly, she turned off her motor and volplaned to the ground, landing within yards of where she went up. The *New York Herald,* the only paper to mention the event, wrote: "She has postponed her next altitude flight until warm weather."

Little is known of Bernetta's activities in the next several years. An undated special to the *New York Herald* indicated movies would be made of her flying the Moisant monoplane, which would be used to instruct future aerial pupils before they go up. Apparently she flew for her own sport for a while before giving it up completely.

An unidentified newspaper clipping in 1913 related her thoughts under the heading: "Woman Aviator Regrets It." The article quoted Bernetta's belief that "aviation is dead." Citing the lack of government interest or assistance and the misplaced emphasis on getting rich rather than love of the sport or the idea of doing anything for posterity, the article was a painful comment from a serious flier. Pointing to European countries that were doing wonders, she noted they were not trying to make money out of aviation. The governments were paying the toll, "but not for spectacular purposes." They were experimenting and giving assistance. Miller hated to see the country "that made flying possible allow other nations to excel us in its perfecting."

From time to time, Bernetta wrote about her early experiences and corresponded with Elizabeth Hiatt Gregory, a journalist interested in women's role in aviation from the earliest days. In a 1935 letter, she suggested that Gregory might do an interesting article from the psychological standpoint on why "so many women went into the game and out so soon. . . . Did they find it too expensive as I did or did they make enough to retire? I doubt that they lost nerve." Then later: "Of course in those days, there wasn't so much that a woman could do unless she had tremendous backing and so many men expressed themselves as not wanting to see a woman shovelled up." Miller was cheered by Amelia Earhart's performance. "Fortunate she to have a husband who is interested and ready to greet her at every arrival."

During the First World War, Bernetta, her love of adventure and desire to be useful still intact, served overseas with the YMCA as an accountant, then moved to the front, assigned to the 325th Regiment, Eighty-second Division. Sent to the Toul sector of France, she "rendered the greatest services before and during the St. Mihiel offensive, caring for the wounded in the advance field hospital. She was in the Argonne during the last offensive." The French government honored her with the Croix de Guerre, and the American military recognized her services with a citation.

Following the war, she worked at educational institutions, notably as bursar for the American College in Constantinople (now Istanbul) for seven years, before returning to America in 1933. She tried freelance writing, but the Depression economy made this difficult. That same year, she found a job as bookkeeper at St. Mary's Hall-on-the-Delaware, a school for girls, in Burlington, New Jersey, where she remained until 1941.

Years later a colleague at the school wrote her impressions of Bernetta Miller. Unquestionably, "she was an individual!" A tall woman with short hair, she might have been considered plain except for "her smiling, friendly manner." She cared little for dress; she would never be "modish." Her friends learned she had traveled all over Europe, liked beer, and had a passion for oriental rugs. She was a collector and connoisseur of antique orientals, which, as needed, she shampooed on hands and knees.

One day, a story buzzed around the school that Bernetta had been an aeroplane pilot, the second woman in America. When a colleague confronted her—had she ever been a pilot?—her face became expressionless for some seconds, then she relaxed and nodded her head. Was she really the second? "No," she replied. "I was the third." In the conversation that followed, it was apparent she did not miss flying. For excitement, she thought stunts in a Chris-Craft "lots more fun!"

In 1941, Bernetta became assistant to Dr. Frank Aydelotte, director of the Institute for Advanced Study at Princeton. She remained there until her retirement in 1948, ending a career of more than twenty years in education. She lived quietly in New Hope, Pennsylvania, until her death in 1972 at eighty-six years of age. She was almost blind in later years, and the beloved rugs were her security. She sold some, one at a time, to the Philadelphia Museum of Art for its fine collection.

Bernetta Miller, fifth licensed woman pilot in America, closed the door on her early career when aviation failed to offer real advancement. Her education, interests, and a wish to be useful carried her to distant parts of the globe, which she explored avidly—on the ground. For her, the skies held no more fascination.

FLORENCE SEIDELL AND MRS. RICHBERG HORNSBY

Four more women won pilot's licenses before the end of 1916: Florence Seidell, Mrs. Richberg Hornsby, Dorothy Rice Peirce, and Helen Hodge Harris. They all broke out of the accepted role for women of their generation. Because they had sufficient financial help, they were able to fly for their own amusement, without the need to pay their way.

Florence Seidell, born on June 15, 1885, in Lebanon, Kansas, received license No. 258, having passed her tests on June 20, 1913, at Griffith Park, Los Angeles, flying a Curtiss pusher. Glenn L. Martin, who had taught her to drive her first automobile six years earlier, gave her lessons in the early months of 1913 at Newport Bay, California, on a hydro-aeroplane. (Martin had a second school for land aeroplanes at Griffith Park.) Florence made the cover of *Aero and Hydro,* March 8, 1913, carrying a passenger over Newport Bay. The daughter of a wealthy family, Florence flew solely for her own amusement.

Mrs. Richberg Hornsby's story is similar. Born on November 26, 1887, in Chicago, she trained at the Wright School in Dayton, where she passed her tests on June 12, 1914, to win license No. 301, the first woman graduated by the school. She and Marjorie Stinson were the only two women trained at Dayton before the First World War. Mrs. Hornsby, the daughter of a Chicago lawyer, had married two years before she took up flying, but was separated from her husband. Again, the story ends there.

DOROTHY RICE PEIRCE

On August 17, 1916, Dorothy Rice Peirce (later "Sims") qualified for license No. 561 at Mineola, New York, the tenth American woman to become a pilot. She trained on a Wright biplane, and with luck and some skill she passed her tests.

Dorothy was born into a family of characters on June 24, 1892, in Hollywood, New Jersey, according to Aero Club records. The family's hallmark was doing what they liked, when they liked. Her book, *Curiouser and Curiouser* (1940), with an introduction by George Kauffman, confirms the freewheeling home atmosphere, where children dropped out of school because they disliked it to pursue at home with tutors whatever interest caught their fancy. Both parents were musical, but the children would have none of that. Dorothy, by turns, took up skating, motorcycling, and painting. Eventually, she turned to flying.

She met her first husband, Waldo Peirce, in Spain, where she was studying art. The war came, and Waldo stayed in Europe to drive an ambulance. Dorothy went home, resolved to get into the war. She would fly!

She went to the Wright office inquiring about lessons—two hundred minutes for two hundred dollars—but then discovered the school wouldn't take her. Dorothy was determined and badgered the staff for four hours, until the office manager gave in. Robert Rinehart was her teacher, and in due course Dorothy soloed on August 17, 1916, and won her license. According to Dorothy, she was good at flying because of her sense of balance learned from cycling and skating.

She bought a used aeroplane, powered by a Gnome motor, that was built by a farmer in New Jersey, and set about looking for passengers to take up. Her mechanic, a solemn Swede named Bangs, tended to discourage would-be riders, asking, "You're not going to go up with *her*, are you?" As a result, passengers were hard to come by.

Even harder was finding people who would take her wish to fly for the military seriously. Turned down by the navy and the army, she visited Theodore Roosevelt at his home on Long Island. He was "very sweet except for the details." Rocking in his favorite chair, he said "no" to everything Dorothy proposed. Women should not go to war; they should not fly aeroplanes. Dorothy next tackled General Leonard Wood, who was understanding but said the matter was out of his hands; he couldn't get her into the military.

In the meantime she had met Lawrence Sperry, son of Elmer Sperry, inventor of the gyroscope, who had made a self-flying gadget he wanted to market. He was happy to ride with Dorothy. On one particular flight, to show his confidence in the gadget, he walked out on the wing of the aeroplane. The machine fell eight hundred feet into ten feet of water in Great South Bay, a tangled mess of wires. Dorothy broke her back and was in a cast for six weeks, but she didn't blame Sperry. The two had spent considerable time together and were talking marriage and a flight to Europe. As soon as she was on her feet, Dorothy divorced Waldo, but plans for the European flight fell apart, and the romance cooled.

Columbia University, eager to organize a flying unit, had contacted Dorothy, while she had an aeroplane, to see if she would teach young men to fly. She would be happy to do so, but before official papers were signed, the mothers of the Columbia students bought an aeroplane and Dorothy was no longer needed.

One good thing came from that experience—Dorothy met Hal Sims, a wounded airman back from France and the adviser for the project. He was much taken with Dorothy in spite of her ignorance of mechanics and the technical side of flying. They married, Hal went back to France, and within weeks the armistice ended the war. Dorothy's flying career ended too.

She returned to painting, exhibited in New York City, sculpted, played championship bridge, and was a world traveler. One has the feeling that she learned to fly because it was new and exciting—possibly she had visions of flying in France—before moving on to the next pursuit. Her parents had always encouraged her, certain she had genius, but, as an adult, Dorothy admitted she was never sure what her genius was. She was never dull.

HELEN HODGE HARRIS

Helen Hodge Harris, the eleventh American woman pilot, won license No. 633 after completing her tests on November 12, 1916. She claimed two distinctions: first woman west of Chicago to win a license (she was unaware of Julia Clark and Florence Seidell), and the last American woman to receive a license before the war.

Born in Omaha, Nebraska, on August 2, 1892, she became interested in flying in 1916, seven years after marrying Ralph Newbre in Oakland, California. She tried to train at the Christofferson School in San Francisco, was turned down because of her sex, and refused to take no for an answer. She was accepted, finally, as a student, provided she took the same courses as the men. Consequently, Helen studied engines, aeroplane construction, and the theory of flight as it was at that time. Her actual flying lessons began with Frank Bryant on a Curtiss-type biplane on the field at Redwood City. Having won her license, she flew mainly for her own enjoyment. During the war she taught cadets to fly and made an occasional exhibition flight for the school.

On one such flight in a pusher before a group of dignitaries, the motor mount broke and the motor fell out of the aeroplane. The cool-headed pilot landed the powerless aeroplane by "taking the controls in her hand and climbing out on the front wheel to nose it down." Helen was uninjured and finished the exhibition in a machine new to her and the school, the China Tractor. She had the kind of confidence great aviators possess.

After the death of her first husband, Helen moved south and three years later married Frank Harris in Los Angeles, where she became supervisor of a machine shop making special aeroplane tools and finishing equipment. Directing a workforce of twenty men and fourteen women, Helen could operate lathes, milling machines, and precision grinders if needed, thanks to her early training.

She died in Pomona, California, in 1967, a staunch believer to the end that "nothing is impossible."

These were not the only women flying by any means. Newspaper accounts from the period indicate that others were taking to the air, but they were not serious professionals. They enjoyed the sport of flying the same as driving an automobile, horseback riding, or golf. Some, like Mary Sims Heinrich and Jean Doty Caldwell, were earnest students but gave up aviation to please a husband or family. Inez Eye studied at the

Walden Monoplane Company on Long Island; she learned to fly but never got a license.

Geneve Shaffer Parsons claimed to have flown an aeroplane, built by her brother, Cleve, in the San Bruno hills near San Francisco in 1909. Cleve was an aviation enthusiast and founder of the Pacific Aero Club. The flight was a onetime occurrence. Some five months later, Geneve made a balloon ascension that ended in the drink near San Francisco. At this point she gave up aerial adventures to please her worried mother and is unknown in the record books.

Other young women were flying on the plains of the Alameda near Oakland in Silas Christofferson biplanes. Among them were Helen Gray, Barbara Miller, and Helen Audeffred. Flying was the in pastime among the social set, with this added fillip: There was a "subtle thing about it that makes one feel something above a mere human being." Helen Audeffred found this appeal irresistible. However, none of these young women qualified for the Early Birds.

HILDER SMITH

Hilder Smith, like Blanche Stuart Scott and others, flew for several years and didn't bother to win a license. She discovered aviation when her husband, Floyd Smith, decided to build an aeroplane after performing for five years on the trapeze and high ropes in a circus.

Hilder and Floyd grew up within thirty-five miles of each other in Illinois, but it was in California, when she was sixteen, that they first met. Floyd was an aerialist with the Flying Sylvesters, an occupation her father frowned upon, but in spite of his opposition, the two young lovers married, and Floyd began to teach Hilder the art of trapeze performing. She was soon a member of the act.

Then in 1911, Floyd decided he wanted to build an aeroplane and try a new kind of aerial performance. He studied aeronautics for a couple of months and began construction in January 1912 at Santa Ana. (The clown from their aerial act lived there.) Hilder worked as mechanic.

The Smiths made their first flight in June, after practicing for five days in a field in Santa Ana. Hilder—Floyd always called her Sis—was a willing passenger on most of the flights. The field was not perfect— roughly two blocks by three blocks with trees and wires surrounding the open space—and the machine had to circle several times to clear the trees and wires, but it flew. The motor that powered the machine came from Glenn Martin, who was also working in Santa Ana. When the farmer who owned the field appeared one night demanding five dollars a day for its use, the Smiths flew their aeroplane the next morning to Griffith Park in Los Angeles, about forty-five miles away, flying most of the trip in fog. It was a remarkable feat for a first aeroplane flight.

The couple were soon making appearances throughout the Midwest, on five hundred dollars borrowed from Floyd's mother. It was a picaresque existence, with motor problems, a drunken mechanic, crashes, and dishonest show promoters. After one misadventure too many, Floyd discovered the problem with his motor, made the needed adjustment, and became his own mechanic from then on. This experience led to employment with Glenn Martin as a mechanic. In 1914 he was promoted to chief pilot and, as usual, Sis was involved.

Martin, hired to put on a show for the opening of the Los Angeles Harbor, wanted a young woman to parachute from an aeroplane at the celebration. Sis made a deal: She would do the jump and in return she could fly Martin aeroplanes as long as "she didn't bend them." According to the agreement, Hilder was taught by Arthur Burns, flight instructor for the Glenn L. Martin Aviation School at Griffith Park. Flying a Martin pusher biplane, she soloed during the summer of 1914, and, in turn, took up other students as passengers.

In the next several years, Hilder flew various Martin machines, including the TT biplane with a Curtiss OX-5 engine, which qualified her for membership in the OX-5 Club, a group of pioneer aviators. A letter from Art Burns testified she had indeed flown that machine with that engine to take her girlfriends up for rides. Other testimonials, establishing when she soloed, made her eligible for the Early Bird Society, for whom, in later years, she verified membership applications in the Los Angeles area.

Hilder could repair wings and shape struts with the best of aeroplane builders. When trapeze work was just a memory, she remained an avid aviation fan. She was, unquestionably, a can-do woman.

ALYS McKEY BRYANT

Alys McKey Bryant was a woman to be reckoned with. Of stocky build, she could box and she was self-reliant, intelligent, and a whiz with anything that required the use of her hands. Born on an Indiana farm, on April 28, 1880, one of three children left motherless while young, she learned mechanics from her father, an inveterate tinkerer. The family moved to Boise, Idaho, where her father owned the first electric car in town. As a schoolgirl, Alys wrote an essay describing an imaginary flight across the country from New Jersey to California in an electric-powered craft. She had no idea of aeroplane travel at that time, but on her first glimpse of an aeroplane, she recognized its potential.

In 1911, Alys was teaching home economics in California, a science she had learned at boarding school, and she was among the cheering crowds at Pasadena when Calbraith Rodgers landed at the end of his cross-country flight on November 5. The following year an advertisement in a newspaper for a woman pupil to learn flying caught her eye. The ad was placed by Fred Bennett, who managed the Bryant Brothers Aerial Show. The brothers—John, Henry, and Frank—made their home at Palm Springs, with a flying field in the side yard. Alys applied and was chosen because she had driven a motorcycle, a feat that impressed Bennett. Before instruction could begin, however, the Bryants' aeroplane had to be repaired following a bad crash. Alys pitched in and proved very handy with bamboo, steel tacks, piano wire, and the muslin used to cover the top surface of the wings.

By fall, the machine was ready, and Alys practiced in the single-seater, following instructions from Johnny Bryant on the ground. The machine was a Curtiss-type pusher with an old sixty-horsepower motor, the type Curtiss used in his 1909 flight down the Hudson. Alys once said the motor had been used by every flier in southern California; the aeroplane was definitely a home-built model. By December, Alys had soloed without benefit of an Aero Club observer—there was only one on the entire Pacific Coast at that time. Alys never had the opportunity to be observed, according to her Early Bird application, but she had plenty of witnesses to her flying ability.

In 1913, Bennett booked the Bryant show for appearances in the United States and Canada. With a number of exhibitions scheduled in the Northwest, the Bryants moved operations to Seattle, on the filled ground at Harbor Island. There, by April, Johnny and Alys were readying their machine for appearances and making flights to demonstrate their ability to the sponsors of the upcoming Potlatch celebration. Johnny's night flight with flares lighting the sky proved a sensation. Unsuspecting viewers thought it was a comet of "most extraordinary behavior."

A happy Alys McKey Bryant at the end of a successful flight in Vancouver, July 1913. She taught home economics in California before deciding to learn to fly.

INTERNATIONAL WOMEN'S AIR AND SPACE MUSEUM, INC.

In May, Alys flew her first exhibition flight for money at the Blossom Festival in North Yakima, Washington, followed by the Rose Carnival in Portland, Oregon, in June and the annual Seattle Potlatch in July, to celebrate the arrival of the first shipment of gold out of Alaska. Then it was on to Canada. At the end of July she flew for Edward, Prince of Wales, and his brother, George, at Vancouver, before moving to Victoria, British Columbia, where she chalked up two honors: first woman to fly in the Pacific Northwest and first woman to fly in Canada. (Eileen Vollick was the first Canadian woman to win a pilot's license, No. 77, in 1928.)

The constant proximity of the Bryant fliers had a romantic result: Alys and Johnny became husband and wife on May, 29, 1913, in Boise; the summer would be a long celebration of flying. Alys became something of a celebrity and was interviewed by the newspapers where she appeared.

At her first public exhibition, the *Yakima Daily Republic* described her as "athletic, loves outdoor sports, bikes, motorcycles" and she had "learned everything" about the mechanical parts of an aeroplane. Determined to be her own mechanic, she "trusts nothing to so-called experts," believing that many fatalities are due to pilot's "lack of knowledge of airships and their parts." Not too surprising, she was certain that women had a role to play in aviation as well as men.

By the first days of August, the Bryants were in Victoria in readiness for the exhibition on the 5th. Alys was the first to go up at Victoria, discovering immediately that a hard wind from the Pacific was buffeting the machine like a feather. After sixteen minutes in the air, she gave up her plan to circle the Parliament buildings and came down, telling reporters afterward, "I don't want a ride like that again. It was the roughest, toughest and most fearsome flight I have so far experienced."

The next day Johnny flew over the center of Victoria at about eight hundred feet in the teeth of another strong westerly wind. As he dropped downward to about four hundred feet for a landing in the harbor, the machine suddenly went into a dive. Bryant was seen struggling with the steering controls; the machine bucked up for an instant, a wing crumpled, then the aeroplane drifted and fell heavily on the roof of the Lee Dye Building in the Chinese block, some five hundred feet from the water. Apparently Bennett had advised Bryant not to fly with the added weight of the pontoon for a water landing, but the thousand-dollar fee was forfeited if he didn't fly. Alys, watching the disaster from the Marine Building, ran toward the spot where the machine went down. When told by the police chief that Johnny was dead, she collapsed.

Newspapers the next day featured a story by Bennett, stating that the crash was due to Bryant's good nature. In Vancouver a heavy woman had insisted on having her picture taken seated in the aeroplane. Climbing into the machine, she lost her balance and threw her full weight against the steering column, causing a curve-shaped bend in the column. The column was straightened, but in the rush of shipping the aeroplane and adjusting a new motor in Victoria, Johnny had neglected to reinforce the tube with more metal.

According to Bennett, as Johnny came down from eight hundred feet, the pressure of the wind pushing against the wings caused the steering column to go. His attempt to level the aeroplane from its downward plunge by seizing the control for the elevating plane and pulling up had been too vigorous. The machine came up into the wind "with a fearful leap"; probably a strut snapped off, the supporting wires gave way, causing a wing to collapse, and the machine fell downward heavily. Bryant was dead at the scene.

The following day, his body was shipped to Seattle, then on to Los Angeles, accompanied by Alys and Bennett. The thousand-dollar fee owed to Bryant shrank: Four hundred dollars was forfeited for flights not made, and a sum was deleted to repair the damage to the house where the accident occurred. The balance paid to Alys was about three hundred dollars, according to newspaper accounts.

Bryant's manager was shaken by the pilot's death and the loss of the aeroplane. When Alys indicated she would continue to fly, Bennett said for publication: "Alys McKey Bryant is the best woman flier in the world today, but she will never lose her life flying for me. Now that Johnny is dead, I fear she will become reckless and she has been too game and too brave for me to permit her to fly any more." He didn't know Alys very well.

The months and years after Johnny's death were difficult for Alys. There is a question about how much flying she did, but apparently she did take to the air again. In October, a *Seattle Daily Times* article revealed she planned a flight around the Smith Building in Seattle, to be filmed by a movie crew showing the movements of the controls as the machine circled the building. If she flew, it was at Harbor Island; there is no record of a flight around the Smith Building. Alys had told the *Times* reporter the lure of the air was too strong; like Beachey, she couldn't give it up.

In November, before Alys left the Seattle area, the *Seattle Sunday Times* carried an article on her "sensational stunt under water." Dressed in full diving gear, she went down in the West Waterway to attach a heavy chain cable to a huge pipe the Finch Deep Sea Divers were removing to make way for new supply pipes. She was down for twelve minutes, performing operations as directed by Captain Finch, with a diver's head telephone. The Finch operation was close to the hangar on Harbor Island; Alys had made friends with the divers and was interested in learning a new skill, one that she could perform when needed.

The following July, the Potlatch Girl was back again for the 1914 festival. According to a Seattle newspaper article, friends were urging her to quit. "It's my profession—my work," was her answer. She would try for an altitude mark with the men; the current record of more than sixteen thousand feet was held by Silas Christofferson. Her machine was described in full—a headless biplane, a Christofferson-Curtiss model built for climbing, powered by an eighty-horsepower Hall-Scott engine with a special carburetor that adjusted to atmospheric changes.

The Seattle press was full of hype. Alys, sounding uncharacteristically morbid, was quoted as wanting to go like Johnny. It was better than being injured and living a half-life for years. Like most fliers, she didn't think of danger when in the air. She was tense beforehand, but once in the machine and in the air "I am perfectly calm." Asked about a role for women in aviation, she was not optimistic. "Most women fear high altitudes and space. That is fatal to successful flying." True or not, Alys was not like most women—neither were her sisters who took to the air. Despite the press play, there is no record of Alys's flying at Seattle. She was scheduled to fly at Wallace, Washington, on the Fourth of July, but poor weather and an anxious manager scratched that appearance. It seemed to be a pattern.

The following year Alys worked at the Benoist Aircraft Company at St. Louis, then at Sandusky, Ohio, where she served as an instructor and did some flying. In 1916 she worked briefly as an instructor at the Scientific Aeroplane Company flying school at Stratford, Connecticut, then next appeared visiting her brother, in Virginia. Alys offered her services as an air scout to the District of Columbia National Guard. According to the *Washington Post,* she refused to believe she would be discriminated against because of her sex: "Her record surpasses that of many masculine aviators." All true, but the National Guard replied there was little chance of service for a woman except possibly in case of war. (The military action on the Mexican border was not considered a war.)

Alys worked briefly at an aviation plant in New Jersey, where, for seventeen and a half cents an hour, she supervised fourteen hundred women covering wing frames with fabric. She left in disgust and went to Ohio, where she worked again with Tom Benoist building aeroplanes—she may have tested new models—before joining Goodyear Tire and Rubber Company during World War I.

The *Akron Sunday Times* featured her on June 30, 1918. Describing her various energetic pursuits (including boxing), the article revealed that Alys once said she could eat eight meals a day—"She looked it," commented the reporter—but was now surviving on three to help the war effort. Her attempts to serve in the war—she applied six times to different branches of the government—were unsuccessful. The government's policy of "men only" in the military was especially annoying to Alys because she knew women were perfectly capable of replacing men to fly the new aerial mail routes. Dressed in a jumper and overalls, Alys provoked quite a bit of comment in the Goodyear lunchroom. (Despite the obvious practicality of pants, the appearance of a woman in a divided skirt was enough to rate a headline in many newspapers. Pants were still shocking.)

With the war's end, Alys had big plans. The *Sandusky Register* reported that she hoped to put the city on the aviation map by taking over the plant of Tom Benoist, who had died in a streetcar accident, and build aeroplanes. Alys anticipated an aviation boom; when that happened, she hoped to be ready. In the meantime, she was working on motors and parts, as she had done for Benoist.

The East End Bay, off Sandusky, was ideal for airboats. She had Benoist's big boat and hoped to have it flying by June 1, along with another. She had a contract to carry passengers from Cedar Point to different locations, which could be a successful operation, but her first interest was making Sandusky an aviation center. In August, the *Cleveland News* reported that a taxi service between Cedar Point and Cleveland, a sixty-mile distance, would be run by a woman. Alys had received permission from the Sandusky city commissioners for the proposal, with stations at Bayview Park, Cedar Point, and Put-In-Bay. If needed, a station at Cleveland would be built, with expansion to Toledo and Detroit in time. Alys could carry as many as twelve passengers in an airboat, and she hoped to have three machines ready shortly.

Unfortunately, she was ahead of her time. Lacking a pilot's license and financial backing, and with aeroplanes to be had everywhere after the war, her plans failed to jell. When next we hear of her, Alys was constructing Washington, D.C.'s first airport to open an aviation service, near the site of the old Hoover Field, in 1921. She cleared trees and brush and leveled the ground with a tractor; it was hard physical work. This aviation venture was short-lived, however. Her pilot and partner killed their first passenger in a crack-up.

In the early 1930s, Alys was photographed working at the Aerological Division of the U.S. Weather Bureau. This should have been a permanent job, but, during much of the 1930s, she earned a living making jewelry and cosmetic products, which she sold to local department stores and throughout the South.

In 1934 she worked with Paul Garber repairing what was left of the original *Vin Fiz,* the aeroplane Cal Rodgers used to fly across the country. How much of the machine was authentic is debatable. Alys thought two or three parts at most, but the *Vin Fiz* name on the rudder fin looked like what she had seen years before at Pasadena.

In 1938 she received a happy remembrance from Canada—the Philatelists of Vancouver sent her an air-mail cachet commemorating the twenty-fifth anniversary of the first flight made in Canada by a woman. She was thrilled and touched. Writing to her neighbors to the north, she said: "During the 25 years that have slipped away I have never lost my interest in aviation. Although WINGS have given me everything—and have taken from me—everything but my own life, my love for them has never diminished and now my one thought—one prayer—is that WINGS may be used NOT for destruction, but for making more friendly and understanding relations between the nations of the earth." She had warm greetings for the pioneer fliers everywhere: "There is between us a bond incomparable; for every barnstorming flight was made with the thought and hope of making at least ONE person AIRMINDED . . . and we did succeed."

Alys was sixty-one when the United States went to war again in 1941. She had reached an age when most women begin to think of slowing down. Not Alys! For two years she battled to go to work doing what she did best, building or repairing aeroplanes, refusing to accept the fact she was considered too old. Finally, TWA hired her to work in the Inter-Continental Division, Hangar No. 2, at Washington National Airport. Alys was jubilant. "It isn't how many years one has lived, but how one has lived those years" that mattered. Alys worked ten hours a day, eight on Sunday, and proved she could do "a better job than the men."

Her job called for doing a little bit of everything and, as she wrote to a friend, "the nice part is that no one has to tell me how to do it." She read blueprints, made parts from prints, riveted and welded to repair or create new parts; the work was hard and constant, and she loved it. She was especially pleased to show her superiors that age "isn't always the bugaboo it is supposed to be." She marveled at the engineering designs for the machines she worked on, was delighted to have lived to see the amazing progress in aviation. Regretfully, war had brought it about. She was confident, however. "We shall win—but at what a price."

When the war ended, Alys put away her toolbox. "Moms," as she was known during her days at National Airport, held one dream for most of her life: to earn money to buy an aeroplane, for "that's the only sensible way to travel." At her home in Washington, she sewed, sold cosmetics and jewelry, gave massages, did whatever might earn money. In spite of her optimism, something always kept her from her dream, though heaven knows it wasn't for trying.

Alys McKey Bryant died on September 6, 1954, at seventy-four years of age. Friends believed she was born with wings. She spent seventy-four years proving they were right.

LILY IRVINE

Lily Irvine, British born, married the American James V. Martin in England in 1911 and left that country before earning her pilot's license. Both she and her husband trained at the Grahame-White School at Hendon, but it was in America that Lily made her mark as a flier and did her most important work.

James Martin, while a student at Harvard, had founded the Aeronautical Society there and promoted the first air meet at Boston in 1910. His meeting with Grahame-White at that meet led to his studying in England, where he met Lily. Born in Durban, South Africa, in 1891, Lily lived in Newcastle, South Africa, for most of her childhood before immigrating to Britain. As a young woman she horrified her mother by wandering about Hendon Aerodrome in grease-smeared overalls to learn aircraft construction.

A great-niece, Helen McCurdy, has written that Martin claimed for his wife, Lily, the honor of being "the first English-speaking woman to operate an Aeroplane—the first woman to fly in America." Not quite accurate on either count since Blanche Stuart Scott and Bessica Raiche were both flying aeroplanes in America in 1910, and Hilda Hewlett was certainly operating an aeroplane at Brooklands, England, in 1911. However, it made good copy.

Following their marriage in 1912, the couple came to the United States. *Flight* reported that Lily made a fine flight over London before leaving to catch a westbound boat. Back home in America, James Martin made exhibition flights to raise money for a planned transatlantic flight, the grand ambition of many aviators. Lily appeared with him regularly and flew exhibitions on her own after her initial debut in Boston.

The *Boston Post* was glowing about her performance: "Mrs. Martin Clinches Title to Queen of the Air." The size of the Farman machine led the reporter to wonder if the slight woman could master "the monster" in the air. She could and she did, sailing through space with "the grace of a bird." The *Post* reported that word of her flight quickly spread outside the field, and hundreds of eager spectators hurried to the field.

Her career launched, Lily appeared around the country for the next several years. She and James traveled to Alaska, where they flew at 10:30 at night in broad daylight, the first aeroplane exhibition ever in Fairbanks. The money earned by such appearances helped Martin build aeroplanes that excelled because of their speed and stability. Lily piloted Martin aeroplanes for several years.

On one such flight at Cleveland in 1914, she flew seventy-four miles in sixty minutes. The crowds gathered on Euclid Beach cheered lustily as the hydro-aeroplane launched from Cedar Point came into view. Lily circled near the excited thousands on the beach at two hundred feet, to give them a close-up view, before landing offshore, exactly between the two white flags that marked the site. Flying four miles more than the prescribed seventy-mile course because of the wind, she had cut ten minutes off the record made by Glenn Curtiss in 1910. Speaking afterward, Lily said, with "a little more favorable wind, I believe I could have made the trip in fifty minutes or less."

In 1914, husband and wife were working with the Aeromarine Plane and Motor Company in Avondale, New Jersey. Martin designed and built hydro-aeroplanes, and Lily piloted them. When the couple's first child was born, she gave up flying altogether. Despite the lack of a pilot's license and the creditability it bestows, Lily proved herself a capable flier.

14

The Challenge Is There

IN 2002 IT IS IMPOSSIBLE to imagine the excitement, the wonder viewers felt in the early years of the twentieth century on seeing an aeroplane skimming through the sky. It was miraculous. And the people who drove those magical machines were of heroic nature—hardly mortal. They were all men in the beginning, which was the proper state of affairs, so most men believed.

The pioneer women aviators, a gutsy group, were never large in number, but their presence was an affirmation of women's determination to overcome the prevailing mentality, which still appears at times: Women don't do that. These women did it, frequently much better than their male peers, for the sheer fun of it.

A casual viewing of Walter Jerven's film *Himmelstürmer,* an archival work of early film from various countries, shows how completely aviation was a man's world. Women were enthusiastic spectators, but they are nonexistent in the film except for brief glimpses of Raymonde de Laroche and Melli Beese.

Henry Woodhouse, an early authority on aviation, writing in *Flying* in June 1913, explained the difficulties faced by the woman who wanted to make a living flying. Foremost was the need to maintain the fragile machine that carried her aloft. "She is the slave of her big, expensive, frail aeroplane," he wrote. Keeping it tuned, a full-time occupation, required a good mechanic and often an assistant, unless the pilot had mechanical training. Her life depended on their skill and diligence, not always a comfortable situation.

Then there was the expense. Moving from place to place was costly and cumbersome, as there was no special facility to handle aeroplane transport in 1913. Woodhouse wrote that women seldom commanded fees equal to those paid to men, and event organizers were notorious for holding fliers to the terms of a contract regardless of weather or other circumstances. A sudden summer tempest could cost the flier her fee, leaving her to pay for transportation out of pocket. Furthermore, fearing the possibility of accidents, many organizers refused to hire women fliers even though the fatality rate among men at meets was predictably higher than the two female fatalities (Harriet Quimby and Julia Clark).

Flying was "a psychological process," according to Woodhouse, dependent on a feeling of confidence. When pilots knowingly went up in machines that had a faulty motor or were otherwise unsafe, they were risking their well-being. Knowing a machine's faults caused mental strain that could be dangerous, leading to panic and a fall. It was far better, Woodhouse thought, for a flier to be oblivious of a machine's limitations, hardly a safe situation, which surely contributed to the accident rate in early aviation.

Woodhouse's article failed to acknowledge the competency displayed by early women aviators, most of whom flew assuredly in their fragile machines, knowing they were as airworthy as possible. They were experienced enough to know from a motor's sound when something was wrong and take immediate action. In an emergency, these female aviators proved they had the quickness of mind to survive, thanks to courage and skill.

"If she has the means and flies for sport" was the best of all worlds for women pilots, noted Woodhouse, who probably thought deep down that women didn't belong in the rough and dangerous life of exhibition flying, the only way open to women who wanted to earn a living in aviation. It would take two wars before attitudes toward women flying began to change, and then only because of necessity.

The press in the early years gave considerable prominence to women fliers, particularly in America, where so much of aviation was more entertainment than science. The first appearance of a woman in an aeroplane

was news, especially her costume. As women performed more spectacu-
larly, the press reported in depth. Ruth Law's and Katherine Stinson's
distance flights and aerial acrobatics had good coverage. In Europe,
women shared news space with men equally, but their fewer numbers
and venues for exhibition meant fewer articles about women. The French
journals were the exception; the interest there centered on costume and
attitudes. The major aviation journals in England and America were
evenhanded in writing about women fliers; they appeared on covers, and
their activities were reported along with those of the men.

It is surprising, therefore, to read fact books for early aviation that
have no mention of women in the early years. Did their authors not
know, or did women fail to meet certain standards? It's as if women
pilots in America began with Amelia Earhart, the one woman mentioned
in most sources. The last thirty-some years have seen a change, however.
A casual reading of standard aviation surveys will find the names of Harriet Quimby, Katherine Stinson, and Ruth Law, a definite improvement.
Elsewhere, there has been a similar change in writing about aviation
history, spurred, perhaps, by women doing the writing. French and German writers have discovered some of the fascinating women who flew
before World War I and rescued them from oblivion.

In the years between the wars, women flew across continents and
oceans, set records, and raced in women's events, but the prevailing attitude about women in the growing commercial-aviation industry had
changed little from that of the World War I military. Helen Richey, hired
over eight male competitors to fly for Central Airlines in 1934, quit ten
months later when a Department of Commerce ruling barred her from
flying in bad weather. At the same time, the pilot's union refused her
application for membership.

Helen taught students to fly for the air force in World War II, then
flew in England with ATA (Air Transport Auxiliary) and in the United
States with the WASPs (Women's Airforce Service Pilots). In spite of this
record, she found doors closed in commercial aviation when the war
ended. Despondent, she committed suicide in 1947.

Today the scene is more promising for women wishing to make a
career in aviation. At least four universities around the country offer four-
year programs that train women and men for careers in this field. Nora
Sullivan, a recent student at Purdue University, said that in her class of

sixty-five to seventy students, ten were women. The program is tough—training hours have increased dramatically from the three or four hours of the early years—but at the end of two years and sixty-some hours of flight time, students generally earn a private pilot's license. At the completion of the four years, with simulator experience on various types of aircraft, the graduates earn an air-transport license, which often means immediate employment on commercial airlines. A woman as first officer or captain on a transatlantic flight is no longer unusual—a recent flight had all women in the cockpit.

Federal Aviation Administration statistics show that women who fly commercially represent almost 5 percent of licensed pilots, earning comparable pay with men in particular positions, and their numbers in other aviation positions are slowly rising. Women work in airline transport, as mechanics, repair people, air-traffic controllers, ground instructors, flight engineers, and flight instructors, thanks to federal laws that have opened doors for women in aviation. Reluctantly the military services have taken women into their ranks, but the numbers are small compared with civilian aviation. At NASA (the National Aeronautics and Space Administration) women number 33 percent of total employees, almost 18 percent of the scientists and engineers, and 23 percent of the astronauts, according to statistics for the year 2000. Estimates for the next five to ten years call for fifteen thousand pilots to replace those retiring from the cockpit; women who are trained will share that opportunity. The adventuresome women who climbed into the rickety bamboo-and-wire contraptions of yesterday would not be surprised. They might wonder: Why did it take so long?

Blanche Scott, the first American woman to go up, accidentally or not, revealed in an interview in 1940 the spirit that motivated so many early women fliers: "If I were a young girl now, I don't think I'd fly unless I could be a pioneer in space. I just don't want to do things that have already been done."

Appendix: The Fliers

Name	License Number	Date
FRENCH		
Raymonde de Laroche	No. 36	March 8, 1910
Marthe Niel	No. 226	August 29, 1910
Marie Marvingt	No. 281	November 8, 1910
Jeanne Herveux	No. 318	December 7, 1910
Marie-Louise Martin Driancourt	No. 525	June 15, 1911
Béatrice Deryck	No. 652	October 10, 1911
Jeanne Pallier	No. 1012	September 6, 1912
Hélène de Plagino	No. 1349	June 4, 1913
Marthe Richer	No. 1369	June 4, 1913
Carmen Damedoz	No. 1449	September 5, 1913
Hélène Caragiani	No. 1591	February 6, 1914
Gaétane Picard	No. 1653	July 10, 1914
Thérèse Peltier	Unlicensed	

Name	License Number	Date

FRENCH

Mathilde Frank	Unlicensed	
Mme. Aboukaia	Unlicensed	
Lottie Brandon	Unlicensed	
Mme. Beroul	Unlicensed	
Mme. Copin	Unlicensed	
Mlle. Dindineau	Unlicensed	
Mme. Dorival	Unlicensed	
Suzanne Bernard	Unlicensed	
Denise Moore	Unlicensed	

BELGIAN

| Hélène Dutrieu | No. 27* | August 23, 1910 |

GERMAN

Melli Beese	No. 115	September 13, 1911
Charlotte Möhring	No. 285	September 7, 1912
Martha Behrbohm	No. 427	June 4, 1913

CZECH

| Bozena Láglerová | No. 37# | October 10, 1911 |
| | No. 125** | October 19, 1911 |

SWISS

| Elsa Haugk | No. 785** | June 6, 1914 |

---

*Later licensed also by French Aero Club
#Licensed by Austrian Aero Club
**Licensed by German Aero Club

Name	License Number	Date

HUNGARIAN

Lilly Steinschneider	No. 4	1912

ITALIAN

Rosina Ferrario	No. 203	January 3, 1913

RUSSIAN

Lydia Zvereva	No. 31	August 8, 1910
Eudocie V. Anatra	No. 54	October 3, 1911
Lyubov Golanchikova	No. 56	November 19, 1911
Eugenie Shakhovskaya	No. 274**	August 16, 1912
Helena P. Samsonova	No. 167	August 13, 1913
Sophie A. Dolgorukaya	No. 234	June 5, 1914
Nadeshda Degtereva	Unlicensed	

BRITISH

Hilda Hewlett	No. 122	August 29, 1911
Cheridah de Beauvoir Stocks	No. 153	November 7, 1911
Winnie Buller	No. 848***	May 3, 1912
Lilian E. Bland	Unlicensed	
Dorothy Leavitt	Unlicensed	
Spencer Kavanaugh (Edith M. Cook)	Unlicensed	
Lily Irvine	Unlicensed	

**Licensed by German Aero Club
***Licensed by French Aero Club

Name	License Number	Date
AMERICAN		
Blanche Scott	Unlicensed	
Bessica Raiche	Unlicensed	
Harriet Quimby	No. 37	August 2, 1911
Matilde Moisant	No. 44	August 17, 1911
Julia Clark	No. 133	June 11, 1912
Katherine Stinson	No. 148	July 24, 1912
Bernetta A. Miller	No. 173	September 25, 1912
Ruth Law	No. 188	November 20, 1912
Florence Seidell	No. 258	August 20, 1913
Mrs. Richberg Hornsby	No. 301	June 24, 1914
Marjorie Stinson	No. 303	August 12, 1914
Dorothy Rice Peirce	No. 561	August 23, 1916
Helen Hodge Harris	No. 633	November 12, 1916
Mary Sims Heinrich	Unlicensed	
Jean Doty Caldwell	Unlicensed	
Geneve Shaffer Parsons	Unlicensed	
Hilder Smith	Unlicensed	
Alys McKey Bryant	Unlicensed	

Notes on Sources

BEFORE AMELIA EVOLVED from a variety of sources—newspapers, personal accounts, correspondence, journals, and numerous books—all most helpful in describing the unusual women who braved the skies and the period in which they lived. Where possible, the following abbreviations are used: LOC (Library of Congress), NASM (National Air and Space Museum), MAE (Musée de l'Air et de l'Espace, Le Bourget). I have identified clippings and articles as accurately as possible, but some are undated and/or unidentified in the source collection.

CHAPTER 1

For material on the early aviators, the biographical files at NASM, the Royal Air Force Museum at Hendon, and MAE were invaluable. Clippings, articles from journals and personal accounts, and some revealing photographs were wonderful inspiration. Grahame-White's criticism appeared in the *American-Examiner,* 1911, no date for the day. Kruckman's comments came from the *New York American,* May 14, 1911. The source of Harry Harper's comments is his 1929 book, *Twenty-five Years of Flying.* Heath and Murray's remarks on why women make better pilots than men are from their book *Woman and Flying.* The *New York Times* supplied the quote on excluding women from flying, the day after Quimby's crash. *Flight* was essential for keeping abreast of day-to-day developments in aviation.

CHAPTER 2

The biographical files at MAE were essential to write about French women aviators. In addition, the archives contain the prominent aeronautical journals since aviation began, which have numerous articles on the French lady-birds.

Raymonde de Laroche

An undated article, "Flying in the Presence of the Czar," from the Marjorie Stinson collection at LOC, is de Laroche's account of flying in Russia. It was translated into English for American readers; the newspaper is unidentified. Harry Harper's article "The Intrepid First Lady of Flight" appeared in *Flying* for March 1957. *Aeronautics* described de Laroche's activities at the Heliopolis meet (February 10, 1910) and the Budapest meet (June 16, 1910). The London *Times* covered the Rheims meet on succeeding days, with a full report, on July 9, 1910, of de Laroche's crash. The *Daily Mail,* an early supporter of aviation, also reported the accident, with activities at the meet. *L'Auto* for October 26, 1909, was the source of an interview with "la Première Femme-Oiseau" and an account of de Laroche's accident, on July 9, 1910. The *New York Herald* reported de Laroche's award for damages on April 19, 1912. The French and American press devoted considerable space to accounts of her death in 1919. Marie-Josephe de Beauregard's *Femmes de l'air* (1993); *Les Aviatrices* (1993), by Bernard Marck; *Memorial des pionniers de l'aviation, 1909–1921* (1998); and *Vingt cinq ans d'aéronautique Française,* vol. II (1934) were useful sources. Gilbert Deloizy and Armel Brault at MAE shared information on de Laroche's private life and her friends in artistic circles.

Hélène Dutrieu

The MAE biographical file on Dutrieu is a fine source for copies of journal articles, newspaper clippings, personal writings by the aviator, and photographs that reveal a young, enthusiastic woman who enjoyed what she was doing. The January 8, 1910, *Flight* showed Dutrieu standing beside the Demoiselle she was learning to fly, wearing a "special aviation costume." *L'Aérophile* was another dependable source for what French women were doing in aviation. Dutrieu's flights in England and America were reported in the press of both countries, the *Times* and the *Daily Mail* in England in 1910, the *New York Times,* the *New York Herald,* and the *New York American* in September 1911. Her accident at Le Mans was news, and the *New York Herald* reported it on August 29, 1911. "La Première Pilote Belge," by A. Van Hoorebeeck in an undated journal article summarizes the flier's career; a similar article appeared in *Aero-France* for July–August 1961. The French journals found Dutrieu a sympathetic subject in the years after World War II, for her contributions in realizing "the bird-like dream of Icarus" (*Air Revue*, April 1956). Copies of these articles are in her MAE file, including her own account of beating the women's records. *Les Ailes* published an interview with her on April 5, 1958, and reported her reception of the insignia of the Légion d'Honneur in the presence of Henry Farman and Gabriel Voisin (December 3, 1955). Copies of obituaries from French, English, and American newspapers are contained in the biographical file, but they must be read with care. The books listed previously as sources for de Laroche also contain material on Dutrieu.

Marie Marvingt

Marvingt's long life, her many accomplishments, and her indefatigable work for different causes has created a mountain of source material. The biographical file at MAE is a beginning, the Association de Documentation Aéronautique is another good source, as is the city archives in Nancy, France. The work by Marcel Cordier and Rosalie Maggio, *Marie Marvingt: La femme d'un siècle* (1991), is a must-read. Marvingt's MAE file is chock-full of copies of articles from journals and newspapers describing the exploits of this unusual woman. Copies of her writings are included, some in her own handwriting, in French and a few in English, including her comments on how she conceived the first *avion sanitaire*. Other writers—Edmond Petit, Jacques Boetsch, and Michel Daurat among them—also detailed her long, exuberant life. *L'Aérophile, La Revue Aérienne,* and *Icare* provided fulsome articles depicting her athletic feats, ballooning, aviation ventures, and science accomplishments. The December 25, 1910, *La Revue Aérienne* summarized her career to that date—more than most people accomplished in a lifetime. *Flight* reported her aviation activities regularly, notably August 12, 1911 (the landing in the *boule* game), and August 19, when she was hailed as winner of the Coupe Fémina. (This was in error. Her flight was a record at the time, but Dutrieu would later beat it and win the prize.) *Le Grand Livre du Sport Feminin* (1982), by Françoise Laget and Serge Laget, has little information on Marvingt but includes a wonderful picture of her being carried in triumph by the ground crew after flying a record fifty-three minutes. Marvingt styled herself the "fiancée du danger"—the title of her memoirs, which have disappeared—but an outline of her life, dated June 22, 1948, with handwritten notes, available at MAE, is a good replacement. Gordon Ackerman's article "Fiancée of Danger," from *Sports Illustrated,* June 26, 1961, captured this extraordinary woman.

CHAPTER 3

Marthe Niel, Jeanne Herveux, Marie-Louis Driancourt, Jeanne Pallier, and the rest of the French women aviators have files at MAE, which help detail their careers. Articles from *L'Aérophile, La Vie Illustrée,* and *La Revue Aérienne* all provided good information, as did the dependable *Flight,* with its weekly accounts of women's activities: training for the Coup Fémina, solo flights, Jeanne Pallier's spectacular flight with a passenger, and even Mathilde Frank's plans to fly the Channel. Jeanne Herveux's file contains notes from an interview about her auto-racing days, a brief biography, and a copy of the contract she signed with La Société de l'École Nationale d'Aviation, plus photographs and promotional material. The deaths of Denise Moore and Suzanne Bernard are noted. Bernard's file is slim, but articles prompted by her death are eloquent reminders that a woman's death was considered more terrible than that of a man in the public mind. Clippings from French and American newspapers are available on many of the women in this chapter. Marck's *Les Aviatrices* (1993), de Beauregard's *Femmes de l'air* (1993), and Schmitt's *Die Ladys in den fliegenden Kisten* (1993) were useful sources.

CHAPTER 4
Melli Beese

Melli Beese has been discovered in the last twenty years. Articles in a variety of journals have told her story, most of them based on Adalbert Norden's romantic treatment, *Flügel am Horizont* (1939). The January 22, 1982, *Zeit* magazine provided a good account, with pictures; the March 1994 *Flugzeug,* the January 1986 *Fliegermagazin,* and the January 1994 *Luft-und Raumfahrt* were helpful. A longish article by Hans Ahner, part of a Luftpost exhibition in Dresden, was a good source, but the best was Beese's account of flying in the pioneer days at Johannisthal—"Unser Flugplatz—in Memoriam"—from the May–June 1921 *Motor.* It's the source for the chapter title. Barbara Spitzer's book, *Melli Beese: Bildhauerin, Pilotin—eine ungewöhnliche Frau* (1992), from the Treptow Museum, was invaluable for setting the record straight on several points. Robert Gsell's book, *25 Jahre Luftkutscher* (1936), offers a brief glimpse of Beese; Peter Supf's *Das Buch der deutschen Fluggeschichte* (1935), is an excellent history of early German aviation, with comments on the women flying at that time. Günter Schmitt's two books, *Als de Oldtimer flogen* (1980) and *Die Ladys in den fliegenden Kisten* (1993), were helpful. Werner Schwipps's three works were good sources for flying in the pioneer days: *Kleine Geschichte der deutschen Luftfahrt* (1968), *Riesenzigarren und fliegende Kisten* (1984), and *Schwerer als Luft* (1984). Hellmuth Hirth's *Meine Flugerlebnisse* (1915) was the source for his comments on women flying. Georg von Tschudi's *Aus 34 Jahren Luftfahrt* described conditions at the Johannisthal meets. Joachim Wachtel's *Die Aviatiker oder die tollkühnen Pioniere des Motorflugs* (1978) devoted a chapter to women aviators. The September 20, 1911, *Flugsport* gave a description of Beese's test flights. Berlin newspapers provided details on her competition—the *Berliner Tageblatt* was very good— and her death, which was noted in the *New York Times*.

Other German Fliers

Information on Charlotte Möhring, Martha Behrbohm, and the other women who won licenses in Germany is very limited. There are a few articles with personal comments available at German museums (publications unknown), and there are brief mentions in the German press. An article by Anneliese Dieffenbach, publication unknown, was the source for Behrbohm's *Rundflug* with Georgi, as well as Behrbohm's comments on aviation when she was an older woman. Möhring's notes to Peter Supf, from the Deutsche Museum, provide brief details of her career. Günter Schmitt's book was very helpful in identifying German women who won licenses, as was Willi Hackenberger's book *Die Alten Adler: Pioniere der deutschen Luftfahrt* (1960).

CHAPTER 5

The Russian aviators are much less documented than the other European fliers; there is room for more research on the subject of early women pilots. Alan Durkota's book, *Imperial Russian Air Service* (1995), has a helpful chapter on the first women pilots, but errors with the photographs give one pause. The officer's comment on Zvereva's flying ability is from Durkota. Christine A. White's 1991 paper, "Gossamer Wings," was very useful, as was an article by Edgar Meos in the winter 1975 *Cross & Cockade*. The Meos article is the source of the salacious information on Shakhovskaya. *Flight* printed news of Russian activities, as did *Aeronautics* and *Flying*. (The facts are often at odds.) Günter Schmitt's book, *Die Ladys in den fliegenden Kisten,* has a section on Russian women that was informative. Peter Supf's book, *Das Buch der deutschen Fluggeschichte* (1935), establishes Shakhovskaya and Golanchikova at Johannisthal in Germany. Michel Gregor's article in the December 1939 *Sportsman Pilot* described the sometimes dangerous life that some of the women experienced while flying exhibitions in Russia in the early days.

CHAPTER 6
Hilda Hewlett

The Hewlett family in England shared information on the young Hilda and her later years, her marriage to Maurice, her intense interest in aviation, and her partnership with Gustave Blondeau. Maurice's letter to Hilda stating his unorthodox view of marriage vows is from his letters (1926) in the Imperial War Museum. Hilda Hewlett's notes for a speech on aviation and the role of women were provided by the family. Information on the Farman school at Châlons came from an unidentified newspaper clipping, dated April 16, 1910. Grahame-White's comments were printed in *Flight* and the *American-Examiner.* Mrs. W. K. Clifford's sketch of the Hewletts appeared in the *Saturday Review of Literature,* May 1, 1926. Michael Goodall's article "The Graceful Bird," printed in the Brooklands Museum magazine, *The Spirit* (autumn 1998), served as a good overview of Hewlett's career. *Flight* followed the progress of her career through 1911 and 1912; the Hewlett-Blondeau construction company is featured in the December 7, 1912, issue. "Flights of Fancy," by Patrick Loobey, printed by the Wandsworth Borough Council, was the source for details on the partners' factory on Vardens Road, labor disputes, and the figures on the output of aircraft during World War I. *Flight* published Hewlett's letter regarding the Royal Air Force and the aviation industry on January 31, 1914. Comments on aviation and the war came from her booklet "Our Flying Men"; notes on woman in aviation came from her observations. An article in the *Bay of Plenty Times,* May 8,

1999, "A Magnificent Woman (and Her Flying Machines)"—was very useful. The *San Francisco Chronicle* (March 30, 1919) had a front-page article on Hewlett when she traveled through on her way to New Zealand. Hewlett's article "London to Batavia by Air" appeared in the January 25, 1933, issue of *Aeroplane.*

Other British Fliers

Cheridah de Beauvoir Stocks's brief career was covered in news releases in *Flight.* The Hendon archives has her license certificate but little else. Both the English and American press noted her licensing (*New York Herald,* the London *Times,* and *Daily Mail*). A most attractive young lady, she was photographed regularly in the aviation journals. The May 15, 1914, *Flight* published a long account of her accident with Mr. Pickles. Follow-up articles on her recovery and work during the war appeared on July 19, 1913; November 22, 1913; September 10, 1915; October 15, 1915; and December 31, 1915.

Information on Winnie Buller comes mainly from *Flight.* A small article on March 31, 1912, explained her decision to train in France; her work at the Caudron School was noted and her war work was recognized in November 1914. *Aeronautics* featured her in the November 1912 issue, with a longish article welcoming her to the British aviation world.

Peter Lewis's article in the January 23, 1964, *Flight International* was an excellent source of information on Lilian E. Bland. J. W. Freeman, writing in *Aviation News* ("First Ladies of the Air," March 17, 1988), gave a briefer summary of this extraordinary woman's work. Best of all were the articles in *Flight:* the construction of the *Mayfly* (July 30, 1910); she flies (September 10, 1910). Bland wrote a step-by-step guide to constructing the aeroplane, complete with diagrams.

Michael Goodall's book, *Flying Start* (1995), provided a brief history of Brooklands, the schools working there, and some of the personalities who flew. Mrs. Gavin was mentioned as flying there on a glider machine in 1910.

CHAPTER 7
Blanche Scott

The best source for information on Blanche Scott was the biographical files at NASM. Scott's file is fairly full; she was a natural PR person. There are copies of articles on her automobile trip across the United States, on her accidental first flight (the date changes from September 2 to 4 to 6), and on her subsequent career in early aviation. The September 9, 1967, *Sports Illustrated* ran an article on her, "The Lady Flew," by William Gottlieb; the May 1954 *Aero Digest* published Scott's account of the first flight; *Chirp,* the publication of the Early Birds, credited her with flying on September 2; a *Smithsonian Studies* article provided highlights of Scott's career; the May 10, 1947, *Collier's* ran a short article on Scott by Ernest Jones. Clara Studer's *The Life of Glenn Curtiss* (1937) was helpful with details of Scott's training at Hammondsport; a personal-data form provided useful information on her family and early education. Clippings from Marjorie Stinson's papers at LOC were useful, but they were not always identified. The February 24, 1912, *San Francisco Chronicle* had an account of the Third International Aviation Meet at Emeryville where Beachey flew in a dress; the *New York World Telegram* for January 28, 1937, hailed the Early Birds and credited Scott as "first woman to fly plane." The *Rochester Democrat and Chronicle* welcomed her home in July 1935. (The date on the copy in her NASM file is missing.) The September 12, 1955, *U.S. Flying News* discussed Scott's efforts to aid the Air Force Museum in Dayton, Ohio. An article by Gay Pauley in the *South Bend Tribune* for October 2, 1964, described Scott's career. Her January 13, 1970, obituary in the *Evening Star* (Washington, D.C.) contained the quote "Most of us got killed."

Bessica Raiche

Bessica Raiche's story relied heavily on the account of Catherine Stull (Bessica's daughter) filed in the Raiche biographical file at NASM. Stull's information corrected repeated errors in accounts of this remarkable woman's flying and medical careers. Other sources were an article, "America's First Flying Sportswoman," in the June 1931 *Sportsman Pilot,* and clippings, most of them undated, from the Marjorie Stinson Collection, LOC, detailing Raiche's first flights (the *Globe*), her appearance in pants (the *Washington Post*), minor accidents, her presentation with a medal by the Aeronautical Society of New York, and the Dr. Johnson quote on a woman flying, from the April 22, 1932, *Washington Times.*

CHAPTER 8

Harriet Quimby has been the subject of many articles and at least two books; in addition, a study center named for her does research on women in aviation. Sources of information are many and varied. On her early years, Henry M. Holden's book, *Her Mentor Was an Albatross* (1993), was helpful, as was an undated article by Jean Hubbard from an unidentified newspaper in Arroyo Grande, California. Quimby's writing for *Leslie's Illustrated Weekly* was very useful, with weekly articles on a variety of subjects during 1910 and 1911, including "Women as Automobile Enthusiasts." On flying, there were articles on the International Air Meet at Belmont Park (October 1910), "How a Woman Learns to Fly" (May 25, 1911; August 17, 1911), "How I Won My Aviator's License" (August 24, 1911), "An American Girl's Daring Exploit" (May 16, 1912), "New Things in the Aviation World" (June 6, 1912), "Exploring the Airlanes" (June 22, 1912), and "Flyers and Flying" (June 27, 1912). The *World Magazine* published a Quimby article on August 27, 1911, in which she admitted wanting to be "the first American woman to fly" and her delight in reading about herself "for once." *Fly Magazine* published Quimby's Channel-crossing account in June 1912. "American Bird Women" was Quimby's last contribution (*Good Housekeeping,* September 1912); Elizabeth Hiatt Gregory's "Woman's Record in Aviation" appeared in the same issue. The New York and Boston newspapers were full of Quimby, from her first mysterious appearance on the field at Nassau Boulevard in 1911 until her death on July 1, 1912. The April 1912 *Aeronautics* and Earle Ovington's letter in the August 10, 1912, *Scientific American* discuss faults in the Blériot aeroplane design. A. Leo Stevens's article "On the Death of Miss Quimby" appeared in the August 1912 *Aeronautics.* Lygia Ionnitiu's "What Harriet Quimby Saw at the Nassau Boulevard Aerodrome," for the *Harriet Quimby Research Conference Journal,* 1996, provided conjecture based on newspaper reporting. "Who Knew She Flew?" which appeared in *Stamps and Coins* (April 19, 1991), announced a stamp for Quimby. Other useful sources included "Miss Harriet Quimby," by Samuel S. Whitt, in the spring 1973 *National Aeronautics;* "Wild about Harriet," by Terry Gwynn-Jones, in the January 1984 *Smithsonian* magazine; "Beauty and the Blériot," by Weston George, in *Aviation Quarterly,* vol. 6, no. 1, 1980; "Harriet Quimby, America's First Woman Pilot," by Hugh Powell, in *American Aviation Historical Society Journal,* winter 1982.

CHAPTER 9

For the early years of Matilde Moisant, Doris Rich's book, *The Magnificent Moisants* (1998), was a good source. As with Quimby, the New York newspapers covered Moisant's progress as an aviator, her licensing, and her participation at the Nassau meet. The Moisant scrapbooks at the Garber Facility of NASM are a rich treasure. Her interview at the Oral History Research Office, Columbia University, was helpful. The Marjorie Stinson Collection at LOC provided numerous clippings, good for describing the period and Moisant. When Moisant began exhibition flights, there were press reports at the stops on her schedule—Mexico City and Guadalajara (the *Mexican Herald* and *El Imparcial,* November 16–22, and December 5–6, 1911), New Orleans (New Orleans *Times-Picayune,* March 11–12, 1912), Shreveport (*Shreveport Times,* March 15, 18–19, 1912), and Dallas (*Dallas Morning News,* March 25–27, 1912)—until the crash at Wichita Falls, Texas, when she walked away from flying.

CHAPTER 10

The Marjorie Stinson Collection, LOC, was an important source for information on Katherine Stinson; NASM, less so. LOC includes a chronology of Katherine's career with family information, a short bibliography, copies of magazine articles, clippings from newspapers around the country, copies of aviation journal articles with news of Stinson, *Billboard* news, and coverage of her trip to the Orient, with photographs. The collection is impressive. Her first loop-the-loop is noted (*Chicago Tribune,* July 18, 1915), as are the night flight at Los Angeles (*Los Angeles Times,* December 18, 1915) and the Chicago–to–New York City flight (Chicago and New York papers, May 23–30, 1917). *Aerial Age* featured her on the cover (June 21, 1915) and noted looping (August 23, 1915) and use of the new tractor machine at the Michigan Fair (September 13, 1915). A reporter's ride with Stinson appeared in the August 16, 1914, *Kansas City Star* (Missouri). Flights through the West and South were recorded by local newspapers—the *Tucson Citizen* (November 3–5, 1915), and the *Mobile Register* later in November. "Aviation as an Attraction," by William Pickens, was published in *The Billboard* (December 18, 1915). The New York papers (May 20–27, 1916) headlined Stinson's flight at Sheepshead Bay. *Flight* (August 9, 1917) covered Stinson's career, including the Red Cross flight. The San Diego–San Francisco flight was reported in the *San Francisco Examiner* (December 12–13, 1917). John Underwood's *The Stinsons* (1969) was a good source of information on both Stinson women, as were books by Charles Planck (*Women with Wings*, 1942) and Edward Jablonski (*Ladybirds: Women in Aviation*, 1968). The *Curtiss Flyleaf* (July 1918) described Katherine's aerial mail flights in Canada; *Stamps* (December 9, 1933) detailed her aerial mail flight in Helena, Montana. *FAA Aviation News* (November 1971) featured an article on Stinson: "The Flying Schoolgirl." A copy of an obituary from the *New Mexican*, July 10, 1977, is in Stinson's LOC file.

CHAPTER 11

References for Ruth Law are many and varied. NASM's biographical file is a start. Two articles were especially helpful: "A Lady's Flying Past," by Emily Watson (no publication identified), and "Flying as It Was," by Law, in the *Sportsman Pilot* (undated). Both contain her personal comments. Law's interview with the Oral History Research Office, Columbia University, was another source for many of her quotes, descriptions of unusual incidents, and the trip to the Orient. Most useful was the press coverage. The *New York Journal* covered her first flights at Saugus, Massachusetts, as did the *Boston Herald;* one can trace her career by reading what newspapers had to say wherever she exhibited—the East, Midwest, or the South. The aviation journals covered her activities, notably: *Aerial Age Weekly* (loops at Daytona Beach, Florida, January 17, 1916; the dinner honoring her, December 18, 1916); *Flying* (the record distance flight, December 1916; dinner in her honor, January 1917; the Liberty Bond appeal, August 1917; "Recruiting by Aeroplane," February 1918). The Chicago and New York City newspapers (November 19–21, 1916) reported the record distance flight, as well as Law's war work (1917, 1918). Her comments on French aviation are from the *World* (February 19, 1917); those about her return from Europe, the *New York Times* (April 4, 1917). "Go Get the Kaiser" appeared in the *Chicago Sunday Herald* (July 22, 1917). Lines of poetry in the Lynn obituary (*Lynn Item*, December 5, 1970) were written by Mrs. Douglas Robinson, the sister of President Theodore Roosevelt, on the occasion of the 1916 dinner.

CHAPTER 12

The Marjorie Stinson Collection in LOC is the primary source of information on the flier and her period. She once planned to write a book on early aviation and did considerable research. The biographical file on Marjorie at NASM is far less informative. Two of Marjorie's articles were most useful; they supplied many of the quotes in this chapter: "Diary of a Country Girl at Flying School" (*Aero Digest,* February 1928) and "Wings for War Birds" (*Liberty,* December 28, 1929). In addition, press clippings provided details about her career and quotes: her first public flight (Brownwood, Texas, *Bulletin,* October 10, 1914); the Stinson school to lease land (*San Antonio Express,* January 18, 1916); and the crash at Cleveland (*Cleveland Plain Dealer,* September 5–6, 1916). The *San Antonio Express* and *San Antonio Light* were especially good for reporting on activities at the school and Marjorie's flying career (she plays Santa, her movie work, her membership in the U.S. Reserve Corps). *Aerial Age Weekly* printed regular notes on her activities. Stinson's personal correspondence provided not only family details but also insight into her thinking on a variety of topics.

CHAPTER 13

The accounts in this chapter relied heavily on the biographical files at NASM. These pilots did not make a big splash in the aviation world, but they were there.

Julia Clark's file has limited information. When she died, newspaper accounts provided considerable detail about her, but some of the facts are questionable. *Smithsonian Studies in Air and Space* (no date) devoted a page to her. *Flight's* confusion was apparent in the June 29, 1912, issue.

Bernetta A. Miller's file is slightly fuller. She wrote two articles, "How I Learned to Fly" (The *World Magazine,* December 2, 1928) and "First Monoplane Flights for the United States Government" (unpublished, written October 1962), which were helpful. A copy of Mrs. Ruth Bird's letter to Paul Garber provided details about Miller at St. Mary's Hall-on-the-Delaware in New Jersey. Correspondence with Elizabeth Hiatt Gregory was illuminating. *Aero and Hydro* for February 8, 1913, reported Miller's near miss with oil. Newspaper clippings reported her debut flight, her unhappiness with the state of aviation, and her obituary.

Florence Seidell and Mrs. Richberg Hornsby are known because of their license certificates and brief mention in the press. There is no record of their membership in the Early Birds.

Dorothy Rice Peirce (Sims) described her aviation career in a chapter in her book, *Curiouser and Curiouser* (1940). That, her license certificate, a newspaper photo, and a clipping provide the sum of information on her.

The NASM file for Helen Hodge Harris contains brief but good information on her life and flying career. The Aero Club report is there, as is her application for membership in Early Birds, a brief biography, and correspondence from her daughter with pertinent details.

Hilder Smith's flying career is chronicled in copies of three articles, one from the *Sportsman Pilot* (no date), another from *U.S. Air Services* (August 1930), and the third from the *Christian Science Monitor* (no date). Her file also has copies of her lesson log, showing her time in the air, and an affidavit from her teacher, Arthur Burns.

Alys McKey Bryant's file at NASM was a useful start, and newspaper coverage fleshed out her story. There is a biographical sketch, an application for Early Birds, a copy of her reply to the Canadians thanking them for the air-mail cachet, an article from the *Sportsman Pilot* (November 15, 1940), and correspondence with Early Bird members. Frank H. Ellis's books *In Canadian Skies* (1959) and *Canada's Flying Heritage* (1954) were useful sources. Press stories supplied quotes and details about her flying career, especially those in the *Seattle Daily Times* (April and July 1913), the *Akron Sunday Times* (June 30, 1918), and the *Sandusky Register* (May 18, 1919). Obituaries in the *Washington Post* (September 1954) and the *Evening Star* (September 8, 1954) were helpful.

Sources for Lily Martin included a brief biographical file at NASM; the James V. Martin papers at the Garber Facility, NASM; and several references in *Flight*. Among them were flying at Hendon (May 27, 1911), flying a Benoist flying boat from Sandusky to Cleveland (August 21, 1914), and night flying in Alaska (August 23, 1913). Clippings from the *Boston Post* (June 29, 1911) and the *Cleveland Plain Dealer* (July 24, 1914) provided helpful details.

CHAPTER 14

The Helen Richey story had three sources: a *Ninety-Nine News* (April 1978) article, "Helen Richey, First Lady at the Airlines," by Glenn Kerfoot; Ann Butler's article, "She Lived to Fly," in *The Pittsburgh Press Roto*

(October 6, 1974); and the *Miami Herald* (October 5, 1939). *Administrator's Fact Book, FAA* (April 2001) and "The Facts 2001," a brochure printed by Women in Aviation International in Daytona Beach, Florida, provided statistics on women in aviation. The Scott quote appeared in an unidentified clipping in the NASM file.

Bibliography

Ackerman, Gordon. "Fiancée of Danger." *Sports Illustrated,* June 26, 1961.

"Aerial Mail Service in Canada." *Curtiss Flyleaf,* July 1918.

Ahner, Hans. "Melli Beese—die erste deutsche Flugzeugführerin." Dresden: Kulturbund der DDR, Arbeitskreis Luftpost, 1986.

Archdeacon, Ernest. "Mademoiselle Marvingt, Une Sportswoman Extraordinaire." *La Revue Aérienne,* December 25, 1910.

Association pour la Recherche de Documentation sur l'Histoire de L'Aéronautique, Navale. *Memorial des pionniers de l'aviation, 1909–1921.* Paris: Association pour le Recherche de Documentation sur l'Histoire de L'Aéronautique, 1998.

Beaubois, Henry, and C. H. de Levis Mirepoix. *Siècle de L'Avion.* Paris: A. Fayard, 1949.

Beaumont, André (Lieutenant Jean Conneau). *My Three Big Flights.* New York: McBride, Nast & Co., 1912.

Beauregard, Marie-Josephe de. *Femmes de l'air.* Paris: Éditions France-Empire, 1993.

Beese, Melli. "Unser Flugplatz—in Memoriam." *Motor,* May–June 1921.

———. "Melli Beese Fliegerleben Selbstporträt im Telegrammstil."

Beevers, David. *St. Peter's Church Vauxhall, A History.* London: Vauxhall St. Peter's Heritage Centre and the Vauxhall Society, 1991.

Bennett, Charles. "Katherine Stinson Otero: On a Wing and a Prayer." *Santa Fean Magazine,* October 1993.

Bernadi, Fiorenza de, ed. *Pink Line— A Gallery of European Women Pilots.* Aeritalia, 1984.

Bilstein, Roger E. *Flight in America: 1900–1983.* Baltimore: Johns Hopkins University Press, 1984.

Binyon, Laurence. *The Letters of Maurice Hewlett.* London: Methuen and Company, 1926.

Bland, Lilian E. "Positive and Negative Angle." *Flight,* July 30, 1910.

———. "Miss Lilian Bland Flies." *Flight,* September 10, 1910.

————. "The 'Mayfly'—The First Irish Biplane, and How She Was Built." *Flight,* December 17, 1910.

Boase, Wendy. *The Sky's the Limit: Women Pioneers in Aviation.* London: Ospry, 1979.

Boetsch, Jacques. "Une Vie en équilibre." Marie Marvingt biographical file. Musée de l'Air et l'Espace, Le Bourget, France. Publication and date unknown.

Brett, R. Dallas. *History of British Aviation, 1908–1914.* Air Surbiton, Surrey, England: Research Publications with Kristall Productions, 1988.

Brown, Don. *Ruth Law Thrills a Nation.* New York: Ticknor & Fields, 1993.

Bryant, Alys McKey. "Flying as It Was." *Sportsman Pilot,* November 15, 1940.

Buchanan, Lamont. *The Flying Years.* New York: G. P. Putnam's Sons, 1953.

Butler, Ann. "She Lived to Fly." *The Pittsburgh Press Roto,* October 6, 1974.

Clifford, W. K. "A Letter from London." *Saturday Review of Literature,* May 1, 1926.

Commission Histoire, Arts et Lettres de l'Aéro Club de France. *Cent ans avec l'Aéro Club de France.* Paris: Commission Histoire, Arts et Lettres de l'Aéro Club de France, 1998.

Daurat, Michel. "Marie Marvingt, demeure toujours la fiancée du danger." Unidentifed article. Musée de l'Air et de l'Espace biographical file.

Dent, Penelope. "Interlopers with Lipstick." *Aeroplane Monthly,* April 1997.

Dinand, R. "Mlle. Marvingt lance un défi mondial." *Le Figaro,* December 16, 1963.

Dodds, Ron. "When the Canadians Took Over U.S. Flying Schools." *Flight,* February 1969.

Durkota, Alan. *Imperial Russian Air Service.* Mountain View, Calif.: Flying Machines Press, 1995.

Dutrieu, Hélène. "Je bats les records feminins." Biographical file. Musée de l'Air et de l'Espace, Le Bourget, France. Publication and date unknown.

Ellis, Frank H. *Canada's Flying Heritage.* Toronto: University of Toronto Press, 1954.

————. *In Canadian Skies.* Toronto: The Ryerson Press, 1959.

Farman, Henry, and Dick Farman. *The Aviator's Companion.* London: Mills and Boon, 1910.

Federal Aviation Administration. *Administrators Fact Book* (April 2001). Washington, D.C.: FAA.

Freeman, J. W. "First Ladies of the Air." *FAA Aviation News,* March 17, 1988.

Freiherr, Peter. "Melli—zeigte es den Männern." *Fliegermagazin,* January 1986.

George, Weston. "Beauty and the Blériot." *Aviation Quarterly* 6, no. 1, 1980.

Gibbs-Smith, Charles H. *Aviation: An Historical Survey from Its Origins to the End of World War II.* London: Her Majesty's Stationery Office, 1985.

Gibson, Ada. "Women Who Fly." *Aircraft,* June 1910.

Goodall, Michael. *Flying Start: Flying Schools and Clubs at Brooklands, 1910–1930.* Weybridge, England: Brooklands Museum Trust, 1995.

————. "The Graceful Bird: Mrs. Hilda Hewlett, England's First Lady Aviator." *The Spirit,* Brooklands Museum Trust, Autumn 1998.

Gregor, Michael. "Flying as It Was—Early Days in Russia." *Sportsman Pilot,* December 1939.

Gregory, Elizabeth Hiatt. "Woman's Record in Aviation." *Good Housekeeping,* September 1912.

Gsell, Robert. *25 Jahre Luftkutscher; von Luftsprung zur Luftbeherrschung.* Erlenbach-Zurich and Leipzig: E. Rentsch, 1936.

Gwynn-Jones, Terry. "Wild about Harriet." *Smithsonian* Vol. 14, Janaury 1984.

Hackenberger, Willi. *Die Alten Adler: Pioniere der deutschen Luftfahrt.* München: J. F. Lehmanns Verlag, 1960.

Harding, Earl. "Liberty in the Dark." *Service,* July 1951.

Harper, Harry. *Twenty-five Years of Flying.* London: Hutchinson and Co., 1929.

———. "The Intrepid First Lady of Flight." *Flying,* March 1957.

Heath, Lady Sophie Mary, and Stella W. Murray. *Woman and Flying.* London: John Long, 1929.

Herner, Christine. "Melli Beese: Die erste deutsche Fliegerin." *Luft-und Raumfahrt,* January 1994.

Herveux, Jeanne. Reminiscences. Biographical file. Musée de l'Air et de l'Espace, Le Bourget, France.

Hewlett, Hilda B. *Our Flying Men.* Kettering, England: T. Beaty Hart, Bridewell Works, 1915.

———. "London to Batavia by Air." *Aeroplane,* January 25, 1933.

Hirth, Hellmuth. *Meine Flugerlebnisse.* Berlin: F. Dümmler, 1915.

Hodgman, Ann, and Rudy Djabbaroff. *Skystars: The History of Women in Aviation.* New York: Atheneum, 1981.

Holden, Henry M. *Her Mentor Was an Albatross.* Mount Freedom, NJ · Black Hawk Publishing Co., 1993.

Ionnitiu, Lygia M. "What Harriet Quimby Saw at the Nassau Boulevard Aerodrome." *The Harriet Quimby Research Conference Journal* 2, 1996.

Jablonski, Edward. *Ladybirds: Women in Aviation.* New York: Hawthorn Books, 1968.

"Katherine Stinson, First Aviatrix to Fly U.S. Mail." *Stamps,* December 9, 1933.

"Katherine Stinson—'The Flying Schoolgirl.'" *FAA Aviation News,* November 1971.

Keimel, Reinhard. *Osterreichische Luftfahrzeuge,* Graz, Austria: H. Weishaupt Verlag, 1981.

Kerfoot, Glenn. "Helen Richey, First Lady of the Airlines." *Ninety-Nine News,* April 1978.

Korol, Vladimir Vasilevich. *V nebe Rossii.* St. Petersburg: Politekhnika, 1995.

Kruckman, Arnold. "They Lack Coolness and Judgment, Say Their Critics." Aeronautical page, *New York American,* May 14, 1911.

Laget, Françoise, et Serge Laget. *Le Grande Livre du Sport Feminin.* Paris: FMT Editions, 1982.

Laroche, Raymonde de. "Flying in Presence of the Czar." Publication and date unknown. Marjorie Stinson Collection, Manuscript Division, Library of Congress, Washington, D.C.

Lauwick, Hervé. *Heroines of the Sky.* London: Frederick Muller, 1960.

Law, Ruth. "Go Get the Kaiser." *Chicago Sunday Herald,* July 22, 1917.

———. Biographical statement and record. Biographical file, National Air and Space Museum, April 5, 1933.

————. "Flying as It Was." *Sportsman Pilot,* n.d.

Leish, Kenneth. Interview with Ruth Law Oliver. Columbia University Oral History, 1960.

————. Interview with Matilde Moisant. Columbia University Oral History, 1960.

————. Interview with Katherine Stinson. Columbia University Oral History, 1960.

Lewis, Peter. "Lilian Bland and the *Mayfly.*" *Flight International,* January 23, 1964.

Loobey, Patrick. *Flights of Fancy: Early Aviation in Battersea and Wandsworth.* London: Wandsworth Borough Council, 1981.

Maggio, Rosalie, and Marcel Cordier. *Marie Marvingt: La Femme d'un siècle.* Sarreguemines, France: Editions Pierron, 1991.

Marck, Bernard. *Les Aviatrices.* Paris: l'Archipel, 1993.

Margetson, Stella. "Glory in the Golden Wings: British Women Pioneer Aviators." *Country Life,* March 22, 1984.

Marvingt, Marie. "Comment j'ai comçu le premier avion sanitaire?" Biographical file, Musée de l'Air et de l'Espace, Le Bourget, France.

————. "Mon vol de plus émouvant." Biographical file, Musée de l'Air et de l'Espace, Le Bourget, France.

May, Charles Paul. *Women in Aeronautics.* New York: Thomas Nelson & Sons, 1962.

Meos, Edgar. "Amazon Pilots and Lady-Warbirds." *Cross & Cockade* 16., no. 4, 1975.

Morehouse, Harold E. "Flying Pioneers Biographies." Unpublished.

————. Katherine Stinson, NASM, 1971.

————. Alys McKey Bryant, IWASM, 1971.

————. Ruth Law, NASM, n.d.

————. Marjorie Stinson, NASM, n.d.

Norden, Adalbert. *Flügel am Horizont.* Berlin: Im Deutschen Verlag, 1939.

Ovington, Earle L. "The Cause of the Quimby Accident." *Scientific American,* August 10, 1912.

"Pégoud Opens New Era in Aviation." *Fly Magazine,* no. 10, 1913.

Penrose, Harold. *British Aviation: The Pioneer Years, 1903–1914.* London: Putnam, 1967.

Petit, Edmond. "Marie Marvingt." Biographical file, Musée de l'Air et de l'Espace, Le Bourget, France. Publication and date unknown.

Pickens, William H. "Aviation as an Attraction." *The Billboard,* December 18, 1915.

Planck, Charles E. *Women with Wings.* New York: Harper & Brothers Publishers, 1942.

Powell, Hugh. "Harriet Quimby, America's First Woman Pilot." *American Aviation Historical Society Journal* 27, winter 1982.

Quimby, Harriet. "How a Woman Learns to Fly." *Leslie's Illustrated Weekly,* May 25, 1911.

————. "How a Woman Learns to Fly, II." *Leslie's Illustrated Weekly,* August 17, 1911.

————. "How I Won My Aviator's License." *Leslie's Illustrated Weekly,* August 24, 1911.

————. Interview. *World Magazine,* August 27, 1911.

————. "An American Girl's Daring Exploit." *Leslie's Illustrated Weekly,* May 16, 1912.

————. "Flyers and Flying." *Leslie's Illustrated Weekly,* June 27, 1912.

————. "Sky Women." *Collier's,* September 30, 1912.

————. "The Dangers of Flying and How to Avoid Them." *Leslie's Illustrated Weekly,* August 31, 1911.

————. "We Girls Who Fly and What We're Afraid Of." *World Magazine,* July 14, 1912.

Rawles, Obera H. "All Aboard for the Moon" *New York Journal,* May 16, 1936.

Reinhold, Ruth M. *Sky Pioneering,* Tucson, Ariz.: University of Arizona Press, 1982.

Rich, Doris. *The Magnificent Moisants.* Washington, D.C.: Smithsonian Press, 1998.

Roseberry, C. R. *The Challenging Skies: The Colorful Story of Aviation's Most Exciting Years, 1919–1939.* New York: Doubleday & Co., 1966.

"Ruth Law and Her Remarkable Flight from Chicago to New York." *Scientific American,* December 2, 1916.

Schmitt, Günter. *Als die Oldtimer flogen: die Geschichte des Flugplatzes Berlin–Johannisthal.* Berlin: Verlag für Verkehrswesen, 1980.

————. *Die Ladys in den fliegenden Kisten.* Berlin: Brandenburgisches Verlagshaus, 1993.

Schwipps, Werner. *Kleine Geschichte der deutschen Luftfahrt.* Berlin: Haude & Spener, 1968.

————. *Riesenzigarren und fliegende Kisten: Bilder aus der Frühzeit der Luftfahrt in Berlin.* Berlin: Nicolaische Verlagsbuchhandlung, 1984.

————. *Schwerer als Luft: die Frühzeit der Flugtechnik in Deutschland.* Koblenz: Bernard & Graefe, 1984.

Sims, Dorothy Rice Peirce. *Curiouser and Curiouser.* New York: Simon and Schuster, 1940.

Spitzer, Barbara. *Melli Beese: Bildhauerin, Pilotin—eine ungewöhnliche Frau.* Treptow, Berlin: Heimatmuseum, 1992.

Stevens, A. Leo. "On the Death of Miss Quimby." *Aeronautics,* August 1912.

Stinson, Marjorie. "Diary of a Country Girl at Flying School." *Aero Digest,* February 1928.

————. "In the Air." *Washingtonian,* November 1929.

————. "Wings for War Birds." *Liberty,* December 28, 1929.

————. "The Upper Road." *American Motorist* (AAA, D.C. edition), September 1930.

Stroud, Patricia. "Women in Aviation." *Flight,* August 20, 1954.

Studer, Clara. *The Life of Glenn Curtiss.* New York: Stackpole Sons, 1937.

Supf, Peter. *Das Buch der deutschen Fluggeschichte.* Berlin-Grunewald: Verlagsanstalt Hermann Klemm AG, 1935.

Tageev, Boris L. *Aerial Russia.* London: J. Lane Co., 1916.

Tessier, Roland. *Femmes de l'air.* Paris: Correa et Cie., 1941.

Tschudi, Georg von. *Aus 34 Jahren Luftfahrt.* Berlin: Verlag von Reimar Hobbing, 1928.

Underwood, John W. *The Stinsons.* Glendale, Calif.: Heritage Press, 1969.

Villard, Henry Serrano. *Contact! The Story of the Early Birds.* New York: Bonanza Books, 1968.

Vingt cinq ans d'aéronautique Française, vol. II. Paris: Édité pour La Chambre Syndicale des Industries Aéronautiques, 1934.

Wachtel, Joachim. *Die Aviatiker oder die tollkühnen Pioniere des Motorflugs.* Berlin: Mosaik Verlag, 1978.

Watson, Emily. "A Lady's Flying Past." Unknown journal, n.d.

White, Christine A. "Gossamer Wings: Women in Early Russian Aviation, 1910–1920." *Proceedings of the Second Annual National Conference on Women in Aviation.* St. Louis, 1991.

Whitehead, Hugh L. "A Magnificent Woman and Her Flying Machines." *Bay of Plenty Times,* New Zealand, May 8, 1999.

Whitt, Samuel S. "Miss Harriet Quimby." *National Aeronautics,* no. 1, 1973.

Wohl, Robert. *A Passion for Wings: Aviation and the Western Imagination, 1908–1918.* New Haven, Conn.: Yale University Press, 1994.

Women in Aviation International. *The Facts, 2001.* Daytona Beach: WAI.

Woodhouse, Henry. "Pioneer Women of the Air." *Flying,* June 1913.

Quoted and background material also came from the following sources:

NEWSPAPERS

Akron Sunday Times
Alameda Times Star
American Examiner
Arbeiter-Zeitung (Vienna)
Bay of Plenty Times (New Zealand)
Berliner Tageblatt
Boston Herald
Bulletin (Brownwood, Texas)
Chicago Daily News
Chicago Examiner
Chicago Herald
Chicago Tribune
Christian Science Monitor
Cleveland News
Cleveland Plain Dealer
Daily Colonist (Victoria, British Columbia)
Daily Mail (London)
Dallas Dispatch
Dallas Morning News
Deutsche Zeitschrift für Luftschiffahrt
El Imparcial (Mexico City)
El Mañana (Mexico City)
Evening Bulletin (Providence)
Evening Star (Washington, D.C.)
Evening World (New York)
Journal du Dimanche
Kansas City Star
Le Figaro
Le Matin
Le Monde
Le Petit Journal
Leslie's Illustrated Weekly

Le Temps
Los Angeles Times
Mexican Herald
Mobile Register
Morning Telegraph (New York)
New Mexican
New York American
New York Herald
New York Herald (Paris)
New York *Sun*
New York Times
New York World Telegram
Public Ledger (Philadelphia)
Rochester Democrat and Chronicle
Sandusky Register
San Antonio Express
San Antonio Light
San Francisco Chronicle
San Francisco Examiner
Seattle Daily Times
South Bend Tribune
Times (London)
Times-Picayune (New Orleans)
Tucson Citizen
Washington Post
Wichita Falls Daily Times
Yakima Daily Republic

JOURNALS
Aerial Age Weekly
Aero and Hydro
Aero Digest
Aero-France
Aeronautics
Aéronautique
Aeroplane
Aircraft
Air Revue
Aviation News
Aviation Quarterly
The Billboard
Chirp
Country Life

Cross & Cockade
Curtiss Flyleaf
Fliegermagazin
Flight
Flugsport
Flugzeug
Flying
Fly Magazine
Good Housekeeping
Icare
L' Aérophile
L'Air
La Revue Aérienne
L'Auto
Les Ailes
Liberty
Luft-und Raumfahrt
Motor
National Aeronautics
Paris-Match
Santa Fean
Saturday Review of Literature
Scientific American
Service
Sketch
Sports Illustrated
Sportsman Pilot
U.S. Flying News
World Magazine
Zeit Magazin

FILM

Walter Jerven's "Himmelstürmer"—Film Division, Library of Congress

Index

About the Author

EILEEN F. LEBOW, a former teacher, has written several books, including *Cal Rodgers and the* Vin Fiz: *The First Transcontinental Flight, A Grandstand Seat: The Army Balloon Corps in World War I,* and *The Bright Boys: A History of Townsend Harris High School.* She lives in Washington, D.C.